YESTERDAY'S
RULERS

YESTERDAY'S RULERS

The Making of the
British Colonial Service

ROBERT HEUSSLER

Foreword by Sir John Macpherson, G.C.M.G.
Introduction by Margery Perham, C.B.E.

SYRACUSE UNIVERSITY PRESS   1963

To

Carlotta Morgan Heussler
and
Herman Koerner Heussler

Contents

Foreword

As more and more British colonies achieve independence within the Commonwealth, there is a strong and growing feeling amongst members of Her Majesty's Overseas Civil Service, past and present (how quickly the proportions are changing!), that steps should be taken to do for the Colonial Service what Philip Mason did for the Indian Civil Service in his two splendid volumes "The Men Who Ruled India"—that is, to tell the story of British colonial policy through an account of the "faith and works" of members of the Colonial Service. The task would be much more complex than the assignment which Philip Mason carried out so ably, because of the number and diversity of the colonial territories which came under British rule or protection. And the timing is difficult, because, unlike the way of the national press with obituaries, one hesitates to compose the epitaph (even for the pigeonholes) before the subject of it has finally passed away. But it should be done while those whose memories go back fifty years or more are still available for consultation.

Professor Heussler has not, of course, attempted to undertake this task, but his present study of the methods of recruitment and training of colonial administrators during the quarter century beginning in 1920, when the much-loved father of the Service, Sir Ralph Furse, was at the height of his powers and influence, is a most valuable and very timely contribution on a major aspect of the story. How good it is for us to have turned upon us the searchlight of a cool, objective, far from uncritical but—dare I say—basically admiring appraisal by an American who is deeply interested in the Colonial Service and who has a sympathetic understanding, gained at first hand, of the job that its members are called upon to carry out. I only wish that Robert Heussler could have extended the period under study, so that he could have here described, as he has done before ("An American Looks at the Colonial Service," *New Commonwealth,* July, 1960; "Why Study the Colonial Service?" *Corona,* May, 1961; "The British Colonial Legacy: The Colonial Service," *South Atlantic Quarterly,* July 1961), the delicate and demanding task that faces the members of that Service in the final run-in of a dependent territory to independence, and how well most of them respond.

There are some passages in this study which I should like to challenge, but this would relate more to the stresses he gives to certain aspects—rather than to any basic disagreement. A not inconsiderable part of the study constitutes a selective social history of England. (Not Britain!) Such class consciousness as still exists in this changing Britain no doubt strikes an American more forcibly than it does the British people themselves, and this probably colours his view of an earlier period. Whatever may be said about the *source* from which Ralph Furse selected most of the colonial administrative officers between the two wars, the *qualities* that he sought— strength of character, readiness to accept responsibility, care for the people whom the administrator was serving, albeit at times rather autocratically—were surely the qualities primarily needed during that period. I have an idea that Robert Heussler agrees! Personally, I strongly challenge the view that those qualities were to be found then, any more than now, only in a certain social class, or in the products of selected schools and universities. And I don't recognize myself—or a good many of my erstwhile colleagues—in the rather rigid pattern described!

This may be in part because my own early service (nearly half of the whole) was in Malaya, starting as an Eastern Cadet, and because I and my contemporaries who joined the Malayan Civil Service after the First World War were selected not by Ralph Furse but by the Civil Service Commission! When the Federated Malay States and the Straits Settlements Governments reverted to the competitive system after the postwar reconstruction period, the then Governor, Sir Laurence Guillemard, noted on the file:

> "Seen. It is a pity. Although myself a product of the Competitive System I am not convinced that it secures the best results."

Incidentally, Guillemard passed *second* into the Home Civil Service, but this didn't satisfy him. He sat again the next year—and came *first*. I would add that when the selection of cadets for Malaya was eventually entrusted to Ralph Furse, the first batch to be appointed, in 1933, to whom I taught the rudiments of the Malay language on the Colonial Administrative Service course at Oxford, were not at all of one rigid pattern, either in character or in their educational provenance. I was greatly impressed with the selection. Indeed, I can say with confidence that colonial governors trusted Ralph Furse completely and were content to leave it to him to select the right material.

Robert Heussler concedes that when Ralph Furse made suggestions to the Devonshire Committee regarding the changes needed in methods of selection and of training, once the Second World War was ended, he pointed to the need for broadening the recruitment base to meet the challenge of the changing times, but he says that the changes came too late. This cannot be gainsaid, but I suggest that it doesn't make sufficient allowance for the swiftness of the dramatic changes in colonial territories brought about by the last war.

It is very easy to get into an argument about when the British, a race of empiricists, came to realise that the final step in their imperial mission must be the devolution of powers to the component parts of the Empire— more particularly about the date of the realisation that this doctrine could, and should, be applied not only to dependencies inhabited by people of British stock but equally to territories inhabited by people of different race from our own. Certain it is that far-sighted statesmen in Britain, and the finest servants of Britain in the East, recognized the inevitability, and the rightness, of this doctrine more than 150 years ago. I think it is true (and Robert Heussler makes the point) that those of us who were sincerely serving colonial peoples in the period under review, didn't keep this doctrine sufficiently in the forefront of our minds. But there was a good deal of excuse for us. The critics forget that strong feelings of nationalism and the passionate desire for political freedom (what Robert Heussler calls the "nationalist infection") are quite recent phenomena in most of our colonial territories. I can truthfully say that, when I was in Malaya from 1921 to 1937, and when I was first in Nigeria, just before the last war, there was no clamour or pressure for faster constitutional advance. The Second World War, which greatly widened the horizon of the colonial peoples, and the speed-up of communications of all kinds changed the whole situation in a dramatic way. We were not far-sighted enough—we were caught off balance—but in my experience the Colonial Service adapted itself remarkably well to the new situation.

These passing thoughts in no way detract from my

sincere admiration of the penetrating study which Robert Heussler has presented. His final judgment, in the last chapter of the study, is a handsome tribute to the Colonial Administrative Service—the more appreciated because it comes from a shrewd and not uncritical observer. The service to which I had the honour to belong owes him a deep debt of gratitude.

JOHN MACPHERSON

London
June 19, 1962

Introduction

AN immense literature has been written about British colonial policy and administration and surprisingly little about the men who expressed policy in administration. There are, of course, many studies of individual pro-consuls: it is as a service that they have been given inadequate attention. We have general studies by Sir Charles Jeffries and Sir Alan Burns, two men who have the knowledge which comes from long and direct responsibility in this sphere.* The special characteristics of Professor Heussler's present work are detachment, thoroughness, and selectivity. All these require some explanation.

The detachment is neither from a vast distance, nor from superior eminence: it results from both his nationality and his experience. Professor Heussler has qualities of heart as well as head which have enabled him to enter with imaginative understanding into the more human and idealistic aspects of colonialism without being drawn away from his usefully external viewpoint. For myself I have found it a stimulating if sometimes uncomfortable experience to follow the probing light thrown by this American mind as it passes over a subject much of which has been left by us British in the shadow of the unquestioned.

About the thoroughness there is more to say. Those of us for whom the Colonial Service filled a large part

---

* C. Jeffries, *The Colonial Empire and Its Civil Service* (Cambridge: Cambridge University Press, 1938); Sir A. Burns, *Colonial Civil Servant* (London: Allen and Unwin, 1949).

in our lives must be grateful not only for the comment but also for the lively and detailed picture upon which it is based. For this is not one of the hundreds of academic theses composed in studies and libraries out of the relevant records and then loosened up for publication. The essential work on the records is there, but few students of foreign institutions have been able to spend so much time out in the field of their studies. In Professor Heussler's case this field covered almost the whole of Europe's dependencies and ex-dependencies, some of which he visited not once but many times. It was from the skies as a U.S. Army Air Force pilot that he began to view the world and to make contacts with his British opposite numbers. Work for an oil company posted him to China and Hong Kong and this was followed by assignments in aerial photography in parts of the West Indies, nearly all of tropical Africa, the Arab States and the Mediterranean, and all of ex-British Asia. In 1959 Professor Heussler came to England and to Oxford as a Fulbright scholar, determined to study the British Colonial Service whose work he had so often encountered in his travels. In Britain he interviewed large numbers of Colonial Office officials, active and retired, academic workers in Commonwealth affairs, and other informants. Everywhere, I know, he made a great impression by his understanding, both deep and wide, of their problems and by his seriousness of purpose. As a result he was everywhere given the maximum of information and access to the records. In 1960, as an associate director of a Ford Foundation survey to determine the possibility of attaching American graduates to colonial governments for training, he took time off to revisit much of tropical Africa—I saw him at work in Tanganyika—and Southeast Asia, and he reached Borneo and Fiji. He estimates that in the course of these travels he interviewed 150

British colonial civil servants and perhaps another fifty non-British. It would, indeed, be difficult to imagine an approach which so fully combined the documentary, the human, and the geographical sides of a large aspect of modern government.

Professor Heussler was faced with many intricacies and obscurities in his extensive study. But he was helped by one great simplification. He might have expected that, as is usual in the history of British institutions, the policy behind the formation of the Colonial Service would have to be disentangled from the activities of a succession of ministers and officials, expressing the subconscious standards and the unspoken purposes of their class and nation. But he found something very exceptional in the British record. Not only had one man directed the recruitment of the Service for the entire twenty-five years under review, but he had done so according to clear principles and by means of a sustained and brilliant administrative campaign. This man was Major Sir Ralph Furse, K.C.M.G., D.S.O., M.A., Hon. D.C.L., Oxford—unusual and significant combination of titles!—and he has confessed that he owes his success less to Eton, Balliol, and Oxford than to his early training as a cavalry officer. For by a fortunate coincidence the present study has been preceded by the vividly personal recollections of this official. These should certainly be read alongside Professor Heussler's book, since much of this is a description and commentary upon Furse's life work.*

I must confess here that in commenting upon the subject of this book I cannot claim complete detachment. As the pages which follow may suggest, both Sir Ralph and Sir Douglas Veale, the former Registrar of Oxford University and another main actor in these events, were

---

* *Aucuparius: Recollections of a Recruiting Officer* (London: Oxford, 1962).

my admired friends and colleagues, and I was involved both in helping to plan the courses for the Service in Oxford and in teaching these courses in colonial history and administration.

Turning now to Professor Heussler's selectivity, he has cut a section out of a very large field by imposing upon himself four limitations. Firstly, he has selected the quarter-century following 1920 for his period, covering the years when the Colonial Service grew to its brief maturity both in size and in clarity of vocation. Secondly, he has confined his attention mainly to the administrative cadre of a service which was rapidly extending its ancillary social and technical branches. Thirdly, he has concentrated his attention upon the aspects of recruitment and training, though with a clear sense of the wider horizons to which these aspects pointed. Fourthly, among the three universities which were centres for training— Oxford, Cambridge and London—he has concentrated upon the records of the first in its relations with the Colonial Office.

To some it might seem at first sight that the second and third of these limits have unduly narrowed the subject. But if no understanding of the British colonial empire would be possible without a study of the men who were the distant and scattered agents of their country's policy, it follows that the administrators must demand first attention because they were for many years almost the only agents and remained the dominant branch of the Service until the later years brought their ever-widening concept of the scope of government. Such a service does not come into existence by any autonomous process similar to natural growth. Recruits have to be attracted, assayed, appointed, stationed, promoted and, later, perhaps retrained and transferred. All these intricate operations should be carried out under the direction of some

guiding principles. They will certainly reflect the governing *mores* of the society within which they are conducted.
Professor Heussler's concentration upon the two first
processes of recruitment and training is justified since,
although by the intelligent administration of administrators the best use can be made of given human material,
there are limits to what can be done to change and
develop the material itself.

We are confronted in this book by a major theme,
one that was bound to strike forcibly upon an American
mind but which, until recent years, was largely taken
for granted in Britain, especially in civil service and professional circles. There was the determined and largely
successful effort of Furse to make the administrative
branch of the Colonial Service what the writer calls
an elitist corps. Today a majority both of Americans
and of British will almost certainly regard this as a serious
criticism of the Service. When I look back over the thirty
years during which I have been involved in teaching for
the Colonial Service and also in studying its work overseas, I realize now that I took this aspect for granted.
It needed this book and Furse's own recollections to
reveal its significance and also the single-minded tenacity
with which Furse pursued his aim.

Those who criticise this policy should re-examine
their own reasons. They should measure the speed with
which education has spread in Britain and with it the
assertion of social and political equality and observe that
it has been a natural, perhaps a necessary, part of this
assertion to condemn the concepts of a "ruling class"
and a "public school type." They should reconstruct
both the conditions of the early interwar years and the
different ideas then prevailing and study the character
of the need which Furse was trying to meet. His Service
needed a steady recruitment of men who combined a

high, though not necessarily the highest, intellectual standard with the desire and the stamina to face an adventurous life in strange, distant, and sometimes dangerous conditions. An unusual combination of qualities was needed—courage with adaptability; firmness with sympathy; enterprise with reliability; obedience with authority. In lonely stations, far from the restraints of European public opinion and supported by no lavish remuneration, the officer must remain dignified and incorruptible. Moreover, with whatever margin of individual qualities, the members of this increasing corps must share the same standards of conduct and manners sufficiently to allow them to understand one another. They must act, when dispersed over wide and testing regions, upon similar principles and in pursuit of the same almost unspoken purposes. Officers of the Colonial Service needed a pride in their Service, derived from an almost indivisible devotion to their own country and to the people they felt they were serving. The book describes how by recruitment and training this need was largely met in what was, in the years concerned, the most obvious and reliable way. This was from the public schools and the two ancient universities from which most of the boys from these schools proceeded. For it was in the confident, athletic, and privileged—but not too privileged—class that the necessary combination of qualities could most often be found.

There is one special point I would add from my own experience of the work of training. Although the Colonial Office, as Professor Heussler shows, was in a sense the employer of the university in this work, there was never to my knowledge even the suspicion of interference with the freedom of those engaged in teaching. I was myself engaged in the most controversial of our subjects, colonial administration. I was, and was known to be, critical of some aspects of our colonial policy, especially in areas of white settlement. I used the opportunity, even after the difficult challenge of African nationalism had begun, to discuss these difficult issues. As far as I know neither I nor any of my colleagues who may have used their freedom in this way ever received official criticism or caution. If such criticism ever emanated from a colonial government it was smothered in the Colonial Office before it ever reached us. I think that, in general, the influence of the university teachers would often have tended to question rather than confirm accepted ideas of colonial policy. It is a tribute to the liberalism of the Colonial Office, and its respect for the British tradition of academic freedom, that this remained possible until the end, in places the somewhat difficult end, of its rule. It is, perhaps, also a tribute to the officers that they did not resent this doubtless sometimes rather unrealistic handling of their life's work. Certainly they never seemed to me to belong to a uniform type. If the second courses sometimes contained men whose conformist minds had become further rusted through the exercise of power and the effects of isolation, I can remember few classes which were not enlivened by others with open and questioning minds.

It will already be clear that from the starting point of recruitment this study leads on to wider considerations of the British social structure. In the background, moreover, lies the whole question of imperialism, now called colonialism, upon which world opinion, stimulated by the sudden awakening of African political consciousness, has so vigorously reversed an acceptance as old as the historical record. The past is now seen in the highly coloured light of the new political emotions of our time and it is not possible at present to find any agreed standards by which to judge the record of past, and passing, colonial rule. It is much too soon to judge how far the emancipated peoples will consciously or unconsciously use the colonial foundations for their new political erections and, if they do use them, how serviceable they will prove. This is not to say that no preliminary attempts can yet be made to weigh the mistakes and the achievements of colonialism. In Western countries students of this subject are right not to reserve all judgment. They analyse and record and in the process devise at least provisional standards by which to weigh both the intentions and the achievements of the men of their own age. In making his record, Professor Heussler is thorough and lively: as a judge he has the necessary moderation and personal and national detachment. Dealing with an often obscure but central part of the whole subject of colonial rule, this book is likely to remain one of the most convincing parts of the evidence in a controversy which much of world opinion has turned into a prosecution.

MARGERY PERHAM

Nuffield College, Oxford
June, 1962

Author's Preface

In her Introduction Miss Margery Perham, Senior Fellow of Nuffield College and distinguished authority on colonial administration and history, discusses the relevance of this study to wider aspects of imperialism-colonialism. Such was always meant to be its frame of reference. There is also considerable treatment of social organization. Because a number of knowledgeable, experienced people in England have read and commented on the book in manuscript I am aware of certain fundamental misunderstandings. These arise, it seems to me, out of differences in British and American histories, cultures, occupations, and experiences. Given these profound dissimilarities, it is inevitable that points of view will diverge and honest men find themselves at variance, even when the same body of fact is recognized and when there is a substantial amount of common knowledge. I must note here that I do not suffer from the illusion that access to the colonial service was limited to dukes, marquises, and the occasional quick-footed earl. Nor do I think that candidates were barred who had not been to Eton or Winchester. When I refer to "the civil service class," "the ruling class," "the upper classes," or, rarely, to "the aristocracy," I speak in the *political,* not the social, sense. Britain in the interwar years did have a group of people that participated in governing the Home Islands and overseas dependencies more than did other groups. Aside from lineage, titles, and money, there was an identifiable ruling group. Especially this was true by comparison with the United States in the same period.

That the colonial service was recruited mainly from cadet branches of this group strikes me as immaterial to the central point: that the ethos of the ruling classes was the ethos of the colonial service; that the lead given by Eton and Winchester was followed by the school where the typical colonial civil servant went.

Furthermore, no opprobrium is attached in these pages to the ruling classes as such or to their activities. One does not seek to evade the scholar's duty of evaluating, in the last instance. But before that stage is reached I am concerned with description, not with praise or blame.

There is perhaps another pertinence. This book attempts to place in historical perspective an approach to assembling and preparing for duty a steady stream of officials for work outside their own country. The United States is now as much concerned with this type of recruitment and training as Britain once was. The career positions differ greatly. But there is an essential similarity: both the old colonial service and the various corps now representing the United States abroad wanted and want people capable of functioning in unfamiliar environments. Were the British right to focus on internal resources as identified in unscientific, in fact blatantly intuitive, personal interviews? Were they right to leave training, for the most part, to the college of hard knocks? Is it right to look for a "good man" who will do well at whatever he attempts? Hopefully this book will provide a contrast for American personnel officers who now use scientific methods, psychological tests, lectures on something called "The Overseas American," and orientations which devote as much time to knowing oneself and one's country as to learning about other lands and peoples.

In these anteroom pages, too, Sir John Macpherson and I offer the reader materials for a good-natured debate or two. Sir John, former governor-general of Nigeria

and the only career colonial civil servant to become head
of the Colonial Office, accuses me of admiring his former
Service. This is right, in that I greatly admire many in
its ranks. In fact the egg was hatched in well-remembered
talks with administrators in the jungles, deserts, and islands of the colonial empire. I am not objective. My regard for these men does not remove the fact, however, that
I salute their *accomplishments* more than their *aims,*
various as the latter have always been. Nor do I think that
Sir John's loyalty to Scotland would lead him to deny
that the colonial service was made by a most English
Englishman, to English measure, with Englishmen always a majority in its far-flung cadres. A relatively recent innovation, the word "British."

Those who made my work easier are too many to list
in this place. I must thank a few to whom my debts are
greatest.

Among scholars I think first and foremost of Miss
Perham, who gave indispensable encouragement, intellectual sustenance, and such tangible support as intro-
ductions to knowledgeable people. Professor Harold
Sprout of Princeton read and helpfully criticized the
original manuscript. Professor George Stuyvesant Jackson of the University of Maine at Portland and Sarah
White Jackson of Westbrook Junior College made a
heroic safari through the entire typescript in an attempt
to find common ground where the English language and
I might meet and come to terms. Mr. Lionel Smith of
Mesopotamia and Edinburgh taught me valuable things
about the overseas British and how they got that way.
Sir Douglas Veale opened certain cellar doors beyond
which there lay a number of clues to the Whitehall-Ox-
ford collaboration mentioned in the following chapters.

Legions of civil servants gave patiently of their time
and advice. Sir Ralph Furse, the central figure of the

book, submitted cheerfully to verbal and written questions in great quantity. Later he extended this generosity by reading the entire manuscript and saving me from innumerable pitfalls. Sir Arthur Benson also took a vital part in this educating and salvaging work. Harold Ingrams, H. E. Newnham, A. N. Strong, and A. D. Garson all gave me invaluable aid and much enjoyment in the process.

Because the terrain of the colonial service is, still, so extensive, I am mindful of the vital assistance of three tolerant and generous past employers—C. E. Meyer, Lowell Thomas, and Stephen K. Bailey—who enabled me to seek out the colonial service on its own ground.

I thank the editors of the Syracuse University Press and the Oxford University Press for many kindnesses and Mrs. G. H. Borst, indefatigable colleague, for typing the final draft. It is a pleasure to have this opportunity of recording my gratitude also to the Warden and Fellows of Nuffield College for giving me a quiet place to work in and for making me a member of their Senior Common Room.

ROBERT HEUSSLER

Moscow, Vermont
October, 1962

YESTERDAY'S
RULERS

CHAPTER I

Before 1914

FEW expressions in geography and politics have given rise to so many misconceptions as the terms describing the territories associated with Great Britain during the last century and a half. Histories and newspapers are studded with imprecise references to "colonies," "dependencies," "protectorates," "dominions," and more recently "mandates," and "trust territories." Today all remaining units of what used to be called the British Empire are grouped together as the Commonwealth of Nations. The modern term is as misleading in its connotation of unity and similarity of status within the whole group as were the older terms, "British Empire," or "Commonwealth and Empire."

In these pages we will be concerned with the political units spoken of in British documents until 1947 as "the Colonial Empire" and thereafter as "the Colonial Territories." Even under the former heading it is necessary to be specific with reference to times and places in order to make clear which areas are involved in the staffing responsibilities of the Colonial Office in London. India was never involved, having been under its own department of state. "The White Dominions," Canada, Australia, New Zealand and South Africa, were self-governing and did not therefore concern the C.O. from the staffing point of view. Other territories shown as British on world maps had special relationships either to London or to larger imperial units. Thus Burma was for a time governed from India and later by a separate office in London. Aden was an appendage of India until the 1920's. The Sudan, legally a condominium of Britain and Egypt, was the civil service responsibility of a special London office. *Ad hoc* arrangements have been made from time to time for the staffing of countries such as Egypt and Iraq for which Britain had temporary responsibility. The other territories governed by Britain during the years of the present century are lumped together as the Colonial Empire, although within this group there has always been wide variation in type of government and in C.O. responsibility.

Four major geographical groupings may be listed for purposes of describing the Colonial Empire: 1) the West Indies and Atlantic group, 2) the Mediterranean and Middle Eastern, 3) the African and Indian Ocean, and 4) the Asian and Pacific group. With reference to the provision of staff from Britain, this list must be narrowed down still further before the geographical domain of the colonial service is identified. The first group, Bermuda, the Bahamas, the mainland colonies of North and South America, the West Indies, the Falklands, and the St. Helena group were not a large staffing problem for the C.O.; governors, other high-ranking officers, and technical staff were sent out from Britain. But social and educational development in many of these territories was such that the majority of their administrators were locally recruited. In the Mediterranean, Gibraltar and Malta were governed as military bastions and did not require significant numbers of civil servants through the C.O. Cyprus, although also a military base, did take small numbers from the Home Islands from time to time. So did Transjordan and Palestine when Britain had responsibility for administering them between the wars. Aden became a crown colony in 1937 and received a handful of C.O.-recruited cadets thereafter.

Africa is by far the most important area, and indeed the name "colonial service" normally suggests administration in tropical Africa more than in any other part of the world. The West African colonies took the lion's share of C.S. recruits, East Africa being second and Central Africa a poor third. Small numbers went to the High Commission Territories of South Africa (Bechuanaland, Basutoland and Swaziland), to Zanzibar, Mauritius, the Seychelles, and Somaliland. In Asia the former "Eastern Cadetship" colonies of Ceylon, Malaya, and Hongkong came under the recruitment umbrella of the C.O. in the 1930's. The Pacific Islands, notably Fiji, the Solomons, New Hebrides, and the Gilbert and Ellice group, made small demands on the C.O., and the Borneo territories under Britain's wing took an occasional recruit, usually by transfer from a larger colony nearby.

The colonial service was thus overwhelmingly an African service and secondarily a Southeast Asian service. The important colonies in its history are Nigeria, the Gold Coast, Kenya, Uganda, Tanganyika and Northern Rhodesia in Africa, and Malaya and Ceylon in Southeast Asia, although the last two have histories falling mainly outside the purview of the rest of the service. Colonies which figured prominently in the annals of the C.S. but lacked the quantitative importance of the others were Sierra Leone and the Gambia in West Africa, Somaliland in East Africa, and Nyasaland in Central Africa. Southern Rhodesia, although legally bound to Northern Rhodesia and Nyasaland in the 1950's, recruited its own civil service. In Asia, Hongkong completes the list of colonies whose importance was not reflected in the numbers of civil servants sent from Britain to staff their administrations.

The complexity of this imperial vista is indicated further in the frequency with which it is necessary to qualify generalizations. The C.O. supplied the governors but did not provide the rest of the services of Jamaica and Trinidad, for example. Sarawak was not a British colony, yet the C.O. occasionally helped its ruler by supplying a cadet. Aden and the Southeast Asian dependencies were part of the C.S. picture, but only later on when the service had passed its prime. Even in the African dependencies, which have been named as being of primary importance and which took large numbers of recruits from the C.O. all during the interwar period, there was so much diversity in human conditions and economic circumstances that the scale and character of government were nowhere the same. This was true partly because Britain acquired her colonies piecemeal over a period of centuries and partly as a result of political attitudes which her administrators brought to their tasks. A third prominent cause of differences was the presence of British settlers in some colonies and not in others. Colonial administration, in the words of an interwar secretary of state, showed a consistent "autochthonous evolution and diversity of experiment in each separate dependency." [1]

For reasons to be examined in the following chapters the Colonial Empire was decentralized to a degree that no other empire in modern history even approaches. No matter how strong her power was at a given place and time, Britain did not undertake a policy of assimilation or cultural imperialism as did the French and the Portuguese. Nor did she attempt paternalism on a scale comparable to Belgium's or Holland's. British methods were practical and empirical. Her administration was everywhere characterized by reluctance to force her own ways upon non-British peoples. In the early 1900's she ruled Northern Nigeria through institutions which were found in existence, while at the same time the French across the borders began a systematic policy of Frenchification centrally directed from Paris. The contrast between British and Dutch methods in Malaya and Java respectively was also striking. British policy and impact in any particular place, in brief, have been determined by a mixture of local circumstances and British capacity, the latter being comprised in turn of available power and of intent. To gauge the nature of her intent an examination must be made of the social system which produced Britain's officials and the educational determinants of specific policies.

Two effects of autochthony in the Colonial Empire may be mentioned in passing. It meant, first, that the civil service of each dependency had a character of its own from the beginning. Throughout the interwar years the term "colonial service" had for the most part only a legal integrity. A truly unified service in the French sense, one in which officials are transferred from colony to colony and continent to continent, has often been proposed and striven for. It has never become a reality. Secondly, the peoples living in each separate British colony have developed, willy-nilly, more according to their own cultural impulses than have natives of French or Belgian dependencies. This has sometimes been attributed to conscious British policy. Rather, in these pages, it is seen as the result of partly conscious but mainly intuitive and haphazard factors. Whether governed by direct or indirect rule, over a long period or for a relatively short time, and whether or not they lived among settlers, the natives of British dependencies developed more internal resources towards the competence of self-rule than did natives elsewhere. Notwithstanding autochthony, they shared an exposure to the British governing ethos, which was, for all the contradictions of domestic social practice, one which had always adapted to demands for more representative political forms.

The responses of the British to the wishes and developing capacities of natives in their colonies have been such as to necessitate a constant interrelating of changing conditions in the colonies with developments in the Home Islands. A retired civil servant who governed one colony and served in three others divides colonial history into three periods: an exploratory phase, one of settled administration, and a phase of transferring authority to native leaders.[2] In Victorian times most colonies were still in the first phase, especially their up-country areas. Health conditions were generally bad; government was minimal and primitive; the C.S. was small, widely scattered, and subject to many variations in conditions of service. The recruitment system, if it can be called that, was informal. The division of discretion between the C.O. and colonial governments was seldom clearly made, and staff turnover was high. That the expression "Her Majesty's Colonial Service [could] claim a century of authority . . ." as of the 1930's is true enough in the legal sense,[3] but it was simply a blanket expression covering all civil services, including those of such widely differing "colonies" as Canada and the Gambia. As a collection of civil services similarly recruited in the United Kingdom and then posted throughout the Colonial Empire to undertake roughly comparable administrative duties, the C.S. is a phenomenon of the present century. The last major expansive phase of European imperialism took place in the 1880's and 1890's. The C.S. may be described as Britain's organizational response to increased governmental responsibilities resulting from her acquisitions in that period.

C.O. documents referring to events in the nineteenth century, before the last expansive phase and while administration was still largely experimental, show a consistent informality and lack of system. In 1868 an official who had been acting governor in the Gold Coast and who had been forced to retire due to "the noxiousness of the climate" wrote to the secretary of state requesting another appointment.[4] At that point he had been unemployed for four years. The minister's private secretary commented that the former official was a "well meaning gentlemanlike man with some small amount of talents fitted for a small place" and recommended that he be given "the usual answer." [5] This was that if an opening occurred he would be advised. Other applicants failed to receive even this minimal encouragement. In 1869 a private secretary replied to an application by expressing "his Lordship's regret that he cannot make any promise as the vacancies are very few and the list of candidates is already long." [6] Former officials and their relatives fared no better than young men applying for their first positions. The widow of an official who had been "for twenty years captain of the Port of Demerera" petitioned the Duke of Buckingham repeatedly and without success on behalf of her son.[7] She not only failed to obtain a position for him but also failed to enlist the C.O.'s aid in securing a pension promised but never paid by the government of her husband's former colony.

Those with friends in power were sometimes more fortunate. One Thomas Sidgreaves mentioned in a letter to the Minister that he knew a Mr. Holland in the C.O.[8] Asked about this, Holland advised his chief that "the writer is a good lawyer and a gentleman (and) . . .

would do very well in any colony." [9] The official position was that the secretary of state would make no appointment without "recommendations from persons known to himself." [10] An applicant with no experience or other objective qualifications therefore sometimes succeeded where ex-governors failed.[11] The form of patronage used throughout Victorian times and called into question only with the arrival of Joseph Chamberlain in 1895 resulted inevitably in unevenness of quality among colonial services. The penniless son of good family, whose classic portrait was drawn by Thackeray in *Vanity Fair,* might or might not have been competent.[12] This was purely a matter of chance and depended on the whim of incumbent ministers and their casually appointed private secretaries. Colonial governments, for their part, had to make do with local revenue out of which administrators' salaries were paid. There was great variation from colony to colony, according to economic facts of life. Standards, in a word, were absent at both the London and colonial ends. The duties, contracts, and quality of officials presented such a confused picture worldwide that imperial unity appears to have depended on little more than common nationality.

The casual, almost absent-minded, staffing system used at the nerve center of the Empire in late Victorian times is recalled by an early appointments secretary:

> My special duty, apart from such things as opening letters and answering the less important ones, was a curious feature of an old order which has entirely passed away. The juvenile Assistant Private Secretary sat in a back room with an unpaid colleague of about his own age, and made (subject to the Minister's assent, which was seldom withheld) *all* the new appointments to the Colonial Service! There were four

large leather volumes, labelled Administrative, Legal, Medical, and T.A.C., meaning "Treasury, Audit and Customs," in which we entered the names, qualifications and credentials of the candidates (colloquially "cands.") in these several spheres; we interviewed them at length, and took careful notes of what we called the "impression" they made; and when a vacancy arose we went diligently through them all and (of course, in the case of legal appointments, with the help of the Legal Adviser) made our submissions, which as I said were usually approved. My unpaid colleagues, first Oliver Howard then Conrad Russell, were good judges of men; we took immense pains and had a good sense of responsibility; I don't think we made many mistakes, and I shouldn't wonder if the system worked as well as another.[13]

Britain could stumble along with a ramshackle system of recruitment and overseas administration as long as the larger imperial units were well governed and while she held smaller colonies mainly as trading posts or naval stations and left the hinterlands unadministered. Competition with France and Germany at the end of the nineteenth century, however, stimulated intrusions into these hinterlands, mainly in Africa. The exploration phase was ending and giving place rather suddenly to the phase of direct confrontation between European and native. Commercial enterprises such as Sir George Goldie's Niger Company and the Uganda Company on the other side of Africa would not be adequate to administrative challenges lying just over the horizon. In 1899 Chamberlain called for a review of all officials throughout the Empire who might be described as belonging to the C.S. His aim was to establish a unified service. The very fact that personnel data were not available for immediate submis-

TABLE 1

IMPORTANT AREAS OF THE COLONIAL EMPIRE

	Date of Becoming a C.O. Responsibility	Beginning Date of Recruitment, if Different	Remarks
West Africa			
*Nigeria	1900		
*Gold Coast	1821		
*Sierra Leone	1808		
The Gambia	1821		Independent colony, 1843. Usually supplied from other W. African colonies.
East Africa			
*Kenya	1905		
*Uganda	1905		
*Tanganyika	1918		
Somaliland	1905		
Zanzibar	1913		
Central Africa			
*Northern Rhodesia	1905	1924	
Nyasaland	1904		

South Africa

High Commission Territories (Bechuanaland, Swaziland, Basutoland)	1885		Under the Dominions Office in the interwar period

Asia and Pacific

*Malaya	1867	1932	
Aden	1928		Became a crown colony, 1937
Cyprus	1880	1935	Became a crown colony, 1925
Ceylon	1802		
Hongkong	1841		
Palestine and Trans-Jordan	1920		
Pacific Islands (Fiji and Western Pacific Group)	1877		Various island groups came under C.O. purview at various times after 1877

Note: Other territories for which the secretary of state had responsibility from time to time but which were not involved in recruitment and training considerations in any important respect were: The West Indies, St. Helena and dependencies, The Falklands, The Seychelles, and Mauritius. The secretary of state did not have responsibility for Sarawak or North Borneo in the interwar period, but the C.O. did occasionally recruit and train members of their services.

The asterisk denotes colonies requiring considerable numbers of staff members on a regular basis

sion to the minister indicates the condition of the C.O.'s staffing machinery at the time. The resulting report showed a total of 434 administrative posts high enough to require staff from Britain, some filled by patronage and some by examination.[14] The majority of these were in the Eastern Cadetship areas and in the West Indies. Africa's needs were beginning to expand, principally in the old colonies of the Gold Coast and Sierra Leone. But in the last years before 1914 the balance shifted to Africa, with Nigeria being taken over as a crown colony in 1900 and the C.O. assuming responsibility in 1905 for enormous areas in East and Central Africa.

Infant governments in Africa were fortunate to experience their first major staff needs at precisely the time when the end of the Boer War made available large numbers of adventurous ex-officers. The first of three waves of "war babies" in the twentieth century entered colonial services in the beginning decade of the century. By the end of that decade, however, the stream of veterans had dried up and African climate and disease had taken a heavy toll. Staffing needs, especially in the vast new colony of Nigeria, were beginning to tax the limited appointments facilities of the C.O. and to overreach the capacity of established sources of recruits, such as military units. Chamberlain's private secretary, who managed appointments along with other duties, sent circulars to Oxford, Cambridge, and provincial universities, announcing C.S. openings.

An informal and small-scale liaison between the C.O. and the major universities had operated sporadically before. More often than not this was confined to correspondence between individual dons and their friends in Whitehall. But in 1892 an Oxford don who had functioned as a go-between in finding positions for graduates helped to establish the Oxford University Appointments

Committee, a placement office which soon extended its contacts from education to government and business as well.[15] An early secretary of the committee was Rev. M. B. Furse of Trinity College, later bishop of Pretoria. The Oxford-C.O.-Africa connection, long an informal one, gradually became more systematized and redounded to the early advantage of the C.S.

TABLE 2

NUMBER OF ADMINISTRATORS ON DUTY IN A
SAMPLE SELECTION OF COLONIES BY YEARS

	1909	1919	1929	1939	1949	Remarks
Nigeria	261	297	488	411	486	
Gold Coast	47	86	142	114	219	
Tanganyika		109	177	179	260	German East Africa before 1917
Kenya	82	118	125	121	170	
Northern Rhodesia			102	109	163	C.O. recruitment began 1924
Malaya	125	242	270	223	226	Additional 30 officers on contract in 1949

Note: In the 1930's the total Colonial Administrative Service averaged 1,500, of whom approximately two-thirds were in rural and one-third in urban posts.

In fact, the numbers of university graduates—mainly from Oxford and Cambridge—seeking civil service appointments grew steadily in the early 1900's. The appointments committee secretary wrote to the C.O. asking for information on available posts in 1908.[16] In its answer the C.O. stressed the "large number of openings for university candidates in administration." [17] At this time patronage positions in the new African colonies could not compete in prestige with those in the Indian Civil Service

and the Eastern Cadetship colonies to which entrance
was by examination.[18] But the very fact that no examination was necessary for the African services made many
unacademic types among recent graduates willing to accept the rigors of careers in newer colonies where there
was the lure of faster promotion opportunity. Two factors, therefore, an unusually large number of openings,
and an increased supply of candidates, created a demand
for better C.O. facilities to undertake recruiting and posting work.

By 1910 the secretary of state had two full-time assistant private secretaries for appointments duties. The
younger of these, who assumed his post in that year, was
R. D. Furse, a recent Oxford graduate and nephew of
the former secretary of the Oxford Appointments Committee. Except for war service in 1914–19 Furse was to
remain principally responsible for C.S. recruitment until
1948 after which he was to serve an additional two years
in an advisory capacity. Major (later Sir Ralph) Furse
thus stood at the crossroads of the Colonial Empire for
nearly half a century. More than any single man he *made*
the C.S. and is deservedly spoken of as its father. His
personality, his outlook on life, and his conception of
the qualities which colonial officials ought to have were
stamped indelibly on the character of the service.[19]

A year before Furse joined the C.O. staff the first
cautious move was made in the direction of formal academic training for recruits. There was talk of establishing a course at Oxford where it might also serve as an
advertisement of C.S. openings. "If the candidates don't
come to us, we must go to the candidates," admitted a
C.O. minute of 1908.[20] But proximity proved a compel-
ling consideration, and the first course was given at the
Imperial Institute in London. There were lectures in law,
tropical hygiene, surveying, economic products, and ac-

counting. Not all recruits took the course, which lasted only two months, and the outbreak of the First World War forced discontinuance of the modest beginning. Despite the establishment of an early precedent neither the 1909 course nor its interwar successors were considered as important as the learning process which began when recruits took up their duties in colonies. Even the C.O. itself took a somewhat patronizing view of the lectures. In reply to an inquiry about a "scheme for training" sent to the C.O. by Manchester Grammar School, a private secretary denied that such a scheme existed.[21] The philosophy of in-service training held undisputed sway, both in England and throughout the Colonial Empire.

Of more importance were efforts to bring about greater standardization in conditions of service. A Tropical Services Committee established in the C.O. in 1910 reviewed the wide diversity of terms under which officials served in the various colonies.[22] Recommendations towards common standards made over the next few years were mostly unavailing, although a rough standard of leave regulations and pensions for widows and orphans was provided for. In the future there would be less necessity for embarrassing inquiries on behalf of senior civil servants who found after distinguished careers that they lacked even the bare minimum living allowance for retirement years in England. The head of an Oxford college, for example, had been compelled to write to a friend in the C.O. asking help for his brother, Sir H. M. Jackson, who had governed three colonies.[23] Dissatisfaction remained a serious detriment to morale, however, and there were waves of resignations in the East African services from 1909 to 1911.[24] In 1911 nine out of eleven applicants selected for that area refused appointment. Again the autochthony of the colonies was sufficient to resist London's best efforts towards even so minimal a measure of unity as would be represented in partial standards of contract. It was, as always, local conditions more than any imperial design that guided colonial administration. Following time-honored principles of indirect rule which were brought to the highest degree of system by Sir Frederick Lugard in Nigeria, colonial regimes exercised as little government as possible. Their efforts were directed at keeping other colonial powers out of their spheres of influence, collecting barely enough revenue to support themselves, and providing a stable atmosphere for trade and missionary work.

The system of patronage operated by Furse and his colleagues in the name of the secretary of state had not changed since the nineteenth century so much as it had expanded in volume. A C.O. memorandum of 1909 is illustrative. Referring to the filling of appointments rendered vacant by dismissals, it sets out the rule that "decisions on the recommendations of the Patronage Committee for the filling of a post are . . . taken in the Department without troubling the Secretary of State." [25] In the nineteenth century no such memorandum would have been necessary, since ministers would have told their private secretaries verbally what procedure to follow or would have left the matter to their discretion. A greater volume of business is hinted at in the phrase "Patronage Committee," another recent innovation. Unchanged in fact was the power of private secretaries to reach decisions on their own. Despite the creation of a Nigerian service from nothing in 1900 to 261 officers in 1909, for example, the failure or success of individual candidates still depended completely on what the private secretaries thought of them.

One of Furse's long-time assistants who eventually succeeded him describes the system as "one of the secrets of the Empire." [26] It is true that the British population at large knew nothing of it. Anyone off the street could ask for a set of application forms, however, and satisfy himself as to the objective selection criteria. What was secret, if anything, and it was not so to a great many people in government and education, were the particular qualities, as viewed by men such as Furse, which were thought necessary and without which men of outward promise did not succeed. Caricatures such as Professor Parkinson's amusing portrait of the C.O. and an occasional autobiographical sketch make the procedure appear frivolously irresponsible. Sir Arthur Grimble, who later governed three colonies in succession, writes of being interviewed by a whimsical old man in a beard, seated in a musty room in the old Downing Street office and seemingly removed in every way from the reality of administration in far-off places.[27] In retrospect a careful and complicated routine appears to boil down to a single circumstance or remark. Recruits, of course, saw only one side of the picture, although some returned many years later to participate in the process and came away with a different impression.[28]

On each candidate considered worthwhile a patronage or "P One" file was assembled. When complete it contained lengthy patronage forms, application forms, letters from referees, and notes by interviewers. In 1909 the forms were on long sheets of stiff paper with the candidate's name at the top and the name of the colony and service for which he was being considered. Then followed a list of questions printed on one side of the form with a space for referees' answers on the other. Their Edwardian tone contrasts with the brisk, abrupt style of contemporary personnel forms. "Will you be good enough to state," asked the C.O., "how long you have been acquainted with the applicant?"[29] The circumstances of the acquaintance are asked for. Is the candidate honest, sober, generally well conducted and healthy? If appropriate, details of previous employment were sought. Is the candidate qualified to undertake the duties of the position? Finally the secretary of state requested any additional details respecting the character of the applicant which referees could supply.

The applicant himself had to fill in long forms giving his name, the date, his father's name and profession and his father's address. "If dead, his name and profession should nevertheless be given," added the form,[30] which also called for age, marital status, and the desired appointment and salary. Educational data asked for were the names of schools and colleges, academic distinctions, and dates of entry and leaving. "If you have obtained any athletic distinctions or have held any position of responsibility at school or college you should state it here," instructed the form. In later chapters it will be shown why such importance was always attached to athletics and school leadership. Finally there were questions about professional and employment qualifications, especially military, and candidates were asked to list the names and addresses of two referees. They were warned that these should be people who really knew them well and that at least one of them should have intimate knowledge of their private lives. "The names of distinguished persons should not be given unless they really know you well; and the names of relatives or of those from whom you send testimonials should not be given." In this way the C.O. would have letters sent through the applicant and others solicited directly. In either case a suspect letter could be checked.

Unquestionably the heart of the system was a combination of testimonial letters and a course of personal interviews in the C.O. itself. References from school headmasters were always of importance. Writing in support of a Lt. J. P. S. Brown, the Head Master of Charterhouse told the C.O. that he was "of the highest possible character (and) got on excellently with his fellows." He was "just the type of boy to occupy later on a position of responsibility." [31] He was offered a post in Northern Nigeria, eventually the most sought-after area in the Colonial Empire. A similar letter from the Head Master of Shrewsbury mentioned that the candidate in question had been head of his house and had had a good influence upon others.[32] He too was offered a Nigerian appointment. The Head Master of Winchester stressed the leadership potential of a candidate he was supporting, noting that the candidate had been "one of the leading boys in the school (and) bore the highest character." [33] Another referee thought it quite enough to describe an applicant as "a good type of . . . English Public School man." [34]

Letters were also received from university dons and staff members of appointments committees. The secretary of the Oxford committee referred the C.O. to a previous applicant, mentioned that another candidate was a friend of the latter and observed that therefore "they are probably birds of a feather." [35] The committee always enclosed its own form, listing, in addition to data requested in C.O. forms, the marks attained by students on various examinations at stages in their university careers. Proficiency in modern languages was also noted and testimonials from dons were included. The latter were erratic in content. "He would be capable of dealing with men," wrote a Lincoln College (Oxford) tutor, "his mind is well balanced, his manners agreeable and in every respect he is a perfect gentleman." [36] In answer to the question whether he knew of any circumstance tending to disqualify a certain candidate, a Balliol (Oxford) tutor replied definitively, "He is a Public School and University man." [37] From a Wadham (Oxford) tutor came the advice that another candidate "would . . . maintain the best traditions of English Government over subject races. . . . He is a gentleman, a man of character." [38] An Oriel (Oxford) don regretted having to say that an applicant in question was more than a little wild at college.[39] Like Furse, the private secretary of the time hardly regarded this as a detriment, however. He noted that the man had settled down since leaving the university and that therefore the C.O. could safely ignore the disparaging letter.[40] Clearly, personal impressions made in interviews were normally more important than testimonials, provided a man's social and educational qualifications were suitable.

A letter from someone well known did not harm if he knew the candidate well. One young man wrote to Field Marshall Lord Grenfell, a family friend, stating frankly that C.S. competition was severe.[41] Only high-level support would give him a real chance. Another wrote candidly that he owed his appointment to the fact that Winston Churchill, then under-secretary for the colonies, knew his brother.[42] He was received by the under-secretary in a Paris hotel where both happened to be. The candidate, Mr. (later Sir Charles) Dundass, ended a long career in 1944 as governor of Uganda. Similar conditions pertained in the Home Civil Service which supplied the C.O. with its officials. Although entry was by examination, the educational system gave great advantages to graduates of certain schools and universities. Once appointed to a branch of the civil service, moreover, a man with friends in high places could be helped with promotions and transfers. A letter written by R. B. Haldane of the War Office to Sir Francis Hopwood of the C.O. is so illustrative of attitudes and practices that it merits quotation in full:

R. D. Furse in 1910.

Major Furse (at left, below) in 1928 in New Zealand during a tour of some of the dominions and colonies.

LEFT: Sir Douglas Veale at a graduation ceremony in the Gold Coast, January, 1957.

LOWER LEFT: Dr. W. T. S. Stallybrass as vice chancellor, 1947 (by kind permission of Brasenose College).

BELOW: Secretariat and district officials at a provincial council meeting, Fiji (by kind permission of the Central Office of Information; British Crown copyright).

Margery Perham in Darfur, Sudan, 1937.

District commissioner at work, Pemba, off the coast of East Africa (by kind permission of the Central Office of Information; British Crown copyright).

My dear Hopwood,

There is a certain Alexander Gray who is a very distinguished Scotch student and passed 2nd for the Civil Service examination in 1905. He was assigned a place in the Local Government Board which was the best thing for him which was then going but he is anxious to be taken in your office. My sister is interested in him because he is engaged to someone she knows about and she has written the enclosed memorandum. Is there any chance for him?

Yours very truly,
R. B. Haldane [43]

It should not be inferred that all or most of the recipients of such favors were incompetents who would not have got ahead otherwise. The case of A.C.C. (later Sir Cosmo) Parkinson, eventually permanent under-secretary in the C.O., shows that early twentieth-century civil service practices, although definitely elitist, were not therefore in the category of raw nepotism. Parkinson had passed eighth in the national competitions for Home, Indian, and Eastern Cadetship services.[44] He subsequently accepted a post in the accountant-general's department of the admiralty but was anxious to transfer to the C.O. A minute was prepared for the secretary of state on the Parkinson case, attention being drawn to letters written directly to the C.O. by the candidate. "In the old days it was considered improper to apply direct for transfer," said the minute.[45] "I am not sure that we ought to acknowledge officially. A hint might be conveyed. I think there is someone in the Department who knows him." A marginal note indicates that such was indeed the case, that in fact a C.O. official had advised the candidate to write. Within weeks the secretary of state, Lord Crewe, received a letter from Lord Rosebery recommending Parkinson strongly. Another letter from the Oxford vice chancellor to Sir Francis Hopwood in the C.O. pointed out that the candidate had taken a "double first in classics," becoming thereby one of the most outstanding Oxford men of his year. Further, it was added, Parkinson had achieved eighth place in the civil service examinations without attending one of the usual cram schools.[46] Throughout the correspondence the accent is on the man's intellectual brilliance, not on his social connections. In fact the latter are shown to flow from the former.

The opinions and comments of trusted friends of the C.O. or of distinguished public men were even more vital to C.S. appointments personnel than to officials who had the benefit of examination grades to guide them. With such letters in hand interviewers did not have to rely solely on their own judgment of candidates who sat before them for perhaps an hour at most. By the time the interview stage was reached, all of the required biographical data had been set against such objective selection criteria as there were. There remained only the exercise of what everyone knew to be unadorned intuition. If interviewers' notes seem banal it is doubtless because they were only a shorthand guide for other interviewers. "A really admirable man, strong, looks one straight in the face," said a note of 1909.[47] He "has had the C.S. in mind now for some months and is keen," observed the same candidate's second interviewer.[48] "He would be a useful man I think," the note continued. "Sound" was the cryptic comment of a third interviewer.[49] Not much more helpful as an indication of criteria for particular kinds of assignments is the note, "A nice man. Would do for administration." [50]

Furse himself showed an early flair for amateur psychology. After an interview in 1911 he wrote that the candidate was "tall, light haired, slim but well built . . . a good open face with a good deal of grit in it . . . a very good athlete . . . brains I expect fair . . . a 4th (fourth class honors degree) . . . but had influenza just before. He has a slightly affected way of shaking hands . . . but made a good impression and is I think really up to (the) East African standard." [51] There were very few hard and fast rules about what kind of man was appropriate for a particular colony. Age was one; candidates for East Africa had to be at least twenty-two and those for West Africa at least twenty-three. Generally speaking, colonial governments established their own regulations in this regard. But the judgment of the C.O. was absolute in appraisal of personal qualifications in each case. The pairing of individual applicants with the supposed needs of colonies was therefore a function of the image of each colony that lurked in the minds of private secretaries.

A question which vitally concerned the C.O. was the motivation of applicants. Why did they apply? In the case of civil service families the answer was obvious. Many candidates had fathers in the I.C.S. or elsewhere. Others, sometimes suffering from misconceptions of C.S. life, sought to join as a means of bettering or doing away with a circumstance of former employment. A Royal Navy officer, for example, applied because his navy pay would not permit marriage.[52] He chose poorly. Apart from the question of pay (the C.S. has never been well paid), no military or civil service could possibly have been less conducive to normal married life than the C.S. Another applicant, an army officer stationed in England, confessed that his regiment was of such low social standing that his position would definitely "lead to nothing." [53] Still another had failed both the I.C.S. and Egyptian service examinations and was making his third try for overseas service.[54] Candidates who had been rejected by other services did not find that this counted against them in the C.O. Furse and his friends were realists. The prestige of the new, mainly African, services in early twentieth-century years was such that the C.O. was glad to get men who were almost up to I.C.S. or comparable standards. The West African death rate, though declining, was still a subject of some misgivings in England. A candidate who was offered a Nigerian post admitted that his parents' opposition had forced him to decline.[55]

Applicants did appear, however, who had chosen Africa deliberately and for reasons other than the failure of previous applications. Lt. J. A. Ballentine, a 1909 applicant, had served in the Canadian Northwest Mounted Police.[56] He had also served in a West African military unit and had become interested in his native troops and their language. Like Lugard before him he was an adventurer who had found that adventure had its limitations and who wanted to do something more constructive.

In view of difficult and often hazardous living conditions abroad, why were so many young Britishers willing to apply? Part of the answer is the British tradition of exporting manpower for many different kinds of overseas activity. The mere fact that ancestors, fathers, uncles, older brothers or friends were serving abroad or had done so in the past was enough to plant in British minds a notion which was not being planted in, for example, American minds during the same era. The large territorial acquisitions of the late nineteenth century created an unprecedented need for staff; the general increase in the home population and the less spectacular but also significant rise in university capacities more than answered the new needs. In the first decade of the twentieth century, in fact, competition for attractive civil service positions both at home and abroad was more intense than ever before. Already, before the First World War, industrialization had produced an incipient class of "new poor" not unlike that which has aroused comment since 1945.[57] When land was no longer the basis of wealth or of influence, the sons of landed or formerly landed families came to depend increasingly upon military and civil service positions as guarantees of continued status for their families.

Whatever the motivation, Furse and his fellow assistant private secretaries regarded an attitude of responsibility as the *sine qua non*. They would rather have made no appointment at all and have left governments understaffed than to have sent out men of whom they were not sure. Ambition to better oneself was no bar. The greatest imperial pro-consuls had often been ambitious men, sometimes consummately so. Furse looked for the man who would direct his ambition in ways that would help and protect native peoples.

After the application process had been completed and the names of successful candidates entered in lists under colonies needing staff, there remained only one further step. The minister had to give formal assent to each appointment. Complete files of all successful applications were taken in to him with the recommendation that they be approved. At the vortex of selection, then, stood two or three very powerful men, some having civil service standing, some privately appointed. Their values were the major determinants of administrative ethics, if not practices, in the Colonial Empire. Recruitment for the C.S. was intuitive and elitist. There was no pre-service training worthy of the name. Even the kind of in-service training which cadets received in their first posts was more a process of conditioning under fire than training in any systematic sense.

This highly informal procedure was responsible for assembling an administrative corps that was by 1914 governing huge populations in vast tracts of nearly every major cultural area in the world. The service of each colony remained apart from the others. Colonial individuality was still enough to make real unity of the C.S. impossible and to relegate poorer dependencies to positions of continuous administrative inadequacy. The Gold Coast's cocoa-supported budget soon gave her civil service one of the best pay scales in Africa, a scale with which Sierra Leone, for example, could never compete. Nevertheless the C.S. as a whole was, inch by painful inch, becoming more respectable and more competent. After 1919 recruitment would again be aided by large numbers of demobilized officers available for immediate assignment. Once again dry years would follow the torrent. But as Britain and the colonies recovered from the economic slump of the early 1920's the C.S. stood on the threshold of its greatest era. Its numbers would increase apace; its duties would deepen in complexity, and it would begin to meet challenges that would have seemed fantastic to the pioneers who had founded the service a scant generation before.

CHAPTER II

Years of Construction

SINCE the beginning of the twentieth century, ministers and their permanent officials in the C.O. had concerned themselves with the disunity of the C.S. Striving for greater unification of the various services, even so powerful a secretary of state as Joseph Chamberlain had bowed to colonial autochthony. The establishment of the Tropical Services Committee had furthered the unity aim, however, as had the first feeble effort at a training scheme in 1909. According to their individual capacities, and sometimes in concert with one another, the colonies made their services as attractive as local revenue would allow. But the results of all this, wrote Sir Charles Jeffries with classic British understatement, "were not entirely satisfactory." [1] The prosperity of the mid-1920's tended to obscure the inadequacy of organizational machinery and methods by which the C.O. supplied the colonies with staff. As always in times of relative quiet, London tended to rest on the oars of tradition and to make do with anachronisms simply because no crisis of sufficient urgency had appeared to challenge them. Precedent, the prime enemy of dynamic administration, was too often and too long allowed to remain sacrosanct.

But if there was no crisis serious enough to bring change, still a cabinet minister of sufficient imagination and drive might occasionally effect it by sheer persuasiveness and persistence. In 1924 L. S. Amery, the second great colonial secretary of this century, came into office. Like Chamberlain, Amery had definite ideas about the Empire and regarded the C.O. as more than a stepping-stone to greater things.[2] With Furse and others in the C.O., both civil servants and politicians, Amery was an imperialist in the tradition of Lord Milner. He had not been a member of the famous "kindergarten," the brilliant group of young private secretaries with Milner during his long, difficult South African proconsulateship in the 1890's. But as Milner's junior colleague during the First War and as his under-secretary at the C.O. afterwards, Amery had drunk deep of the Milner brand of imperialism. He believed sincerely and strongly in the rightness of Britain's mission in the world, her cultural superiority, her civilizing destiny. His attitude was the antithesis of the self-consciousness, guilt, or indifference which has characterized the outlook on the Commonwealth of so many Englishmen in recent times. Amery was neither reactionary nor complacent. Though his Britishness sometimes carried him to absurd excesses, he knew better than most members of the ruling classes that Britain had work to do in the Colonial Empire and little time to do it in if widespread dislocation was to be forestalled.[3]

Although more of a practical politician than Lord Milner, Amery imbibed from his chief a view of politics which emphasized its moral foundations. Milner had said that the Empire would have to be preserved as a moral unity or it would not be worth preserving.[4] A mere power combination, whose individual units went their respective ways in matters of political philosophy and governmental forms, would have struck Milner as a sham. He did not insist on the acceptance by colonial populations of all things English. But if the ruling circles in the colonies, the emerging native elites, could subscribe to the great essences of English government as he saw them—a Platonic bestowal of power on those best qualified by intellect and morality, the rule of law, the independence of judiciary and civil service—then an empire so united could well afford a galaxy of individual cultural patterns beneath a uniform governmental spirit and structure.

Underlying this moral ideal Milner's unity would require a solid, practical foundation. Earlier than most, Milner saw that the separate units of the Colonial Empire would have to be brought into better contact with Britain and with each other so that the future strength of the whole would benefit from vigorous socio-economic development in each of the parts. "So far as the Colonial Empire was concerned," wrote Amery, "I inherited from Lord Milner the conviction that the twin keys to development were improved communications and research." [5] Two instruments designed to serve these policy aims were forged during Amery's stewardship at the C.O.: the first Colonial Development Fund and the Colonial Research Committee, later to do much valuable work under Lord Hailey's leadership.

In the literature of colonialism the question often arises, "Was the new emphasis on colonial development only a reflection of Britain's own economic difficulties and therefore merely the latest manifestation of imperialist exploitation?" [6] The old phase of exploration and establishment of spheres of influence had been bad enough, held some critics, but at least during that phase native populations had been left largely to themselves. "Would not economic development involve far more direct administration than before, with resulting social disruption among

peoples who had not even been consulted?" Amery was
a strong enough believer in the superiority of European
culture to consider the second question ridiculous. To
the first he gave the emphatic answer on many occasions
that economic development in areas which had lain fal-
low for centuries could not fail to benefit both Britain
and colonial peoples themselves, but particularly the
latter.

In point of fact such questions were to remain mostly
academic in many colonies during the 1920's. Amery's
plea that each colonial government contribute one-
quarter of one per cent of its annual budget to an empire marketing board for the benefit of all went unanswered. "Local particularism boggled at even this
modest sacrifice to the common welfare," he complained.[7]
Before 1914 Malaya had preferred to use its tin and rub-
ber revenue for the Royal Navy, and the Gold Coast, later,
had used its cocoa revenue for harbors and schools. No
more convincing proof could be provided that under the
British colonial system, as compared with the Belgian or
French for example, the metropolitan center could suggest
but did not dictate. As native representation in colonial
legislatures increased during the interwar period, the congenital autonomy of the colonies became all the more
pronounced. Development would come; but it would
proceed more according to each dependency's wishes
and capacity than to London's master plan of the moment. The fact that Englishmen were in charge in every
colonial capital did not alter this fundamental condition.

Thwarted temporarily in the economic sphere, Amery
approached the problem of colonial unity at the personal
level. Although, as he explained on the floor of the
House of Commons in 1925, "the character of the Service
in the Colonial Office and in the Colonial Service over-

seas is very different," he felt that members of the two services ought to be more familiar with each other's work and problems.[8] He succeeded in making willingness to serve abroad a condition of entry into those posts of the Home Civil Service which were part of the C.O.'s permanent organization.[9] Shortly afterwards the first C.O. staff members went out to colonies—Ceylon and Nigeria —on temporary assignments.[10] Amery hoped that one of the benefits of the new arrangement would be an increase of knowledge within the C.O. of matters which were not dealt with sufficiently in reports to London from colonial governments.[11] The secretary himself and the under-secretary also visited a number of colonies.[12]

But unquestionably the most significant organizational development tending in the direction of C.S. unity and increased concern for colonial as opposed to dominion affairs in London was the separation of the C.O. into two offices in 1925. Although Amery held both portfolios, the affairs of the Colonial Empire as such were now plainly considered important enough to require an entire department of state to coordinate the development of the individual colonies. As permanent under-secretary of the new and separate C.O., Amery appointed a colonial governor, Brig. Gen. Sir Samuel Wilson of Jamaica.[13] Exchanges of C.O. and C.S. officials were increased. The C.O. was reorganized both functionally and geographically, and specialists were appointed to advise the minister in such fields as economic and fiscal policy, medicine, education, agriculture, and fisheries.

With new organizational machinery provided for, Amery embarked in 1927 on an imperial tour, a global circuit which included visits to all of the dominions and many of the colonies. In most of the latter he was the first colonial secretary ever to set foot on their soil. The tour was a practical demonstration of Amery's new development policy, an opportunity for him to affirm in person his ideas about the more active role in imperial affairs which he wanted the colonies to play. In an era of war, economic instability, and social disintegration, the Minister sought to proclaim a new *Pax Britannica* and to challenge every imperial unit, large and independent, small and backward, to join in making the Empire a fit competitor of the United States and of Britain's rivals in Europe and the Far East. Indefatigable as always, Amery made hundreds of speeches and held private conversations with every statesman and community leader he could reach. His theme was unvarying: a united British Empire could lead the world and need fear no power. Unity, political and economic, was a panacea for all the individual ills then besetting the dominions and colonies, not to mention the United Kingdom itself.

Coming as it did only two years before the greatest depression in modern history, a catastrophe which was to promote economic nationalism of the most damaging sort, Amery's crusade appears tragic and ironic. Flying in the face of the contemporary world spirit, it was bound to fail. Yet it was pursued with intelligence, determination, and vigor. For the colonies, although independence was not what Amery had in mind, it was to contribute to processes of social, economic, and even political development which would facilitate gradual and comparatively painless transitions to self-government a generation later. With regard to the old dominions and India, there was little any British statesman could do beyond urging. But as he turned his attention to the Colonial Empire, Amery was more optimistic. If London could not always have its own way with the royal governors, at least they were all appointed by the C.O. and owed an allegiance to the Home Islands that portended more favorably for the cause of unity than did the growing independent-mindedness of the larger imperial units.

Accordingly Amery took the unprecedented step of calling a conference of the governors in London. The list of representatives—governors or senior officials—from the colonies was impressive. Such famous serving governors as Guggisberg of the Gold Coast, Cameron of Tanganyika, and Clifford, formerly of Nigeria and now of Ceylon, joined a distinguished group of higher C.O. officials and retired governors. Lugard was present and took an active part as chairman of one of the many committees. Amery himself, the driving force of the conference, attended most of the meetings, together with Ormsby-Gore (later Lord Harlech), his under-secretary, Sir Samuel Wilson, and a host of specialist advisors.

As the conference got under way in 1927, Major Furse found himself in a position, for the first time, to present to the heads of the services a review of his recruitment and training problems in the United Kingdom. Previously he had sought the governors' advice individually, usually in correspondence or during their visits to the C.O. But this was his first opportunity to discuss with them in committee the difficulties, methods, and plans of the C.O. selection office. Furse had prepared a long memorandum on recruitment and training which became the opening item on the conference agenda. In a gingerly and almost apologetic vein he began by noting that autochthony rightly resulted in special conditions of service in each colony.[14] On the other hand, the C.O. was compelled to take an over-all view of C.S. matters. In times when communications were still primitive, Furse remarked, it was understandable that each colonial government would concentrate on its own special problems without particular regard for other dependencies or for London. As the middle man, however, Furse himself had to keep pace with developments, especially economic and educational, which were characteristic of the United Kingdom at the time and which unavoidably affected his work.

Furse's memorandum contained an annex showing recruitment figures for the years 1913 and 1919–26 inclusive. These indicated an enormous rise in demand for staff immediately following the war and a virtual stoppage during the 1921–22 depression. Whereas demobilized officers had monopolized openings in the 1919–21 period, the great national universities of Oxford and Cambridge were by 1925 again supplying nearly all administrative candidates. The average annual intake for the postwar years was 411 in administrative and other services.

Quantitatively the record was satisfactory. But Furse was by no means satisfied that the C.S. was getting the quality it would need in order to serve Amery's imperial aims. Partly the fault lay in the image of empire then prevailing in the Home Islands. "There seems to be a lack of enterprise and a tendency to stay at home amongst the post-war generation," Furse wrote.[15] "This has been commented on at the Headmasters' Conference [*i.e.,* of the "Public Schools"] and elsewhere." The wave of national cynicism towards old values was one explanation. Public men who enlisted in the crusade for a new *Pax Britannica* in these years were accustomed to becoming thereby the butts of fashionable literary circles, of the educated young and of the socially disgruntled.[16] But Furse, in speaking of the postwar generation, did not refer to everyone in that age group. As always, his gaze fell on his own social class. "The kind of man who usually proves most fitted," he went on, "needs certain personal qualities and an educational background mainly to be found in the type of family which has been most severely hit by the war." [17]

Continuing to provide definitive comment on British social stratification, Furse then remarked that it was usually the younger sons of these families who went overseas. The assertion is massively documented in Philip Mason's volumes on the I.C.S.[18] The economic imperatives of primogeniture had long made it impossible for younger sons to stay at home and share in the management of family estates and businesses. They went out in droves to the military services, the various overseas civil services, the Foreign Service, overseas missionary work, and international commerce. This diaspora, which reached its height in the late nineteenth and early twentieth centuries, gave rise to John Bright's much-quoted description of the Empire as a "gigantic system of outdoor relief for the British middle classes." [19] Furse makes clear that the class criterion for participation in administration was rigid enough so that he appointed no one if the only available candidates lacked the desired qualities.[20] He even held to the rule in crisis times such as the immediate postwar years when colonial regimes were desperate for staff. Fortunately, the great bulk of the military candidates of those years qualified socially and educationally.

Heralding a time when the qualifications would weaken due to thinning out of numbers, Furse noted that the war had caused the deaths of over 30,000 officers, a disproportionate sacrifice by the civil service class. The war, increasing tax burdens, and the flow of wealth away from the land had by the 1920's sharpened the plight of Furse's class. Many could not afford to send their sons to university and so provide them with eligibility for the civil service positions without which they could no longer be accurately described as a "ruling" class. Worst of all, complained Furse, "business firms are far more alive than they used to be to the value of the type of man we

seek to attract." [21] If the younger son of a "county family"
would now be willing, for economic reasons, to go into a
business firm, and if the firm would take him, a mighty
blow would have been struck at the very roots of the
upper class ethic—the longstanding bias against "trade"
and people in it. To put the matter differently, if enough
members of the old governing families went into trade
and adopted the ethics of trade, then the British class
system would have been markedly changed from its nineteenth and early twentieth century form. The import of
Furse's memorandum was that this was precisely what
was happening.[22]

"It is men with the qualities of leadership whom we
especially need," Furse continued.[23] He was convinced
that such men came usually from certain families and
educational institutions. The assumption was so deeply
rooted in Furse's consciousness and in that of his listeners
that he saw no need to explain it. What is remarkable
is that he was willing to refer openly to a social assumption which was and usually still is avoided by those with
status, referred to self-consciously by those who wish to
rise socially and savagely by others who consider the subject and the phenomenon invidious. He did so, first, as
a means of underscoring the difficulty of his personnel
problems and, secondly, because he could count upon an
unquestioned acceptance of his rationale in the Governors' Conference. In the 1920's the subject of class could
be mentioned, especially *en famille,* if there was sufficient
reason to mention it. Later on, the class assumption and
even the subject itself would be treated with more reticence, except, of course, by social critics. Furse's second
important memorandum, written in the early 1940's,
avoids it altogether.

Having spoken of the difficulties of the ruling families
after 1918, Furse then observed that the return of pros-

perity since 1925 had improved matters. If Britons generally were still lamentably uninterested in the Empire he was nevertheless able to report that recruitment prospects had brightened. In a section of his memorandum frankly entitled "propaganda" he wrote that "full [sic] recruitment will not be secured until the prevailing ignorance with regard to the colonies . . . has been overcome," but that meanwhile his contacts at schools and universities were producing good material.[24] In the years 1925 and 1926 more than thirty men with first and second class honors degrees had applied and been accepted into the C.S. Over the long run, Furse felt, the problem of popular ignorance of the Colonial Empire would be dealt with through the publication of more and better literature on the colonies. For the time being he depended on lectures and informal discussions, especially in the universities, during which C.S. officials on leave in England would be able to speak informatively about life in the overseas dependencies. Typically, however, Furse echewed misrepresentation. The hard life in Africa and Asia must not be glossed over. Such advertising would be undignified and would redound to the disadvantage of the service in the long run. Early resignations by disillusioned men would help no one.

In a remarkably brave sally for a junior official, Furse asked that the main brunt of recruitment, or "missionary" work as he called it, be left to him alone. He preferred the quiet method of personal contacts to some more sensational technique such as putting notices in the press. The latter had been tried, he said, but had not yielded the desired results. (A colleague of Furse's has said that many of those who applied were simply wasting the interviewers' time and their own.[25]) It was far more satisfactory, though more cumbersome, to visit one's own friends in Public Schools, at Oxford and Cambridge and in country houses and clubs in London, and to propagandize for the service personally. Since Furse himself had no civil service status at this time, there was a certain logic in operating a recruitment system that was as informal as his own career position.

Furse described in some detail the steps he had taken since 1919 to attract recruits. Mindful of the strained circumstances of many families, he had seen to it that the better salaries recently provided by colonial governments were brought to the notice of headmasters and university dons. The old-style announcements which had been sent to university appointments committees in Chamberlain's time were improved and supplemented by letters and visits from Furse and his staff. Correspondence was maintained on a regular basis with over a hundred contacts in universities in Britain and the Dominions and with a similar number of Public School headmasters. As an example of the system whereby types of jobs were mated with types of candidates, Furse explained that 19-year-olds from certain Public Schools, many of them boys who could not afford to go on to university, were given commissions in West Indian and Far Eastern police forces.

As a means of conveying to the governors an impression of the complexity of his task, Furse dealt with the methods of his staff in the C.O. He was at some pains to show his hearers how difficult it was to provide a wide variety of colonies, and posts within colonies, with suitable staff from an equally varied number of educational institutions in Britain. Those who have observed how slowly official matters proceed today will appreciate Furse's time problem in an age when they moved even more slowly. Each application was given careful scrutiny and some were circulated to functional and geographical branches in the C.O., so that particular aspects of a candidate's record and qualifications could be evaluated by specialists. Still more time-consuming was lengthy correspondence with those listed as references who had special knowledge of the candidate as a person. Here Furse was on ground which his listeners well understood, whether their careers had been in civil service alone or in both civil and military service. Writing about the clearly demarcated and unquestioned class structure of England between the wars, a C.S. recruit of that era stresses the "complicated hierarchy of values" which pertained in all types of service to the Crown.

An officer in the British Army did not think of himself as being in the British Army, but in this or that Regiment, the social status of the Regiments ranging all the way from the Guards to the East Lancs. So too in the Colonial Service . . . men getting into Sierra Leone considered themselves superior to officers in the Gambia; officers in the Gold Coast considered themselves superior to those in Sierra Leone; officers in Nigeria considered themselves superior to those in the Gold Coast; and Northern Nigeria rated rather higher "socially" than Southern Nigeria. In the North officers had to keep horses and, in my day, were required to play Polo. This could become a foolish snobbery, but normally was harmless, rather like the pride of boys in their schools. It could even have some merit in giving a constructive pride in their Colonies to the officers serving in the bigger and more important Colonies like Nigeria.[26]

In practice the status preoccupation necessitated the writing of letters to teaching and administrative staff members in Public Schools and universities, to clergymen, friends of candidates' families, or to anyone who might know them and at the same time be known to and trusted by the C.O. Since many recommendations came from people not so known and trusted, the process of selection in a given case could involve a careful check of the referees as well as on the man himself. The elitist ethic aside, it is obvious that the system was workable in interwar England mainly because the land area and the ruling class were both small enough to permit it.

To further the necessary personal relationships Furse urged a number of carefully selected C.S. officials to continue visiting their old schools and colleges and propagandizing for the service while there. Here, too, his appeal found a natural response. Old Boy (alumni) loyalties in Britain have always been strong. Colonial civil servants often left their wives and families during leave time and spent a week or so in their old colleges, especially at Oxford or Cambridge. In the Senior Common Room and sitting around High Table after dinner, many a governor or district commissioner had done more for the service in an hour than the C.O. in months of correspondence. Over port and cigars, toasting their feet before fires that crackle in the novels of C. P. Snow, they spoke as no one else could speak of the challenges of Empire, of the hardships and satisfaction of life in the colonies, and of the duty and privilege the college had to send its sons out to rule the little-known colonial dependencies. Their visits often had a direct effect. Potential recruits among the undergraduates were introduced to C.S. men and encouraged to apply. The valuable long-term effect was to familiarize tutors and college administrators with the criteria of character and stamina which were wanted.

There was much talk in the Governors' Conference about the need for better men in both administrative and technical services. Furse insisted that this was not a reflection on past quality but an evidence of new conditions of life in the colonies. The growing emphasis on economic development would have been a weighty consideration by itself. It was now joined by the emergence of native leaders of a westernized, intellectual stamp, where formerly only tribal chiefs had confronted the service. Furse called for higher academic standards, but, characteristically, "without any relaxation of . . . insistence on those qualities of personality and character which are essential to the proper handling of natives." [27] Furse was willing to agree that changes might be necessary in the preparation of officials. But the basic criteria for selection would continue to be founded on the traditional cult of the gentleman.

In discussing needed improvements in staff, the conference gave a good deal of attention to the changing roles of administrative and technical personnel and their interrelationship. As colonial societies became less primitive their social services grew and with them the number of technicians, professionals, and specialists in a variety of fields. The history of the C.S. in the present century is a story of steady bureaucratizing of administrative work as a result of specialization in technical fields. In the old days the lonely district officer had been all things to his people—judge, tax collector, policeman, counsellor, road and bridge builder, even doctor. In most colonies in the 1920's specialists were beginning to undertake some of these duties. Where did the responsibility of the new D.O. begin and end? Who was in charge and in what situations? How much of each other's work did the administrator and the specialist have to know? Conference members were not in complete agreement on answers to these and other questions, but there was general agreement that administrators needed more and better training to perform their increasingly complicated tasks.

This agreement was significant in itself as an indication of changing attitudes towards training for overseas civil service. Most delegates to the Governors' Conference had had no training at all and had felt the need for none. The very idea of going to school to study such a subject as colonial rule was thought absurd. For generations, centuries in some places, young Englishmen had gone out to imperial dependencies untrained, except, in some cases, for grounding in a language. On arrival at their posts they sometimes took part in cram sessions to improve language facility and perhaps to prepare them for dealing with local legal procedures and the like.[28] Most went straight to work under an experienced administrator. They learned by watching superiors and by making mistakes. An old West Africa hand places great value on the latter method, which he calls "the technique of the controlled breakdown." [29] The process of mistake-making, that is, was watched by experienced officials and kept within safe limits. It was in this tradition that Milner's kindergarten was "trained." Clive, Hastings, Raffles, Frere, Lugard, and all the great figures of the past were similarly conditioned. As late as the 1940's a new D.O., arriving at his *boma* in Northern Rhodesia, was told that he would be given immediate substantial responsibility for the largest tribe in the colony, more than a quarter of a million souls. He protested that he had had no training and did not know what the work involved. "You'll find out presently," answered his D.O.[30] Within a few weeks he described himself as being quite at home and gaining daily in self-assurance.

The traditional attitude towards training is illustrated in the remarks of a Ceylon cadet of 1909. "Living in the Glencairn Chummery," he writes, "I learnt a lot from the 'shop' yarns of Southern, Galbraith, Seymour and such, and at dinner tables. But no one ever set out to train me. The Colonial Empire was run . . . by British Public School boys by the light of nature or of their Public

School 'education.' " [31] He went on to say that training was "all socially effected, at dinner tables or at clubs." [32] In discussions and correspondence with the writer, this retired official never fails to comment in bemused wonderment on the strange notion that training could possibly be concerned with anything except the right fork to use and how to drink heavily without showing the effects.

At the base of such attitudes lay the classic British view of politics as an art, which was to be learned by some inexplicable process of osmosis. It had no fixed principles beyond those which every well-bred young man already knew—honesty, devotion to duty, gentlemanly conduct, and a certain respectable amount of industry. Government was minimal in scope and fairly straightforward in content. Its techniques were susceptible of mastery through the regular and not very intense application of common sense. Medicine, surveying, law, or accounting could be taught. Not administration. The material of government, moreover, is people, and in this case foreigners. Because their work was among Orientals or Africans, the men of the C.S. who held this traditional view of politics did so in the conviction, conscious or not, that the masses were essentially inscrutable. Clearly, the only sensible course of action was to follow intuition. How could there be training for this?

Nevertheless, as we have seen, a short course of lectures was begun in London in 1909 for some of the cadets assigned to Africa. Although "rather sketchy," in Furse's phrase, and not given to all probationers, the lectures were a beginning.[33] After the war the plans of Lord Milner, and later Amery, for colonial development had resulted in markedly improved technical services in the colonies.[34] Shortly before his death Milner agreed, at Furse's urging, to chair a committee looking into ways of bringing about such improvements.[35] In 1924 Lord Lovat succeeded Milner as chairman and continued the task of building scientific services adequate to the new image of the Colonial Empire. It was the success of these efforts and not any abstract theory of administrative training which convinced Furse that new formal courses for administrative probationers would be needed. Administrators, that is, would have to be at the very least equal to the level of specialists or the morale and efficiency of the whole service would suffer. The Governors' Conference seconded, with intense conviction, Sir Hugh Clifford's "doctrine" that the administrator must continue to be *primus inter pares* in posts where there were both administrative and technical personnel. The alternative would be anarchy. To perform this function adequately administrators would need the respect of their technical colleagues, and this would not be given freely if the latter were vastly better trained than the former. Furthermore, a notion that government could be systematically analyzed and taught was gaining ground in the universities in concurrence with greater academic interest in the colonies.

Taken together with the second drying up of the stream of "war babies" available for administrative service and the coincident swing back to university candidates, these developments pointed to a more positive approach to training than heretofore. The influence of academic people and ideas should not be exaggerated. Politics was not widely viewed as a science. In the mid-twenties no one, least of all Furse, was thinking of highly scientific courses for C.S. probationers. The essentials were still to be imparted hand-to-mouth on the job. But an administrative course of some kind there would have to be.

During the early years of Amery's tenure at the C.O. Furse had evolved a close working relationship with Oxford and Cambridge, especially with their forestry and agriculture faculties respectively. Also his recruiting activities had broadened his contacts with dons working in other fields such as history and law. After much negotiation the two major universities agreed to the establishment of administrative courses for C.S. probationers, most of whom would be recent graduates. Furse was able to announce to the Governors' Conference that the first classes for probationers had begun in the previous fall, 1926.

An analysis of the course records makes it quite apparent that a desire to move more towards the concept of formal training and a concomitant desire to have something in the nature of permanent propaganda organizations at Oxford and Cambridge were the principal reasons for the founding of the special courses. At each university a Tropical African Service Committee was set up. At Oxford, Furse's own university, the committee consisted of the vice chancellor, the junior proctor (a university official), the head of one of the colleges, an ecology don, and a don whose special field of interest was colonial history. These were joined by Furse and another C.O. representative, both appointed by the secretary of state.[36] In practice the committees were vehicles of liaison between Furse and his friends in the Oxford and Cambridge faculties. Senior university officials seldom attend T.A.S. Course meetings. The principal function of early meetings was to decide what lectures already provided for in the standard university curriculum could be given at special times for C.S. probationers. The C.O. agreed to arrange payments of fees to lecturers corresponding to the extra amount of work involved. Initially the courses ran for two eight-week terms in order to provide for the two groups of probationers accepted into the C.S. in September and December, the selection dates being designed to appeal to recent graduates. Thus a final year undergraduate at Oxford could apply to the C.O. in the spring, take his "Schools" (final examinations for the B.A. degree) and join the course beginning in September or October. Others who had applied late or failed to make up their minds about a career until summer could be accepted by the C.O. in the fall and join the course in January. The cumbersomeness of running two identical courses led to the establishment of a single course at each of the two universities to run concurrently with the normal academic year.[37]

Course curricula provide insights into contemporary views of academic training for service abroad and the status of Oxford and Cambridge vis-à-vis other universities. "There are limits to what can be taught before a man reaches the colony," Furse told the governors, "and time must be given him to find his feet." [38] A cadet's real training, that is, would begin only when he had reached his post, as always. The function of academic courses was to provide a theoretical introduction to colonial government. This tended to be viewed more favorably by secretariat officials than D.O.'s working in rural areas, the latter finding lectures far removed from administrative routine among still primitive peoples.[39] Technical subjects, such as tropical medicine and accounting, were left to the Imperial Institute in London. At Oxford and Cambridge the curriculum consisted of African languages, law, anthropology, agriculture, forestry, and "British Rule in Africa." As Furse commented to the governors, the syllabus was similar to the 1909 version but put greater emphasis on colonial history and anthropology.

The new stress on anthropology reflected the influence of such giants in the field as Professor Malinowski and Captain R. S. Rattray. Rattray, for example, must be credited substantially for the decision of the Gold Coast Government to turn away from purely British forms of rural administration towards greater reliance upon native

authorities inspired by indigenous cultural forms.[40] Prior
to the 1920's most colonial governments had not really
resolved the dilemma of whether to promote westerniza-
tion or traditionalism. Rather they had, mainly by default,
left the decision to native peoples. As the new Oxford
and Cambridge courses began, however, there was a
feeling that colonial governments ought to be more positive about this and that the responsible thing to do was
to build on the existing native base. To this end C.S.
probationers were given an introduction to anthropological principles and encouraged to experiment for themselves in learning about native institutions on arrival in
their colonies.

Professor (later Sir Reginald) Coupland's lectures on
colonial history were meant to give probationers a historical perspective on their future work. He was assisted
by K. N. Bell, the Beit Lecturer in Colonial History and
a member of the T.A.S. committee. It was hoped that
exposure to the sophisticated outlook of such scholars
would help to counteract anti-imperialistic trends in the
England of the time and arm recruits with an appreciation of their country's achievements abroad. No previous
attempt had been made in this direction because there
had seemed to be no need for it. The British have been
less self-conscious about their empire, generally speaking,
than any of the major colonial powers. Occasionally poets,
zealots in Parliament and elsewhere, and career impe-
rializers had attempted to rationalize, defend, or exhort.
But it was not until attacks on the idea of colonialism
became frequent and dangerous, both inside and outside
Britain, that it was thought necessary to reassure colonial
officials themselves. That some of them did in fact feel
need of reassurance is indicated in the testimony of a
retired civil servant writing of his experiences in Ceylon
and Burma in the 1920's: "We were not consciously

actuated, as far as I ever knew, by any design, destiny or dedication. We were of course habituated to a slanderous press [in England] and virulent attacks in the [Ceylonese] Legislature, but we ignored the former and knew that the latter was largely window-dressing. But after a hard day, it was often bitter to be sniped in the back by one's own people at home, to whom England was always in the wrong, and to whom lies and verification of facts were all one mess-up." [41]

Furse, Sir Charles Jeffries, and other C.O. careerists had always believed that the C.S. would only be as good as its faith in itself and in what it was in existence to do. Without a sense of mission the service would be only another place of employment and source of income. The lectures of Coupland, Harlow, Bell, and later Perham were not meant to instill a national superiority ethos or mystique. But it was seen that the era of absent-minded imperialism was over. The 1920's were a time of questioning. Either one asked the questions himself and came up with convincing answers or others would ask and perhaps arrive at explanations less suited to Britain's purposes. "In my day," wrote an official who retired in 1938, "we had not all forgotten Aristotle. I was continually asking, 'what is the end or object of this endeavor?' But no one could or would give me an answer." [42] The T.A.S. course could not give clearly formulated answers such as those received by overseas administrative recruits on the Continent or by certain American government employees in the 1950's.[43] But it sought to stimulate thinking among probationers by reviewing the colonial record and setting out contemporary problems. After cadets had had a few years' experience in colonies, it was hoped, they would reach their own conclusions about why they were exercising power in a foreign land.

It has been pointed out that the T.A.S. committees at

Oxford and Cambridge were not so significant from the standpoint of systematic, European-style training as from that of C.O.-university liaison. As the Oxford committee met for the first time Furse could not fail to be encouraged by his university's response to C.S. needs. The combination of government funds and university resources in research findings and a theoretical background for C.S. experience was a potent one. London-Oxbridge cooperation, and particularly London-Oxford cooperation, was not new. If it was not quite true that England was run from All Souls (the Oxford equivalent, roughly, of the Institute for Advanced Study) the intimate relations between Whitehall and Oxford were perhaps more remarkable than comparable political-educational relations anywhere else in the West. Milner and Amery had been Fellows of All Souls. So had T. E. Lawrence, the man who presented the C.O. with new responsibilities in the Middle East after 1918. If one reviews secondary positions in both the capital and Oxford at a given time the list of distinguished men with a foot in both camps will be long and impressive.

Yet the T.A.S. committees were innovations in one respect. Recruiting for the other overseas services of the Crown had not resulted in the setting up of permanent C.O.-university committees. Entry into the I.C.S. and the Eastern Cadetship services was via the same Burlington Gardens examinations taken for the Home Civil Service. The Sudan Service recruited by interview and the Foreign Service by a combination of interview and examination. Although access to the other services was in fact governed by the same elitist rationale as that of the C.S., none of them had gone so far as to formalize its interdependence with the major universities. Only the C.S., as of 1926, had permanent joint training committees at Oxford and Cambridge.

The recruitment results were exactly what Furse had had in mind when he first raised the question of moving the C.S. training courses to Oxford and Cambridge. In 1926 the number of administrative probationers selected for the C.S. was 107.[44] Of these, 71 were from universities, the rest coming from African military units, from other types of colonial services such as public works, from Public Schools, and via local promotion in colonies. Fifty-four of the 71 were from Oxford and Cambridge. In 1927 Oxbridge accounted for 79 out of 83 university appointments; in 1928 the figure was 84 out of 88, and in 1929 it was 73 out of 89. By the 1930's, recruitment from non-university sources had ceased. In 1937, a typical year, Oxbridge provided 123 out of a total of 157 administrative appointments to the C.S. as a whole.[45] Oxford and Cambridge had in fact the kind of monopoly that can well afford an annual handful of recruits from other universities.

Recruitment has always been a C.O. responsibility, not one to which colonial governments ever made significant contributions by way of suggestion or demand. However, Furse made every effort to involve the governments by consulting officials on leave and through correspondence. At the 1927 conference he asked the governors to keep him supplied with efficiency reports on administrators in their early years so that recruitment criteria and training courses might benefit from appraisal of field experience.[46] Governments would help themselves to improve the efficiency of their services, Furse said, if they gave him maximum advance notice of staff needs. He could relay this information to educational institutions and direct to potential recruits themselves or to their families. Failure to provide such notice had often caused good potential candidates to be lost to the service, either through the encouragement of hopes which later proved false or through simple lack of information until too late. His discomfort as a middleman is apparent in Furse's memorandum. But his full appreciation of the governors' power to cooperate with or ignore the C.O. is also evident in the tone and phrasing of his remarks and suggestions. At times the conference almost takes on the quality of a conclave of independent sovereigns.

Generally speaking the governors were satisfied with Furse's recruitment performance.[47] Lacking facilities, time and money, they were content to leave selection and training to the C.O. Their main concern in the realm of personnel problems was to promote more continuity in administration by reducing staff turnover. Up until the 1920's all colonial governments in the tropics had suffered alike from losses of staff due to illness, dissatisfaction of various kinds and, especially in earlier years, a mortality rate higher than that of the other overseas services.[48] The surprising aspect of the problem is its persistence. A writer commenting on staff turnover in Sierra Leone during the nineteenth century cites phenomena mentioned by another author dealing with Nigeria in the 1930's: bad climate, poor food, low pay and the generally damaging effect on morale of having to be without wives and families for long periods.[49] By contrast relatively better results in India and the Sudan are attributed by historians of their administrative services to higher degrees of continuity based on better conditions of service life.[50] Improvements in medical services and in pay scales, Furse noted, would have immediate consequences for the better. Furse's recruitment work would be helped, and colonial governments would benefit from infusions of better men who would be willing to spend a whole 25–30 year career in their service.

Turning to the perennial bug-bear of disunity, the conference observed that interest in the Eastern Cadetship services of Ceylon, Malaya and Hongkong had declined relative to Africa, a reversal of the usual pattern. The trend was disturbing enough to prompt a question in the House of Commons, which had seldom taken any particular interest in the C.S.[51] As the under-secretary of state said a year later, this development was due in part to competition from commercial firms but more importantly to the fact that leaves were more frequent in Africa and that candidates for Southeast Asia still had to pass civil service examinations.[52] To some graduates fresh from "Schools" the thought of another examination was unbearable. Prestige notwithstanding, Africa without an examination was preferable to Malaya with one. To Furse the interview system of selection was in any case preferable to examinations. Therefore he welcomed the decision of the Governors' Conference to recommend standardizing the entry system for the whole C.S. As an opening wedge the C.O. was asked to send the governor of the Straits Settlements (Malaya) an inquiry whether he would be willing to end the examinations for his services.

Also involved in wider questions of C.S. disunity was the matter of exchanges and transfers between colonies. "Transfers of officers seem to be opportunistic rather than systematic," the conference reported.[53] Three aspects of the problem are especially noteworthy. In the first place senior officers were available for transfer and promotion to another colony when no higher post was open to them locally. Such transfers had in fact occurred often enough to jeopardize continuity.[54] A former member of Furse's staff remembers that good men were transferred to trouble spots whether or not their colonies could spare them, which they usually could not do without straining their whole administrations.[55] This "crisis system" of postings left the lesser colonies in a more or less permanent state of inferior staffing. Secondly, junior officers (usually D.O.'s in rural districts) were subject to such frequent transfer, especially in larger colonies such as Nigeria, that they had to leave their posts before they had been able to become really familiar with their problems.[56] Yet, thirdly, most officers remained in a single colony throughout their whole careers and thus often became somewhat stale towards mid-career. A truly unified C.S. could have avoided this by providing for transfers often enough to freshen individuals' outlooks but not so often as to imperil continuity. To be specific, if an officer served five years, broken by leaves, in a single post he would become well enough versed in its problems to make a significant contribution towards their solution. And if, after his five-year tour, he were transferred to another colony altogether, both he and his two colonies would benefit from the change. As matters stood, in any case, the two kinds of transfers seriously hampered continuity of administration: inter-colonial transfers, usually of higher-level people, were a nuisance, in Furse's view, but only to the colonies losing the men; intra-colonial transfers, secondly, were far too frequent and constituted a major detriment to administrative efficiency in most colonies.[57]

Separate pay scales and retirement schemes had always prevented the implementation of such a policy on a truly imperial level, however. The French had employed the plan in their dependencies, as had some of the other continental powers. Yet Britain's commitment to colonial autochthony was strong enough to keep her administrative services distinct from one another, except at the highest levels, throughout the entire interwar period and afterwards. The only real unity in the C.S. was the common ground of class and educational background, contributing as it did to similarity in attitude and response. "We were all used to the same drill," writes an old Burma hand, "the same secretariat system, the same ritual at Government House, the same service structure, and largely the same problems of education, agriculture and all the many facets of native life." [58] In other respects the conference had to content itself with some progress towards unity in the scientific services and a more equitable adjustment of pensions for senior officers, mainly governors, whose service had been in more than one colony. In discussing the latter, interestingly enough, the American experience with federalism was cited as a precedent.[59]

The conference also addressed itself to the problem of the rising welfare state as it affected relations between administrative and technical officers. The doctrine that administrators should remain first among equals has been referred to above. It is not surprising that a gathering in which administrators were in a majority should endorse that principle. Furse felt that better relations between the two types of officers could be enhanced if they attended training courses together as probationers. The administrator's duty, it was thought, was to come into such close and continuing contact with the local people that he would develop a working grasp of native mentality and custom. Technical officers on the other hand would be concerned as always with their own special projects. In order for the whole governmental machine to work smoothly the administrative generalist would have to judge in concrete circumstances whether proposed specialist activities would fit the social framework and if so how innovations could be brought about most easily. A revolt had broken out among Hindu villagers in Malaya because a veterinarian had inoculated cows without checking first with the D.O. Efficient liaison between generalists and specialists, ideally, would prevent such incidents.

Given general agreement that liaison was desirable, the problem was one of how to promote it. The question was "exercising all Colonial Administrations" in the 1920's.[60] The governor of the Gold Coast was persuaded that liaison would be truly efficient only if authority throughout each colony was decentralized so that each D.O. had a maximum of latitude in facing difficulties as they arose. But, was a specialist to take all his orders from the local D.O.? If so, what was his relationship to his own departmental head in the secretariat? Would D.O.'s be less arbitrary if compelled to submit detailed reports on all actions taken with respect to technical projects? And if this paperwork was done adequately would they have time to come to know their people well enough to perform the prime administrative function of paternalism?

These questions, which the conference could discuss but not answer finally and definitively, were added to by others concerning the D.O.'s urban colleague, the bureaucrat or "secretariat walla" in the capital. The conference was keenly interested in questions on legislative council procedures. In more politically advanced colonies, such as Jamaica and Ceylon, native representation in legislatures was increasing. Administrators nurtured in the authoritarian tradition of colonial government, a tradition necessitated by the early disinclination of natives to take part in their own government, sometimes found difficulties in adjusting to democratic trends. Here again, the anthropological question arose, "Who shall represent native peoples, the traditional up-country chief, or the anti-traditional 'intellectual' of the coastal town?" And, "How are local peoples to be protected from potential or actual abuses at the hands of either or both?"

In the 1920's colonial officials could still discuss such questions as though the choice of alternatives lay with them. In most colonies this was still largely true. But the winds of change were gathering force in parts of the Colonial Empire, and the day was dawning when discussion and decision would decend into the hot arena of practical politics.

The 1927 Governors' Conference had provided a forum for a general review of conditions in the C.S. and an airing of opinion about changes and improvements. Furse had taken good advantage of a unique opportunity to educate senior administrators on the arduous process by which their staffs were selected and prepared for duty. His memorandum and the new courses at Oxford and Cambridge were practical evidence that the C.O. meant to move towards realization of Amery's plans for a stronger and more unified colonial empire. Training arrangements in particular were as well advanced as could be expected, given the antipathy of senior officials to theoretical training and the limited funds available for course work prior to assignment in colonies. Recruitment, however, was still pursued much as it had been in Joseph Chamberlain's day. Furse was still only a private secretary to the minister and dismissable at any incumbent's whim. His staff in 1927 consisted of only four men, patronage appointees like himself.[61] In 1928 Dr. (later Sir Drummond) Shiels, soon to become an under-secretary of state in the second MacDonald government, remarked in Parliament, "The whole question of recruitment for the Colonial Services [*sic*] is a matter which requires attention." [62] Amery did not need the prod. Placing Furse's work on a more normal civil service basis had been on his mind ever since the Dominions and Colonial Offices had become separated.[63] One of his last acts before leaving office in 1929 was to appoint a committee to review means of effecting this. The committee, chaired by Sir Warren Fisher, Permanent Secretary to the Treasury and head of the Home Civil Service, had the following terms of reference:

. . . to consider the existing system of appointment in the Colonial Office and in the public service of the Dependencies not possessing responsible government, and to make such recommendations as may be considered desirable. [64]

CHAPTER III

Brief Limelight

THE deliberations of the Fisher Committee occupied a full year, beginning in April of 1929. Because a general election took place while the committee was meeting, resulting in the replacement of a Conservative government by a Labour one, it might be expected that this examination of civil service access would have become involved in party politics and an ideological split between Right and Left in Britain. The fact that the new colonial secretary was Lord Passfield (Sidney Webb), one of the best known socialist theorists of the day, might seem to have supported such an expectation. Yet, as we have seen, the appointment of the Fisher Committee was only a logical further step in advancing C.O. plans for strengthening the Colonial Empire. The advent of a Labour ministry in 1923 had not affected those plans, nor would it do so in 1929. Amery had been less than completely satisfied with the response of colonial governments to recommendations for unification of the technical services put forth by the Lovat Committee in the 1927 conference. His avowed aim in appointing the Fisher Committee was to "get the problem [of C.S. unity] tackled on a wider front." [1] Would C.S. prestige not be enhanced, Amery asked Parliament, if it could be combined with the staff of the C.O. itself? [2] If this could be done, which system of entry, examination or interview, should be retained to recruit the united service?

In asking the Fisher Committee to examine such questions, was Amery placing the system of patronage in the public dock? To Furse the prospect looked ominous enough to make him wonder whether the committee would not ruin everything he stood for. "We cannot escape the conclusion," they noted, "that if seriously challenged, such a system could not in theory be defended." [3] Furse's methods seemed to be facing indictment on both moral and practical grounds.

"The Colonial Empire has become a problem of the first magnitude," observed the Fisher Committee, "both on the quantitative and the qualitative side. Its geographical area has been largely extended, its wealth is advancing every year, and the duties of government have been increased in number and immeasurably increased in complexity." [4] New conditions in the colonies required a new type of administrator with "special attainments . . . not previously to be found in Colonial service." [5] In its less than specific delineation of the desired attainments the committee carefully abjured any criticism of Furse, his criteria, and his system. In fact they denied that a more objective or scientific system could be devised. Holding that administrative requirements were not as easily described as professional and technical ones, they maintained that "the special needs (of the administrator) are a liberal education, a just and flexible mind, common sense and a high character, and there is no calculus by which these endowments can be accurately assessed." [6] Taking its stand in this way firmly on traditional ground, the committee made clear at once that it would not see the character of the service altered so much as it would see it strengthened in numbers and capacity.

Borrowing a leaf from Amery's book, the committee outlined Britain's political and economic aims in the colonies. She must seek to preserve what was best in indigenous cultures and at the same time "bring to bear the latest results of scientific research on the development of wealth." [7] The moral imperatives of Lugard's Dual Mandate were readily seen in the condition of colonial government at the time. Vast populations in primitive settings depended for their welfare on the judgment and character of small numbers of officials spread thinly over tremendous expanses of territory. If Britain was to fulfill her trust these officials would have to be the best available, and the selection system was therefore a key element in colonial policy.

But what constituted the best? Today most Englishmen would doubtless answer by citing such criteria as university degrees or some kind of testable intellectual potential.[8] In 1929 the first criterion—class—was so taken for granted that it was not mentioned at all. In their praise of Furse's work the committee made clear that they agreed with the views of a secretary of state a few years earlier: "The code which must guide the administrator in the tropics is to be found in no book of regulations. It demands that in every circumstance and under all conditions he shall act in accordance with the traditions of an English gentleman." [9] The British D.O., standing apart from his people and above them, was to be their protector and not, as in French colonies, a confrere and purveyor of superior culture. To the Fisher Committee as to Furse himself it seemed that the necessary qualities would be difficult if not impossible to identify by methods other than those used by Furse.

However, the committee also understood that future recruitment would have to keep in mind the increasing intricacy of colonial administration. "The whole trend," as a C.O. official put it, was away "from the simple and primitive towards the civilized and complex." [10] Economic and financial planning was replacing the old secretariat function of straightforward accountancy. With worldwide communications improving and metropolitan governments moving towards the welfare state and the positive state, colonial regimes would inevitably turn away from caretaker government, whether or not there was protest from below. In the future the C.S. would have to enlist men who could undertake specialist planning in secretariats and also men who would be able to supervise implementation of such plans in rural districts.

The problem of wedding traditional recruitment criteria and new political tasks may be seen in C.O. memoranda prepared shortly after the Fisher Committee issued its report. "The normal field of recruitment for the higher financial staff must inevitably be the Colonial Administrative Service." [11] Many recruits did not find themselves overly attracted to the paraphernalia of materialism, such as bookkeeping. In addition to financial work the new secretariat type was being exposed in the early 1930's to the projects of the expanding technical departments. Education, land reclamation, agricultural experimentation, public works, animal husbandry, and forestry all demanded coordination, which in turn demanded efficient liaison between administrative and technical officers. As has been noted, the Governors' Conference had already discussed this thorny issue. The Fisher Committee heard new evidence of misunderstandings and working at cross-purposes in the colonies. And the C.O. was given another opportunity of explaining the methods by which proposed remedies were being tried out. Administrative and technical probationers were being trained together in England, and administrators were receiving temporary assignments in technical departments of secretariats in the field.[12]

Nevertheless, the Fisher Committee was told, the C.S. was still predominantly occupied with traditional D.O. work in rural districts. Out of a total administrative force of approximately 1,500, fully two-thirds were engaged more or less permanently in this type of career activity.[13] Even when he rose to be a provincial commissioner the typical official tended to retain an outlook more closely attuned to that of his D.O.'s than to that of secretariat officials in the capital. He knew local languages. He still went on trek into remote areas peopled by primitive tribes. He could not help being suspicious of far-off desk officials whose constant demands for detailed reports ate into time available for his main concern—the welfare of his people. Most secretariat officials spent little time in districts and were marked early in their careers for rapid advancement through the higher echelons of staff positions leading to a governorship. They saw service in more than one colony. Their daily rounds included long hours spent on legal analysis and report compilation. As they rose in rank they became members of executive councils and had to participate in legislative council debates with a very different kind of native than the D.O. knew. Under the circumstances it is not surprising that the two types of colonial civil servants, although both were members of the administrative service, were often as far apart in outlook as were many administrative and technical officers assigned to the same post. To the D.O., sweating in his rural *boma,* the secretariat walla might appear to be a pernicious character, consumed with unworthy ambitions, a mere climber, divorced from all that was noble in the service tradition.[14] The secretariat official, for his part, often saw the D.O. as an unimaginative plodder, so preoccupied with local affairs that he was blind to the wider perspectives of colonial policy.[15] Tact and tolerance kept the two working together. But they lived out their careers in different worlds.

The D.O., annoyed at having to give increasing amounts of time to correspondence with the secretariat and to liaison with technical officers in his district, found that a new function—the training of native staff—was also time-consuming. Indirect rule was still the official rationale of district administration in most colonies. But a practical result of the political and economic objectives mentioned by the Fisher Committee was more recruitment of local people for clerical work. At first it was not fully realized in Britain that economic development implied an educative (in this case Europeanizing) function which would defeat the aim of strengthening traditional authorities. The most able and enterprising native clerks preferred working for D.O.'s or, better still, securing a position in urban centers, to serving a local chief. By employing large numbers of these bright young men the C.S. was inadvertently contributing to the decline of chiefly prestige. At the same time encouragement and experience was being given to a growing indigenous bureaucracy which would some day seek to replace both the native chiefs and the colonial power.

Mindful of the rise of this new force, the Fisher Committee addressed itself to the terms by which native officers served. Would they be transferable to other colonies as in the French dependencies? Would they qualify for Oxford and Cambridge courses? There is no sure evidence in the Fisher Report, however, that the full import of rising native participation in government was appreciated. Full self-rule and even secession from the Commonwealth was not in people's minds in the London of 1930. From the vantage point of the 1950's it has sometimes been assumed that public pronouncements by British leaders—some of them going all the way back to the mid-nineteenth century—did reflect a conscious and historically consistent policy towards that end.[16] But visionary statements in England and pick-and-shovel realities of colonial administration have seldom appeared in perfect harmony. Working officials in the field, the eyes, ears, and hands of policy, were sometimes conscious of a duty of trust. The majority did not see themselves, any more than the Fisher Committee saw them, as instruments of colonial dissolution. On the contrary the rising prestige of the C.S. in Public Schools and universities was strong evidence that the service was thought to be facing a long and spectacular future.

The recommendations of the Fisher Committee were not radical nor its findings damaging to Furse's system. Given the membership of the committee this was only to be expected.[17] Sir Warren Fisher, as permanent secretary of the treasury, was a well-known public figure. He was joined on the committee by another member of the civil service commission, R. S. Meiklejohn. Both major political parties were represented by members of Parliament, the Conservatives by John Buchan (later Lord Tweedsmuir) and Sir Robert Hamilton, and Labour by Dr. (later Sir Drummond) Shiels who, when he became under-secretary of state, was replaced by A. G. Church. Sir Samuel Wilson represented the C.O. The C.S. was represented by Sir Hesketh Bell, a former governor, and Mr. (later Sir George) Tomlinson, formerly of the Nigerian Service. Sir Russell Scott of the Treasury represented that awesome body. Committee members from the educational world were Dr. Cyril Norwood, Headmaster of Amery's old school, Harrow, Professor Sir John Farmer of the Imperial College of Science and Technology in London, Sir Walter Buchanan-

Riddell, Principal of Hertford College, Oxford, and recently chairman of the Ceylon University Committee, and H. A. Roberts of the Cambridge University Appointments Board. The committee's secretary was G. E. L. Gent of the C.O., a member of the T.A.S. committee at Oxford.

"I believe," Amery remarked to a House of Commons committee, "that [the Fisher Committee] with its very wide range of interests and of experience ought to be able to give us a very valuable and helpful report." [18]

Amery's hopes for a common system of appointment for both the C.S. and the C.O. were soon dashed. The committee noted the profoundly different work patterns involved and declined to recommend changes in either system of entry. They had in mind the similarity of C.O. duties to those in other Whitehall departments. C.O. officials were bureaucrats who could without undue difficulty exchange places with those in another department in London. As to the C.S., its recruitment system was seen to be based on the needs of colonial administration. If it was indefensible in theory it was also workable and, indeed, admirable in practice. This was not the first time that the majesty of examination systems had been slighted by inference. In 1906, in, of all places, the Oxford magazine supplement on the civil service competition of that year, there was a tongue-in-cheek reference to the rationale of examinations: "It is . . . for the examiners to say [whether] . . . it is possible to obtain good rulers by means of a competitive examination. . . . A study of the marks does not seem to tell one anything." [19] In 1928 the under-secretary of state, returning from a visit to the Southeast Asian colonies, had uncomplimentary things to say about the apparent results of examination entry to those services. He wrote that the system seemed to attract "those who have specialized in classics or pure mathe-

matics . . . [resulting in] the accumulation of an imposing array of miscellaneous uncoordinated information,
none of it complete or profound, about a large number of
subjects." [20] Ability at memorizing and love of words for
their own sake, he felt, were not appropriate to administration, yet these were the attributes of the typical examination walla. The under-secretary observed that officials
in Malaya were less in touch with wider colonial developments and with events in England than were their colleagues in Africa. The latter had been selected by Furse's
interview system.

In recommending that Furse's system be retained, the
Fisher Committee based their decision on testimony elic-
ited from serving members of the C.S.[21] Agreeing whole-
heartedly, the 1930 Governors' Conference deprecated
"any extension of the system of entrance by examination." [22] A glance at the list of officials testifying before
the Committee renders their decision understandable. In
addition to Amery and Lord Passfield there were nine
governors, seventeen members of the C.S., eleven C.O.
officials and representatives of the Crown Agents, other
government departments, and the academic profession.
Major Furse also testified. C.S. officials were persuaded
by experience that the character and personality of administrators were more important, assuming adequate intelligence, than ability to be clever on an examination
paper. Even Passfield, a lifelong exponent of rationaliz-
ing civil service procedures and a congenital enemy of
privilege, agreed. He told one of his permanent staff
members in the C.O. that, although he thought that the
examination was a fair test of certain qualities, his support for it "does not extend to those at the bottom of the
list," a reference to the fact that the Eastern Cadetship
services took mainly those passing lowest in the civil service examinations.[23]

The Fisher Committee thought that a better way to serve the aim of unity was to promote more regularized exchanges between London and colonial staffs.[24] They recommended that such exchanges be increased to the point where no C.O. regional desk officer lacked on-the-spot experience in the area his office was concerned with.

A professor in an English provincial university argues that if Furse's selection procedures were well designed and better able to determine whether applicants had qualifications appropriate to colonial administration than were written examinations, the system was nevertheless biased in favor of the upper classes. He quotes Sir Warren Fisher's sentiment that the class bias charge is irrelevant: "When I am looking at a fellow, really I am not concerned with what his father was: I am concerned with what he is." [25] Opponents of the class system, while they do not question Sir Warren's sincerity, point out that those who were able to try for civil service positions were overwhelmingly from the ruling class. The educational system in England made this inevitable. In any case the Fisher Committee's only comment on Furse's method and office structure in this regard was that every effort ought to be made to "search the widest field for the best candidates." [26] Not only did they go out of their way to praise Furse, but they made specific their agreement with him that "the widest field" did not extend beyond the best schools and universities as defined by Furse.[27] They believed that the Oxford and Cambridge monopoly of C.S. positions was justified by their long tradition of overseas service, the spirit of which was lacking in provincial and Irish universities. The dictum that "favoritism is the secret of efficiency" would have struck none of the Fisher Committee members as outrageous.[28] The class from which to draw recruits for colonial service was that which had experience-conditioned attitudes appropriate to responsible paternalism. To do otherwise would have been wrong and wasteful.

In a larger and less stratified society than England's in the interwar years the personalities of individual bureaucrats would count for less than they did in the C.O. Procedures would be more susceptible of objective description as parts of a rational organizational code and structure. But, in Lord Hailey's words, "The reality of political relations is not (always) fully expressed in the constitutional form they assume." [29] Both before and after implementation of the Fisher recommendations C.S. recruitment was explainable first and foremost by the personality of one man.

Ralph Dolignan Furse, K.C.M.G., D.S.O., D.C.L., was born in 1887 of a county family in Devon.[30] Although he spent some forty years in London and in travels abroad, Furse lives today at Halsdon, his Devon estate, and goes to the City only occasionally. Country life, country virtues, and country people are his ultimate realities. Just as Devon and neighboring Cornwall have escaped much of the urbanization and modernization which have brought such marked changes to English life elsewhere, so Furse himself remains today very largely an unreconstructed Victorian country gentleman. His convictions about people, society, and politics are simple, straightforward, and unshakable. His speech tends to kindly dogmatism about human nature, about right and wrong, and about obvious needs and possibilities. He is not intolerant. On the contrary, he is the readiest of men to listen to opposing views and to face the facts of change. An innate modesty and awareness of his own limitations shine forth in all his descriptions of the role he has played in great events of the past. Yet there is a refreshing certainty and firmness about his basic views which strike an unfamiliar, old-fashioned note in these days of moral fluidity and questioning.

Furse is essentially an optimist and a humanist. His favorable view of human nature goes hand in hand with an unswervingly aristocratic bias in social and political arrangements. Discipline contributes to order. Directions must be given by some and accepted by others or chaos will result. And chaos can only give way to the worst sort of tyranny. Furse would be the last to favor the kind of aristocracy in which heredity is everything and no one can move up the scale. Neither does he believe that the existing stratification should be ignored. Talent will out. Those with ability will advance according to their lights, although it may require a generation or two to reach positions of privilege and prestige. In the meantime those who have been born to privilege will be better able to serve in positions of responsibility because their birth and breeding provide the indispensable ruling attitudes. Furse would completely agree with a retired colonial administrator who writes, "Power was expected to breed tyranny and corruption. . . . I suppose that judgments in such affairs are based on a low view of human nature." [31] Furse was interested in certain families, schools, and universities because he believed that by passing through the kinds of conditioning they provided a man would acquire the needed sense of responsibility. His view of civil service requirements was moral, not scientific.

If there was a religious aspect to Furse's operating ethic, it tended to be institutional rather than theoretical. In England the established church is joined to the Crown in the person of the Sovereign and the orders of chivalry have religious homes and services. A belief in common decency and in the duty of service, however, is more essential to Furse's make-up than is any conventional religiosity. Characteristically, he remarks that Plato has been one of the main influences in his "religious life."

Referring to the fact that Lady Furse runs Halsdon today without domestic help and that he finds it difficult to maintain the place, Furse remarked recently that nevertheless he will "not be the one to haul down the flag." The attitude is characteristic. The world of his youth is gone. It was a comfortable and serene world for the Furses and their kind, one which found the squire in the manor, the younger sons off serving the Crown and the Church, the vicar on his rounds, and the tenantry in their cottages. The disappearance of most of this atmosphere does not daunt Furse. He holds to the old attitudes even though their institutional framework has evaporated. In view of Furse's own spiritual tenacity it becomes more understandable that a later head of the C.O. recruitment office was able to speak of a completely unchanged set of recruitment criteria throughout all of Furse's years and down to 1960.[32]

While at university Furse visited Ceylon. The experience of seeing British rule close up in one of the major colonies made an indelible impression. The trusteeship duty struck his youthful mind as forming the natural counterpart to the obligations of squires to tenants in England. This view was fortified by five years at Eton, the unique Public School which all others still seek to emulate. Eton's class orientation is unmistakable to even the casual observer. Wall plaques to the school's dead in many wars do not refer, as in American private schools, to "the sons of the school," but to "our brother officers." Just as in Christ Church, Oxford, it is assumed that no Old Boy would have been anything but an officer. The ethos of command thus followed Furse through adolescent years and into the university.

At Oxford Furse was a member of Balliol College

where Milner's incredible scholarship is still a legend. He did not do well academically, taking a third class honors degree in Humane Letters. But he imbibed the spirit of Oxford and formed the impression, so vital to his career work, that no other institution quite equalled it in giving men the proper attitude to public service. He saw Balliol as the perfect sequel to a Public School education and an ideal bridge to government service. At Oxford, too, Furse met scores of people who, whether they remained there as dons or administrators or went into government, would be useful to the C.O. later on. Again one notes the smallness of English society in the early years of this century. A friendly and attractive personality like Furse could not fail to make hosts of personal friends who would honeycomb the upper reaches of government within a decade or two after leaving Oxford. Furse is not only a warm person; he has the gift of being able to remember names and faces.

Arriving at the C.O. in 1910 as a patronage appointee of the secretary of state, Furse was one of two assistant private secretaries responsible for recruitment. At his London club, the Savile, he broadened his already considerable contacts.[33] But, unlike many career civil servants, Furse did not lose touch with his school and university. As 1914 approached he was still corresponding regularly not only with Eton and Balliol but with all of the great and many of the minor Public Schools and with Cambridge, London, and several provincial and Dominions universities. The groundwork for the recruitment drives of the 1920's and 1930's was accomplished before the start of the First World War.

Rejected, due to deafness, by all of the conventional services, Furse managed to get to France in 1914 as an officer in King Edward's Horse, a special reserve cavalry unit recruited from all over the empire. His bravery is attested to by two D.S.O.'s and two mentions in dispatches. Again he met a great many people, fellow officers in this case, who would be useful to him later. Furse arrived back at the C.O. as assistant private secretary to Milner, then secretary of state, in 1919. From then until 1948 he alone was in charge of recruitment.

As to the specific form of the work, the Fisher Committee referred to "this special work, special in the sense that it must be done by a staff possessing the special capacity needed both for assessing the personal qualities of applicants and for the wise and sympathetic handling of *persons* as opposed to *subjects*." [34] Furse and his six juniors were not professional psychiatrists. Their methods in 1930 were just as intuitive as those of Chamberlain's time. They relied on assumptions about human characteristics as identified in interviews which were never founded on any formal or professionally recognized method. Furse's objective was to single out certain desired qualities in the total make-up of a normal human being, to judge the genuineness of these, and to estimate their future development under particular employment conditions. The work proceeded empirically. Advice was constantly being sought from C.S. officials. But in the last analysis the relevant selection criteria were entirely subjective with Furse, and no one really pretended otherwise. [35]

Except for the establishment of an appointments board, following the acceptance of the Fisher Report by Lord Passfield, the procedure was tied to exactly the same institutional framework which has been described above. There was the same buff-colored P-one file containing application forms, letters from referees and remarks by interviewers. The process was a bit more lengthy in 1930; more people took part in the C.O., and of course the volume of applications had increased. It was now somewhat more likely that even if a candidate came from a good family his name would not necessarily be recognized by the staff member doing the initial processing. Red tabs bearing the initials "S" of F" (son of father) showed the uninitiated that the applicant's father was or had been in an overseas service. Social qualifications were just as important as ever, perhaps more so, since larger numbers of the socially respectable were now willing to apply.[36] Perfunctory letters from referees received more careful attention than ever as the size of the appointments staff grew. Questioned about their recommendations, some referees had "been known to send revealing replies modifying or even contradicting their former adulation of the candidate." [37]

As colonial administration became more complicated so did the work of pairing men and jobs. As we have seen, Furse persuaded governors to send him advance estimates of their needs with descriptions of particular vacancies. By the time he had narrowed down a batch of applications to perhaps 200 he was thus able to study each candidate's background in relation to known requirements. To have listed yachting as a favorite pastime, for example, was to make it probable that one would be sent to an island colony such as the Solomons. Academic achievement took on new importance in relation to the deepening complexity of secretariat duties in some colonies.[38] But, realizing that successful allocation of staff consisted of fitting available pegs into a large and varied number of vacant holes throughout the tropical world, Furse and his colleagues kept in mind that the plodder was just as needed as the brilliant "flyer" who would rise to the highest levels some day. "We are not only picking governors," noted an interviewer.[39]

By the time a candidate was invited to the C.O. for an interview those who were to see him had studied his papers. In a characteristic equestrian analogy Francis Newbolt wrote, "You cannot judge a horse in the ring by looking at his head and shoulders only." [40] Rule number one for interviewers was "be human." [41] Applicants could not show what they had if they were not first put at their ease. As the popularity of the C.S. grew, the interviewers' traditional concern with motivation became more important than ever.[42] The aspirations of second generation candidates were plausible enough. But the number of *poseurs* was high enough to demand a skeptical eye on all answers to the motivation question in application forms. An otherwise favorable "submission" (file sent to the secretary of state with the recommendation that the candidate be appointed) contained the remark that the man had "read a few books, including one on African conditions . . . so that his ignorance of colonial conditions is not quite so abysmal as that of some candidates." [43]

Newbolt's advice to new members of the recruitment staff identifies the importance attached to outward appearances:

His [the candidate's] physical appearance will, of course, have been noted at once; the cut of his face and the extent, if any, to which he has the indefinable quality of "presence." Colouring, build, movement, poise will have come under review, and even such superficialities as style of dress and hair, health of skin and fingers. But your scrutiny will be directed chiefly to eyes and mouth, for they, whether in repose or in action combined with speech and gesture, may tell you much. You will have in mind the truism that weakness of various kinds may lurk in a flabby lip or in averted eyes, just as singlemindedness and purpose are commonly reflected in a steady gaze and firm set of mouth and jaw. If need be you will search for any signs of nervous disorder, in the knowledge that an even temperament counts at least equally with a sound physique as a bulwark against the strains of a tropical or solitary existence.[44]

Submissions accordingly contained many references to appearances and mannerisms: "Good blue eyes . . . but rather a weak and selfish mouth."[45] His "appearance seemed to me to be a good gauge of his character. He has a strong, open face with greyish eyes and wiry hair. He speaks in a clear, even voice and appears to be essentially a serious man, who knows what he wants and will probably get it without turning aside on the way."[46] "He has a strong face, inclined towards selfishness, and might incline to short temper with fools or uneducated, primitive peoples. I am doubtful if he has the temperament for heartbreaking work with [sic] difficult climatic conditions."[47] "I cannot see him putting himself across to a disinterested or truculent audience. A man must be ready to accept responsibility in our service." (This interviewer was doubtless a C.S. official on leave.)[48] He "lacks personal charm . . . would probably be an efficient but unpopular colonial official."[49] "Heart definitely better than head."[50] "He looks the type."[51]

Intellectual capacity was also to be estimated. Newbolt reminded staff members that the human brain is a progressive organ so that future as well as present capacity must be guessed. Academic marks were relevant but were by no means the sole determining factor.

Interviewers had considerable power over final decisions. A condescending remark, damning by faint praise, a highly suggestive unanswered question, all could raise doubts in the minds of subsequent interviewers. If these did not dispense with the candidate before he reached the final board, they might do so at that stage. An applicant who happened to be head of an Irish clan and referred to himself as "The O'Malley" ran squarely into traditional English condescension towards the provincial Irish. An interviewer signed his comments on the man "The O'Wilson," and the application failed.[52] Another applicant, asked what his father's occupation was, answered that he was an engine driver, and a board member was seen to write "would be good at shunting" on his pad. But very few such candidates even bothered to apply, in the 1930's or before. The C.O.'s social-educational bias was too well known. Newbolt wrote:

> A man's natural qualities . . . derive partly from inheritance and home environment, and partly from school or academical [*sic*] training. If he comes from stock that has proved its worth, generation by generation, in the professions or in public service, if he has been reared in the faith that duty and chivalry are of more account than ambition and self-seeking, if his education has broadened his mind in that faith and taught him the meaning of responsibility . . . then he has . . . many of the qualities for which you are looking. The truth of this is incontestable, and accounts for the fact that a preponderance of men of this stamp, trained at the universities, come forward as candidates for the Colonial Administrative Service, and are successful.[53]

Furse's system was not altered as a result of the Fisher inquiry, but it was thereafter encased in a new organizational structure—the Personnel Division—which the committee thought would be more independent and authoritative. Headed by an assistant under-secretary of state, the division included all functions having to do with recruitment, training, pensions, promotions, discipline, and conditions of service. Furse remained head of its recruitment and training branch and became, with his staff, part of the permanent civil service for the first time. The change may seem more organizational than essential. To the extent that existing staff, ideas, and techniques persisted, it was. But as the work grew in volume, bringing with it greater systematization, the easy informality of former days inevitably faded. Until the end of the Second World War Furse and his assistants were largely successful in retaining a personal approach. But the new patronage was less haphazard than the old, and it functioned within a self-perpetuating and expanding bureaucratic context. "Parkinson's Law" went its inexorable, burgeoning way.

The C.S. appointments board, another outgrowth of the Fisher inquiry, now stood at the end of the selection process. Candidates appeared before the board after satisfying Furse's staff that they had sufficient qualifications. Usually consisting of three men, the board was chaired by a representative of the civil service commission. At least one and usually two members of the C.S. also sat. Alternatively the board's third member might be another official of the civil service commission, a permanent staff member from the C.O. or, occasionally, a complete outsider. The best loved and most quoted of these was undoubtedly Sir Fred Burrows, the former engine driver and railway union chief who ended his extraordinary career as governor of Bengal under the Attlee Government. Burrows, with his working-class accent and tart remarks, was an unfailing delight to the C.O. and C.S. professionals, who took great satisfaction in finding that his judgments of men usually corresponded exactly with theirs. Slouched in his seat at one side of the board chairman, Sir Fred would twinkle and deliver himself of an opinion that was sure to be the talk of the whole C.O. as soon as the session was over: "Speakin' as one as comes, as ya might say, from the lower deck, I shouldn't 'ave thought that last feller was exactly what we need." [54]

In fact, however, the new board made little difference in the system and did not materially alter Furse's power.[55] Submissions were still made up by his staff. It was he who decided which should go to the board and which should not. C.S. members on the board were almost invariably Furse's men, that is, he had picked them for the service originally. In a total of, say, ten submissions, Furse would usually include two which he knew to be weak. C.S. men on the board could not fail to spot these, and tip-offs were unnecessary. The candidates Furse wanted usually passed, and those he did not want usually failed.

Lord Passfield also accepted another Fisher recommendation, that a single colonial service be recognized as such. Neither the committee nor the secretary of state, of course, could establish C.S. unity by fiat. The underlying conditions of colonial autonomy were very nearly as stubborn as ever. But the Fisher Committee felt that more unity could be facilitated gradually through cooperation between colonial governments and the new personnel division. The very proclamation of unity would give the C.S. added prestige, making it a single legal entity, comparable to the I.C.S. This may seem trivial. In fact Furse found that it helped recruitment in Oxford and Cambridge by creating an image of a single, worldwide service. Moreover, the professional and scientific services were fast achieving real unity, even though Passfield's proclamation still left the administrative services of each colony separate. Doctors, lawyers, education officers, agriculturalists, and foresters, passing from one colony to another, and sometimes serving in as many as five or six during their careers, added to an impression that the colonies were held together by more than purely legal ties to the same Crown. Cultural and topographic differences remained. But improved communications were steadily providing a semblance of unity against whose background the minister's formal proclamation had more meaning than would have been the case a decade before. Furthermore, in the 1930 Governors' Conference Lord Passfield himself agreed to chair a committee on C.S. unity which included Sir Warren Fisher, Sir Samuel Wilson, and Mr. Tomlinson, head of the new Personnel Division. By the time this committee reported two years later, however, Passfield's successor as colonial secretary was unable to do more than standardize the system of entry into the still separate administrative services.

By this act the examinations for Ceylon, Malaya, and Hongkong were abolished. Furse was then master of recruitment for all administrative posts requiring staff from England. As a permanent civil servant and head of selection for all, rather than most, of the services, he had made an important advance. As of 1932, when the former Eastern Cadetship services became his responsibility, Furse had survived the departures of ten secretaries of state, three each from the three major parties and one, Lord Milner, who was non-party.[56] The conclusion is inescapable that Furse had unique ability to influence colonial policy and administration through selection of officials for a kind of rule that was still mainly personal. Secretaries of state could exert powerful influence, as Amery's career in the C.O. shows. Some have been depreciated as mere prisoners of their civil servants.[57] Others, due *inter alia* to their own great energy or the zeal of their biographers, have been credited with acts which were really the work of permanent and parliamentary under-secretaries.[58] Furse, though his heart was plainly with the Tories, worked so well with all his ministerial masters that none of them interfered with his functions. Parliamentarians came and went with the regularity of the seasons. Furse, as a former colonial official said, remained "astride the Empire." [59]

Looking back on the C.S. in the early 1930's, three aspects of the situation at that time stand out. First, the result of the Fisher Committee's work was to further Amery's plans for colonial development and unity. Despite continued autonomy in the dependencies, the C.S. in the 1930's had become equal in prestige to any of Britain's overseas services. Its ability to act as an improved instrument of development was greater after the Fisher-inspired reforms than before. Secondly, practical administration in the colonies had become sufficiently complicated to make pre-1930 personnel machinery in the C.O. inadequate. The new personnel division, recommended by the Fisher Committee, was a response to increased bureaucratization in the colonies. The depression forced drastic cuts in recruitment; liaison training of technicians and administrators was still primitive; but with economic recovery in the mid-1930's the C.S. was exercising a kind of government which, in scale and complexity, was well beyond any the colonies had known before. Incipient nationalism would find the C.S. incomparably better prepared, although not enough so, than its predecessor of the 1920's. Thirdly, the Fisher Report confirmed Furse's convictions about selection criteria and left him in an even stronger position to enforce them. The committee's endorsement of his methods was a striking example of the elitist ethic in action.

In 1960 Furse cast his mind back to the work of the Fisher Committee and mused, "The Colonial Service didn't begin with that committee, you know." [60] By the same token, the settlement of C.S. problems proposed by the committee was not to go unchallenged for long. In less than a decade the Second World War had erupted and brought the recruitment and training work to a halt again, as in 1914. With the coming of war, Furse was already thinking of another appraisal of his precepts in the light of far greater demands which he expected another post-war era to impose on the service. It was not the social and academic sources of administrative recruits which would be considered inadequate so much as the rationale and content of training courses. In the meantime the two waystations on the road to C.S. careers had as powerful a hold as ever on Furse and his staff. Faith in the efficacy of their combined formative influence on C.S. probationers was by 1945 undiminished. These were the great English Public Schools and the two ancient universities at Oxford and Cambridge.

"Henceforth the School and you are one
And what you are, the race shall be."
—*Clifton Chapel* [1]

CHAPTER IV

The Public Schools

THE importance of the English Public Schools to the major civil and military services and even to business would be difficult to exaggerate. Their grip on the national imagination is not equaled by that of comparable institutions in any other country among the Western democracies. Their appeal is strong today, although they are undergoing significant changes. In the interwar period not only was the appeal strong, but the Public Schools were fortunate enough to bask in a less critical atmosphere of social questioning than has been the case since 1945.

What were Furse's assumptions about the role of the Public Schools in equipping men for careers in the C.S.? What was the nature of his dealings with the schools? What particular Public School attitudes and attributes were characteristic of colonial officials, and what were their effects on colonial administration?

"As to the Public Schools," writes Furse, "they are vital: we could not have run the show without them. In England universities train the mind; the Public Schools train character and teach leadership." [2] Furse saw the Public School as "the spiritual child [of] the tradition of chivalry." [3] Since to him "the Colonial Service [was] really a crusading service," the importance of Public Schools as sources of recruitment was primary.[4] Colonial officials were not just civil servants with a serious duty to the nation, as were home civil servants in England; their responsibility for protecting and guiding native peoples in primitive societies was unique. They were the bearers of civilization, the custodians of a sacred trust. Mere ability to pass a difficult written examination was by no means adequate as a measurement of capacity for this kind of service. Furse had to be sure that each applicant had demonstrated conclusively in adolescence and early manhood a genuine concern for the less fortunate. The authentic spirit of *service* as duty to those in whose interests responsibility was exercised was most easily inculcated or developed at institutions whose sole ethos had been concerned with such a spirit for generations past.

"The secret of the ethos of a good English Public School," Furse observes, "and how the authorities set about implanting the points of that ethos in their boys . . . is not an easy thing to explain to anyone who has not been to an English Public School. Witness the appalling, ignorant views of such schools held by most British socialists, most of whom never went near such a school. Although there are shining exceptions among Labour men who were never at such a school but have yet learned to appreciate them. And there are also glaring instances of ex-Public School boys who have failed . . . to understand them. Most of these . . . are misfits." [5] The statement epitomizes Furse's attitude towards both the schools and their critics. His faith in the value of the Public Schools to the English leadership class was absolute, instinctive, and practical. It was based as much on experience as on meditation. When he thinks about the Public Schools today, Furse casts his mind back to his own happy days at Eton, not outward, objectively, towards some hypothetical institution or ideal educational theory.

Furse is not foremost among those who would essentially change the character or curriculum of the schools, agreeing perhaps with defenders of the *status quo* who feel that such changes would seriously harm the whole ethos of the schools and, therefore, their ability to play their traditional role in society.[6]

Furse was not unwilling to listen to criticism of the Public School criterion for C.S. selection. A working-class boy who later became a member of his staff in the C.O. used to engage him in spirited discussion of the point.[7] Later on he was to maintain that the C.S. needed broadening.[8] But throughout the interwar period he held sincerely and firmly to the view that a Public School background was the most appropriate. There was no trace of conventional social snobbery in Furse's approach. The comfortable tenure of his own family background would have made such an attitude unthinkable.

As he explained to the 1927 Governors' Conference, Furse and his staff maintained constant touch with housemasters and headmasters in some fifty Public Schools. The heads of many major schools were known to Furse personally. He devoted considerable time to visiting them, coming to know the particular characteristics of masters and schools, and relating these in his mind to the needs of individual colonies. C.S. officials on leave were sent to schools which had proved over the years to be especially valuable sources.[9] These men explained their needs to school officials and thereby planted the seeds for crops of probationers who were still some five or six years under the entrance age. English headmasters do not think only of getting their boys into universities, as do their colleagues in the United States, but also of what the boys will be suitable for in later life. As time went on, Furse and

his representatives found that masters had already identified certain boys as likely prospects, before recruitment
officers arrived on their annual visits.

Slowly the C.O. was able to reduce what Furse called
the "appalling amount of ignorance" in England of conditions in the Colonial Empire.[10] The myth that West
Africa was still a "white man's grave" continued to plague
the service long after medical advances had made careers
there relatively safe and healthy. In correspondence, some
of it with parents of potential recruits, Furse tried to foster
an image of the C.S. as a worthy career objective. He
sought to develop an awareness in educational circles
that Britain's responsibilities in the colonies demanded
the talents of her best young men.[11] This "missionary
job," as he called it, involved Furse in the propagation
of an idea that appealed to an unmaterialistic sense of
obligation. His method of going about it was as always
elitist, for, as we have seen, Furse believed that certain
families who educated their sons a certain way were the
best sources of recruits. The smallness of the country and
the comparatively high degree of acceptance of the elitist
ethic allowed him to proceed in a manner that would have
been considered inconsistent with the basic democratic
thesis elsewhere.

The fading of myths derogatory to life in the colonies
was helpful to Furse. So was the decline of the I.C.S. from
its former position as the most sought-after of Britain's
overseas civil services. A third factor was the 1929 depression which, as a recruit of the early 1930's remarks,
"made young men happy to get a job in the Colonial
Service." [12] Soon the supply of candidates from the best
Public Schools considerably exceeded the number of places
available. By 1930 Francis Newbolt's boast that candidates "were competing with the best youth of the nation
for a popular profession" was essentially accurate.[13] As

often happened in circumstances favorable to a controller of patronage, this situation allowed Furse to draw recruits from a wide selection of schools and to grade them according to his reading of the requirements of particular colonies.

Certain schools had traditions of overseas service which helped their graduates even if the schools' ranking in England was not of the highest. Haileybury was founded for the express purpose of supplying the I.C.S. Its success in doing so made up for the fact that it was not opened until 1862 and therefore lacked the prestige of Winchester, founded in 1382.[14] Marlborough, an excellent school, although not always included in the top eight or nine, also had an overseas tradition. On a visit to the colonies in the 1950's its headmaster was greeted by 21 Old Boys in Singapore, 20 in Kuala Lumpur and 3 in, of all places, Kuching.[15] Schools such as Rossall did not have high social prestige. But they were known as places to which the sons of impoverished gentlefolk were sent, and were therefore well qualified from the standpoint of Furse's criterion of service and obligation. Lugard himself, the son of an impecunious clergyman, attended Rossall. Bedford, for example, Furse came to associate with Far Eastern and West Indian police commissions, because many Bedford parents could not afford to send their sons to university, and among the only posts open to boys of 19 were junior commissions in these forces.

The problem of defining the term Public School is given comprehensive treatment by the present headmaster of Eton in the Fleming Report of 1944.[16] To most Englishmen the term means the eight schools usually listed as the best—Eton, Winchester, Rugby, Harrow, Charterhouse, Westminster, Wellington and Shrewsbury—and such lesser but also famous schools as are members of the Headmasters' Conference and tend to take their lead from the eight.[17] Prominent in the latter category are Beaumont, Bradfield, Cheltenham, Christ's Hospital, Clifton, Dulwich, Felstead, King's Canterbury, Marlborough, Oundle, Repton, Sedbergh and Uppingham. Most Englishmen would grant honorable mention also to Fettes in Scotland and to a handful of other schools such as Manchester Grammar, which has such a high academic standard that, although not a Public School, it cannot in practice be excluded. Manchester Grammar School's High Master is a life peer. Some might also include other schools for special reasons. For example, the school attended by the Queen's husband and now by Prince Charles is often mentioned, even though it was founded in Scotland during the present century and by a German!

The distinguishing features of the Public Schools are their independence of the state school system, the charging of substantial fees—although not as high as those of American private schools—the ability of their Old Boys to reach high positions in the civil and military services, and above all their national prestige. A tiny fraction of the British male population is educated at such institutions.[18] It is this combination of attributes which sets the English Public Schools off from secondary schools elsewhere and gives them a political importance not approached by, for example, the fashionable but less significant New England private schools which some writers imagine to be the spawning grounds of the American national elite.[19]

The civil service tradition of the Public Schools goes back to the founding of the oldest among them, Winchester and Eton, in the Middle Ages. Even then their primary function was the training of ecclesiastical and legal administrators, the career bureaucrats of the day.[20] "Public" distinguished them from classes held in the great noble homes for sons of landed families. Their first students were either the sons of country squires and town merchants or poverty-stricken wards of religious institutions. They tended to be local in appeal and influence. At first there was little class distinction attached to them, their student bodies being a mixed lot in a time when class lines were less finely drawn than after the Napoleonic era and the coming of the Industrial Revolution. But from the first an underlying assumption of the English educational ethos was that book learning was appropriate for those whose careers were to be in government and not for others. While England remained an agricultural and seagoing nation the assumption was hardly questioned. Ploughmen learned their roles by walking behind a team and seamen by going at tender ages on long voyages before the mast. Rather suddenly, however, the country found itself possessed of a class of newly rich industrialists and merchants who had amassed fortunes during the Napoleonic Wars. England had a vast empire to administer, and her old landed aristocracy was insufficient in numbers alone to manage the task unaided.

The nineteenth century saw the founding of most of the Public Schools now considered to be the best. The system is really a Victorian rather than a Medieval product. It reinforced and perpetuated a class stratification evolved gradually in the early years of the nineteenth century, but did not establish that stratification, as it is sometimes accused of doing. The harsh discipline and strict adherence to rules which have come to be associated not only with the Public School system but with the English as a people were thus in large part a function of a Victorian need to recreate and maintain a competent and responsible ruling class. The system has been self-conscious insofar as the class structure has been open at the bottom, for the *nouveaux* were as gauche as they were numerous. Dr. Arnold, usually regarded as the father of the Public School system, enforced a hard regime and ethic because he regarded it as his duty to make gentlemen out of the sons of men whose chief distinguishing attribute was ability to accumulate wealth. The very severity of Public School life created a deep, virtually unbridgeable gap between those who had and those who had not attended such schools. By the end of the nineteenth century the system had seared its traditions deeply enough into the consciousness of the nation so that class lines in England were at peak rigidity. To borrow Professor Reisman's terminology, the ruling class was so tradition-directed that its members did not need to be inner-directed and would never stoop to be other-directed.[21] After adolescence they were virtually immune to any ethical motivation other than their own Public School-imbued ways of thought and action. The very success of the Public Schools, noted the Fleming Report, "tended to encourage the production of a recognized type, loyal, honest and self-confident, but liable to undervalue the qualities of imagination, sensibility and critical ability." [22] Despite the sincere and vigorous efforts of some headmasters to develop the interests and abilities of the individual boy, the Public School system put a premium on the corporate spirit. As civil or military service was the career at which the schools aimed, such a spirit was deemed not only desirable but necessary.

The connection, if it may be called that, between the Schools and the British government has in fact always been closer than that, for example, between American private schools and the United States government. Graduates of the former schools have gone in steady and large numbers into official positions of various kinds since early in the nineteenth century. Official committees of inquiry have taken an interest in the Public Schools and have made recommendations affecting their character and curricula.[23] Some schools have direct ties to the State, the provost of Eton, for example, being appointed by the Crown. In the interwar period the dependence of the government on the Public Schools was especially noticeable. Three-fifths of the applicants who passed the examinations for the I.C.S. in the years 1921–38 had attended Public Schools.[24] For the diplomatic service during the same period the figure was much higher.[25] In the C.A.S. the Public Schools had what was almost a monopoly, and the small numbers of entrants from other types of secondary schools simply served to prove the rule.[26]

A central factor in any explanation of the importance of the Public Schools to the civil service class in England is the assumption, crucial to Furse's thinking, that Public School life is adult life in microcosm. The School is seen to be an anteroom where all the essential conditions of society are experienced in miniature.[27] Like real-life society, the School is presented as a community, some of whose members lead, others of whom follow, and all of whom have responsibilities and privileges. The wider implications of this are that the life for which Public School is preparation is to be male-dominated and authoritarian. The authoritarianism ahead will be mild and benevolent, with the rights of the ruled majority scrupulously observed. But the egalitarian concept is absent. The idea that leaders will rise naturally, according to individual merit, from all classes, areas, and walks of life, is alien to the Public School ethos. Recruitment of new blood is assumed. But neophytes must pass through the established institutional structures and experiences before their capacity to take part in the ruling process can be judged safe.

Believers in the Public Schools do not minimize the importance of family influences. On the contrary most headmasters themselves insist that their boys are essentially formed before they arrive at school.[28] The austere, impersonal relationships which marked English upper-class family life, especially in the interwar period and before, have conditioned boys to look outside the family for sources of affection, however, and for primary objects of loyalty. The remoteness of parents and the transitory nature of relationships with nannies in childhood cut English boys off from their families at an age when French and American children by comparison are mainly family-oriented. It is therefore to his school that the boy of 13 or 14 has traditionally looked for support; he has given his loyalty and affection primarily to the members of the school community, masters and schoolmates, from early adolescence to the time of his entrance to the university. At school he receives the experience of channeling his instincts and developing his innate capacities. There the natural leader, who has already felt the impulse to power, has his first experience of actually exercising power. Natural followers by the same token learn to accept and obey. The leader learns that responsibility to the governed is an inextricable part of the power privilege, and followers come to rely on the comfort and security of being responsibly led. The two attitudes become at school so deeply embedded in the consciousness of every type of boy that an atmosphere develops which, though certainly authoritarian, is nonetheless relaxed and characterized by an accepting and voluntary spirit. Here again the force of tradition-direction obviates other-direction. There is no perverseness in the claim of one headmaster that English society is actually more democratic than American.[29] The latter, he feels, must rely on more authoritarian sanctions in fact, if not in theory, due to the chaotic societal results of the egalitarian assumption. Leaders are insecure, and followers are suspicious and resentful. However this may be, the loyalty of Englishmen to their Public Schools is remarkable. The wife of the former headmaster of Eton remarks that even she and her husband, with decades of intimate experience of the school behind them, are continually surprised at the volume and intensity of demonstrations by Old Boys of their feelings for Eton.[30] Commemorative dinners, visits to the school continuing well into old age, attendance at athletic events, the wearing of ties, and other gestures give constant evidence that school days are remembered with pleasure. When Lugard disembarked at Lagos to assume the governor-generalship of Nigeria he was greeted with, among other things, a handmade sign, held aloft by an official, reading "Floreat Rossalli." An entire volume of verses by Furse's father-in-law, Sir Henry Newbolt, is devoted to Clifton, the poet's Public School. In England it is commonplace to find that people will be unsure of where major public figures have had their higher education, but most will know which Public Schools they attended. Everyone knows that Sir Winston Churchill was at Harrow, but many are vague about where he went from there. Of the three major stages in the development of the character and capacity of the typical English civil servant—family, Public School and university—there can be little doubt that the Public School stage exerts the most lasting and coherent influence.[31]

In attempting to identify some of the more important characteristics of Public Schools it is well to mention in passing the three criticisms of the Schools most often encountered in England itself.[32] The first is social snobbery, which some writers have described as being an outgrowth of the Public School system.[33] American observers of the English scene find special difficulties in appraising the phenomenon of snobbery, one which has in any case tended to generate more heat than light. One difficulty is that in America anyone who stands apart or above is often thought to be snobbish. In pre-1945 England this definition would have been more or less meaningless. It is perhaps more helpful to define the quality as an attitude which assigns to oneself a social position which is not accepted as such by others and a concomitant attitude of disapproval, arrogance, or condescension towards people to whom one feels superior. Even today Englishmen will recognize this attitude as being characteristic of the socially insecure, especially, by definition, those seeking to rise socially. To the extent that British society has been mobile its rising elements have been open to the charge of this kind of snobbishness. Indeed, one colonial official of the 1930's laments the entry of some, though not many, "fake gentlemen" into the C.S.[34] But Britain, although changing socially in the interwar period, was less amenable to fast and pervasive social mobility than a less stable society such as Germany, for example, or one without an aristocratic tradition, such as the United States. The Public Schools, especially those in which Furse was interested, were still comparatively secure from the standpoints of both their own attitudes and the attitudes of non-Public School classes towards them. The average C.S. probationer of the 1920's or 1930's, along with other Public School products of that period, would have thought it absurd to raise the question of whether or not he was "better" than a non-Public School boy. He was not better, but totally different. His background, position, career function, and future were all different from those of, say, working class boys of the same age. Comparison was not profitable. This attitude may have been morally reprehensible or socially archaic. It was not snobbish in the sense here defined.

The second charge most often brought against the Public Schools was that they contributed to homosexuality by segregating their students from the opposite sex at an age when the sexual consciousness awakens. Being socially disreputable, the charge is difficult to evaluate, although it has received serious public attention in recent years.[35] A scholarly approach to the subject by a medical specialist notes the evaluative difficulties but advances the tentative opinion that, apart from normal adolescent homosexuality, which is transitory, exclusive homosexuals will adhere to their preferences regardless of environment.[36] According to this view the Public Schools may have been a retarding but probably not a permanently corrupting influence. Where the C.S. is concerned it is sexual segregation and not adolescent homosexuality which exerted a relevant influence on the Public School-trained colonial official. Even assuming that homosexuals would have chosen a career in colonial administration—a dubious assumption at best—it is not likely that the bent would have escaped notice, or that, if it did, Furse would have accepted applicants so inclined. But the habit of living in exclusively male company for years on end, even after marriage, and the ability to do so without debilitating effects on morale, was absolutely crucial to C.S. careers. The all-male aspect of Public School existence was therefore of the utmost importance. The life which C.S. recruits faced was often such as to make normal existence impossible, especially in bush stations where D.O.'s had to be without their families for long periods. They did not enjoy this, but neither did they complain unduly of the deprivation. The spartan conditioning of Public School years, socially inappropriate as it may have been, undoubtedly buttressed the stoic traditions of the C.S. in a way that normal schooling, of the American kind, for example, would not have done.

The third prominent criticism—authoritarianism—has already been alluded to.[37] The American student of English institutions finds that the traditions of the two countries are different enough, in both theory and practice, to make discussion of authority and the exercise of power especially susceptible of misunderstanding and confusion. A technique or concept considered natural in English Public Schools might well strike the product of an American high school as being insufferably tyrannical. An example is the method whereby prefects—the nearest American equivalent being members of the student council—are appointed by headmasters after discussion with those masters who are most likely to know the boys under consideration. Popular elections are unknown. To believers in Public School methods the office of prefect is too important and responsible to be exposed to the corruption of demagoguery which elections would entail. Adolescent boys are too immature to be able to pass judgment in such matters, which must therefore be decided for them by experienced members of school staffs. The "benevolent dictatorship" of the prefect system and the relationship between masters and boys in Public Schools was a potent force in the upbringing of colonial civil servants and a determining factor in their attitudes towards their eventual career duties. So unquestioned is the authority of masters and prefects that the social atmosphere in Public Schools appears quite relaxed and friendly.[38] There seems to be no self-consciousness in the vague little hand salutes given by boys to the headmaster or provost of Eton as they pass by. The authoritarian character of the system is unmistakable. Yet its acceptance and ease of operation require that it be judged within the context of its own value structure and not by a standard alien to it. The prefect system and other authoritarian aspects of Public School life contributed to order and were therefore considered fair and just.[39]

When asked to delineate the selection criteria of the C.S., Furse and all senior officials in both the C.O. and the C.S. who were consulted emphasized first and foremost a natural talent for exercising responsibility.[40] As nearly as Furse could enforce it, the criterion and the Public School background which he considered to be its necessary conditioner, were mandatory. Colonial officials of the interwar years were a mixed lot where personality, talents, shortcomings, and sometimes even background were concerned. But in the judgment of those who selected them they had in common that passion for ruling which Santayana and other acute observers of the English scene have identified as a distinctively British national trait.[41] In the words of a well-known retired headmaster who served as an administrator in Iraq, "responsibility is the breath of life to a Britisher." [42]

To Furse the best sign that an applicant might make a good colonial administrator was the item "School Prefect," or better still, "Head Prefect" in his *curriculum vitae*.[43] The C.O.'s extraordinary confidence in the prefect type can only be explained with reference to the prefects' position in the Public School system. Boys in the 15–18 age group in American schools, public or private, are given nothing approaching the authority exercised by prefects. They rather than junior masters are the primary instruments of discipline in English Public Schools. Only in the rare instance when a prefect's discipline fails is the intervention of a master thought appropriate.[44] In houses (dormitories) prefects supervise daily schedules including hours of rising, retiring and studying, meals, many social events, and the activities of extracurricular societies. Prefects are usually looked up to by other boys; they may also be feared or resented depending on their personalities and the subtlety with which they hold sway. With team captains in American sports they share the unique prestige which athletic prowess ensures. Some among them may also be academic leaders. But all are chosen for an air of authority which in the judgment of masters allows them "to get people to do what they do not necessarily want to do" in the best interests of the school.[45] This quality in fact is evidence enough for headmasters that a boy has what is called "character." Those who have it are given natural, ungrudging allegiance. Their leadership is thought to be right and proper and is usually accepted without resentment. In effect the prefect is the glory of a scheme of things which is described as "the distinguishing feature of the English Public School system." [46]

The pertinence of the prefect system to colonial administration is obvious. A ruling rather than a primarily bureaucratic service, the C.S. set great store by leadership qualities in its recruits from the earliest times. Leading fags at school was like leading natives in Africa or Asia. The character and integrity of prefects and D.O.'s determined in similar ways, so Furse believed, their respective effectiveness in personal leadership. One form of paternalism led naturally to another. In both situations it was not physical force that was often required or used but the force of example. In both situations too the accent was on order and justice within a context of order, not on mass participation. Non-English observers will protest that the prefect system was insufficiently concerned with individual liberty and with active participation by the majority in societal decision-making. The English answer is that there can be no liberty without order and no order without strong leadership.[47] The two attitudes are basic to the very different British and American brands of democracy.[48]

Another Public School-imbued characteristic of colonial civil servants was their aloofness from the people they ruled. The friendship and affection which most D.O.'s felt for their people did not cause them to merge themselves with colonial societies any more than similar feelings negated the class system in England. The Public School boy was set off from the rest of English society. That this was the result of social practice rather than of

legal sanctions made it all the more effective and resistant
to change. To a degree, specific rules of Public Schools
defined the reality of apartness: those, for example, which
forbade boys' going into certain areas of the towns where
their schools were located.[49] More important, however,
was the working essence of the class system. Friends and
confidants were drawn from one's own class. One married within his class, joined clubs within it, brought up
children within it, and gave it a lifelong loyalty that was
in some ways stronger than one's loyalty to the nation.
To the adolescent English male of the civil service class
his Public School was the institutional embodiment of
the unspoken class ethic. When he became a colonial official he naturally took his class assumptions and practices with him. The importance of hierarchy, precedent,
and correctness in social and career procedures was carried forward from the time when Dr. Arnold and other
headmasters had had to drill them into the untutored
minds of the rising *nouveaux*. The domestic social hierarchy transferred its spirit to the colonies. Officials
found native aristocrats worthy of one kind of treatment
and other natives worthy of another. This was not dis-
crimination in the usual unsavory sense but simply a matter of following habit and the line of least resistance.
Officials in Northern Nigeria buttressed instinctively the
hierarchy which they found in existence there; so did
their colleagues in Malaya, Uganda, and the Aden Protectorates. The attitude of officials towards other native
peoples, those over whom indigenous aristocrats ruled,
was not unlike that which they maintained from childhood towards the lesser orders at home. One ruled over
the people and protected them from local and foreign injustice. Otherwise one lived apart.

The Public School attitude towards duty was similarly
transferred to the colonial context. It had military and

religious overtones. In the forecourt of Fettes stands an enormous bronze statue of a youthful Fettesian wearing the kilted officer's uniform of a highland regiment. The figure is shown to be mortally wounded in battle. Breathing his last the young officer is depicted holding his baton aloft, pointing it forward. The statue's inscription reads, "Carry On!" From Furse's point of view this spirit was precisely what was needed in the colonies. Although colonial officials did not usually have to face a violent death, the tropical conditions in which they worked called for a kind of courage and resolution similar to that demanded of officers in combat. A former D.O. writes:

There were no refrigerators, so that food either came out of tins or was what one shot locally. There was little fruit excepting for a few weeks of the year, and although we made great efforts, we found it difficult to grow vegetables excepting for a few months. This meant that everyone was suffering more or less from chronic malnutrition. Then there was the climate. West Africa was particularly bad, and we, of course, had no air conditioning and no fans; there was no electricity in outstations (where junior officers spent most of their time). Junior officers, in addition, spent much of their time in any case in touring, and so in living in tents or in grass-and-mud rest-houses. The combination of heat and malnutrition [explained why] . . . there were few people who started their unsavory dinner without having had an appetiser of whiskey followed by a gin or two. Then there was the incidence of disease. . . . We all took quinine every day against Malaria. That usually prevented Malaria, but it made Blackwater Fever, fatal in about fifty percent of the cases, fairly common. There were no prophylactics against a variety of other diseases, such as Yellow

Fever. The mortality or invalidity rate was of course high. I don't know what the figures are but I doubt if more than fifty percent of the men appointed to the West African colonies continued for the twenty years necessary to get a pension. Finally there was the very important fact that most of the men were bachelors or grass widowers. Even those with wives were allowed to have them out for about only six months in an 18 month tour; and in those days (1930's) European children were not allowed in West Africa at all.[50]

For a well-educated man of good family to bear up year after year under such conditions he had to subscribe to a code of obligation, Furse felt, that was utterly inflexible. Public Schools contributed to this in various ways. In most schools the chapel was physically and morally the center of the community. To the civil service class in England Anglicanism has long been more than a religion in the strictly theological sense. It was a framework of ethical and political loyalty, a nationalistic and social institution. To this day the favorite reading of the Provost of Eton in chapel service is, "Let us now praise famous men"—also, significantly, the theme of a series of pamphlets published by a former governor on the history of the C.S.[51] To prefects, accustomed to performing their duty to other boys in school and accustomed also to the stern gaze of masters and the admiring gaze of fags, duty in the colonies was the logical continuation of a familiar ethic under new conditions. Junior officials, newly arrived in colonial posts, were aware of the eyes of a proud imperial past upon them, not to mention the eyes of their immediate superiors. In meeting challenges the D.O. was aided not only by his own inner resources, which may or may not have been adequate, but by a long-standing stoic tradition. Against such a background the social and psychological sanctions of failure were far less sufferable than the rigors of tropical heat and disease. Furse knew from his own experience that no group in the Empire understood this better than the Old Boys of the major Public Schools.

Single-minded and unflinching in the performance of duty, Old Boys were just as single-minded in their attitudes towards any phenomenon or movement which was unfamiliar or irregular to them. If they were incorruptible they were also unreceptive to criticism and unimaginative in the face of changing circumstances. Up to 1920 in most colonies this was not particularly important; in fact it can be argued that the attitudes of the prefect were exactly what was needed to bring order to primitive, tribal anarchy. Colonial government was such as to demand more persistence in the face of hardship than adaptability to changing circumstances. It was the native who had to adapt in earlier years. As long as the D.O.'s main task was to oversee primitive peoples the rigidity of his Public School education stood him in good stead, or so the C.O. believed. While local aristocrats held power, or at least maintained the appearance of ruling, the Public School-trained D.O. was well cast in the role of advisor and real authority. The often dissolute native chief needed nothing so much as a strong, decisive outsider to support otherwise impossibly inadequate indigenous political institutions. What counted was the "drill," *i.e.,* the set pattern of government handed down by one generation of officials to its successor. Nothing aided neophytes so much as their experience as prefects, experience in which single-minded loyalty to existing forms was more important than an imaginative ability to devise new forms.

The stereotyped procedures of Public School life in fact were and are one of its principal distinguishing features. This seemingly redundant observation is given meaning by a remark made to the writer some years ago by a Public School boy commenting on American education. "Everything you do in America seems so experimental," he said. The English educator tries new techniques with reluctance, at least by comparison with his American counterpart. Curricula at the better Public Schools today differ only slightly from their pre-1945 forms. There tends to be a bit less emphasis on classics, but only a bit.[52] An average of about 13 hours a week is still devoted to classics, and the new elective work in special fields is not taken very seriously.[53] The Wall Game is still played at Eton; the Pass is still swum at Bedford before a boy may remove the white button from his school cap; masters must still ask permission of the headmaster to leave the school grounds in many schools, even for a short time; the old songs are still sung; the willow switch is still brought down smartly on the bare buttocks of offenders against precedent, and, most importantly of all, traditional attitudes persist in conscious or unconscious defiance of the passage of time. If British society wants to go in a direction antithetical to Public School traditions, writes a headmaster, let it.[54] The Schools will then be bypassed and will have to wait in the shadows until the rest of the world returns to its senses. There is a right way and a wrong way. A certain amount of eccentricity of a sort is expected and tolerated. But not the kind that runs counter to basic beliefs and rules of conduct. When word reached England that Leopold of the Belgians was dealing with the Nazi conquerors of his country, Lord George Scott was heard to remark in baffled dismay, "But he was at Eton!"[55]

For the C.S. this long conditioning in the stereotyped ways of an entrenched class system meant that new recruits would have little psychological adjustment to make. Hardship there would be. A new culture would be confronted. But there would be no jarring surprises in learning what one was expected to do. One's superiors, from the Governor down to the D.O., were all, like oneself, products of the same system. By the age of 21 basic assumptions were so deeply ingrained that everyone knew what to expect. Few written rules were necessary.[56] Everyone was an Old Boy. The C.S. had a degree of cultural homogeneity comparing favorably with that of any international civil service in history. The level of consensus among officials was an essential ingredient of stability in the colonies and of such uniformity as there was.

The subject of the influence of Public School training on C.S. character and morale must also include mention of an important sub-type regularly produced by the educational system and funneled into the C.S. This may be called the organization eccentric. His presence in the C.S. distinguishes him from the lonely, Thoreau type of eccentric who remains a law unto himself and scorns active participation in worldly affairs. Yet his eccentricity is such that he rarely reaches high rank in the Service and indeed prefers not to. Only when the attainment of high office does not interfere with the way of life he wants to lead does he tolerate it. The organization eccentrics have always been an important minority in the C.S. Every colony has had its examples of the type. In Nigeria one still hears stories of "Rusty" Buckle.[57] Buckle stayed happily in a remote bush station long after his contemporaries had been promoted and posted elsewhere. He preferred being sole lord of his inaccessible domain to serving in a more bureaucratic and less individualized post. His love of his people and his indifference to authority were legendary. On one occasion a message was sent to him direct from Government House (the Governor's residence) which read: "His Excellency is displeased with your report," to which Buckle replied, "Glad His Excel-

lency is pleased." Back came a correction, "For 'pleased,'
read 'displeased.' " And Buckle replied, "For 'glad,' read
'sorry.' "

The archetype organization eccentric in colonial history is undoubtedly T. E. Lawrence. Brilliant, a lone
wolf, careless of rank, rude to higher authority, tireless,
courageous, and forever something of an enigma, even
to those who knew him well, Lawrence could not have
been less conformist. Yet he performed herculean tasks
of group activity and leadership so successfully that he
was offered a title and a governorship. Spurning these,
he did accept a colonelcy and later an All Souls Fellow-
ship because these admittedly organizational positions
offered maximum scope for his talents with minimum
group involvement. His eccentricity did not prevent Lawrence from being socially useful.

The organization eccentric gravitated naturally to the
C.S. in the interwar period. He came from Furse's em-
battled civil service class, itself becoming something of
an eccentric in English society in these years. Modern industrialization and urbanization were anathema to him,
as were the *nouveaux* who epitomized these trends. He
cared little for money as such; he preferred the country
to the city and was usually quite happy in an exclusively
male society. Loneliness was welcome to him, or at least
was preferable to the sickeningly conformist and materialistic suburban society which he felt had taken over
his country. The C.S. offered escape. It was a peculiarly
attractive kind of escape, one in which the organization
eccentric could serve out a career of socially constructive effort without prejudice to his personal tastes.

The unique contribution of the Public Schools to the
forming of this type was to tolerate any sort of eccentricity so long as it did not violate the tenets of gentlemanly
behavior which all members of the civil service class re-

garded as essential. The American high school system, with its emphasis on sports, adolescent dating, and extra-curricular clubs, and its comparative intolerance of the "brainy" student, is much less receptive to the kinds of personal and group eccentricity which are found in English Public Schools. The boy who prefers poetry to rugger, or lonely hikes in the mountains to vacation dances, is not uncommon and may even be respected in the school community. Ordinarily, the headmaster of an American private school would not dare appoint the brightest boy in his school as head prefect, unless the boy happened to have some other claim to distinction, such as athletic ability, which would make his appointment acceptable to the student body. In England, by comparison, this is the usual thing, and students accept it as right and proper.

Once accepted into the C.S., the schoolboy eccentric found himself in an environment even better suited to his antisocial bent than was Public School. The writer has encountered many such types in the Aden Protectorates and in other colonial posts remarkable for their remoteness.[58] Many who man up-country stations in parts of Africa, Borneo, and British Guiana are similarly true to the type. They were never in a majority in the C.S. as a whole. But they have been a prominent and important minority. Their unsocial Public School backgrounds made their lonely lot easier to bear than has been the case with Americans in comparable positions.

A measure of the hold which Public Schools maintain today on English society is the fact that high taxes, austerity, and the appearance of "the new poor" have not damaged their position. On the contrary, as a headmaster puts it, "The Affluent Society has bought the Public Schools." [59] No sacrifice is too great for upper-class English parents to make in order to assure their sons of places in good Public Schools. In the 1920's and 1930's, when a great many Public School boys aimed at careers of service to the state, the Schools were the formative institution *par excellence*. For the C.S., as for other civil services, Public School mores were taken out of whole cloth, transferred to new environments and subjected to new challenges. Even more than Oxford and Cambridge, important as these institutions were, the Public Schools exerted an influence on colonial administration, and therefore on the British colonial legacy, which nationalism in Africa and Asia will not dispense with overnight.

"Privacy after years of public school."
"No wonder looking back I never worked.
Too pleased with life, swept in the
social round. . . ."
"For while we ate Virginia hams
Contemporaries passed exams."
—*Summoned by Bells* [1]

CHAPTER V

Oxford

FOR colonial civil servants Public School was the basic conditioner. Thought processes of school days went on to university along with one's schoolmates. There they were added to and complemented by new ideas and concepts. The university offered more freedom. Graduates were more sophisticated and mature than their friends who did not go beyond Public School. Still, university life was the last step in a continuum of formal education rather than a totally new experience.[2]

The average colonial official spent four years at the University—three in the normal undergraduate course and one in the C.A.S. course. Adequate description of the institutional milieu from which probationers entered the C.S., therefore, requires discussion of student life at the two English universities from which such a large majority of C.S. officials came in the interwar years.[3] The spirit of an Oxford or Cambridge education must be examined in the perspective of its influence on administrative assumptions and procedures. Analysis of relationships between Furse and university authorities will furnish additional perspectives on English society and education in the two decades before 1939. The C.A.S. course itself must be viewed within the Oxford and Cambridge

107

context rather than as a phenomenon apart from the main stream of higher education as were comparable courses in Europe at the time.

The emphasis in these pages will be on Oxford to the almost complete exclusion of Cambridge. The similarity of life at the two institutions justifies this, as do identical C.A.S. courses and relations with the C.O.[4] Moreover, comparable numbers of probationers entered the C.S. from each university in the period under review.[5]

Over and above its purely academic features, Oxford as a state of mind and a way of life has always been sufficiently distinctive to provoke voluminous comment.[6] The jealousy of other British universities is approached only by the slavishness with which many try to copy Oxford. Abroad, especially in the Commonwealth, and even in countries no longer politically associated with Britain, Oxford is as much a mother of universities as Westminster is of parliaments. The pride and vanity of the place are in keeping with its towering reputation, and the notion that a university cannot rest forever on the laurels of age seems to filter through but slowly to Oxford's dons. The classic Oxonian is portrayed as urbane, skeptical if not cynical, civilized to a fault, rude, intellectual, and not a little smug. The institution has been accused for years of both decadence and corruption. It would be hard to say which is more scathing, the criticism of her own sons or that of outsiders. Yet today Oxford remains unique not least in the intense loyalty of her offspring.

Colonial civil servants looking back on their years at Oxford see it as a needed interim of relaxed living, lodged between the harsh discipline of Public School and the stern realities of career life. Undergraduate days appear as an idyllic pause in an otherwise mercilessly rushing life stream. As a place and an attitude Oxford seems to have been able to defy time. This has brought her much criticism as a backwater, out of touch with modern industrial society.[7] To Furse, however, the university was precisely the right place for the intellectual training of gentlemen.[8] The founding of a special vocational institution, more closely attuned to contemporary social developments, was viewed with disapproval by both Furse and his Oxford associates. University education was reading the classics under the direction of cultivated men, developing close and easy relations with one's teachers, and imbibing the spirit of a well-bred and erudite society in which kings will be at least a little philosophical and philosophers on better than speaking terms with kings. This was the Oxford celebrated in the memoirs of Buchan and of Sir David Kelly, the blessed place where there was time enough to think and talk for a few years before going out to rule the world. To be comfortable such an educational atmosphere had to be relaxed; there had to be enough teachers so that every student could talk with his tutor often and in a leisurely way. If surroundings were to be genteel and conducive to thought, both dons and undergraduates would have to be decently housed and freed of menial chores. Servants were called for, and well-stocked college wine cellars. All this was so costly that it was beyond the reach of all but gentlemen and a few worthy scholars who would be subsidized by a gentlemanly tax structure. It was an elitist educational pattern, not one designed for mass utility.

Despite the hammer blows of the industrial revolution, the greatest war in history, and a devastating depression, Oxford was still that sort of place in the 1930's. The three-year undergraduate curriculum followed by the average C.S. probationer was heavily weighted with classics and modern history, with specialization during the third year in law or politics.[9] There was minor interest in other fields such as literature and geography.

Subjects drawing the fewest men of all were languages and science. When the Public School emphasis on classics is recalled, the continued stress on that field at Oxford meant that classics cannot have failed to exert a powerful and lasting effect on the consciousness of officials. Precisely what form that effect took in each case is of course impossible to gauge. But the neglect of science and the near monopoly of classics was bound to leave its mark on colonial administration. Classical references in the conversation and correspondence of colonial officials testify to at least a superficial impact.[10] In conversations and written exchanges with administrators the writer has gained the impression that at least the rough outlines of Greek and especially Roman thought had been retained. One must avoid the temptation to be over-specific about this. It is enough to note that the study of classics formed a prominent part of the educational experience of C.S. probationers and that more concrete subjects such as chemistry did not. Classics were part of growing up, along with Public School discipline, cricket, and the social whirl at Oxford. A mildewed volume of Plato appears on the shelf of a remote district office in the West African jungle. The odd veteran will refer to classical reading in his memoirs or will perhaps throw in a bit of Greek to impress those who cannot read it. But education, in the words of a retired headmaster, is what is left when you have forgotten everything you learned at school and university.[11] It is the residue that sinks deeply and perhaps imperceptibly into the consciousness. This is an infinitely varied matter. No two men will use their formal education in exactly the same way. The English classical education is seen as part of a way of looking at life and living it. It was rigorous mental exercise. Negatively it may be claimed with more precision that such a curriculum left little room for the kinds of social science specifics which were to be recommended later on.

Outside the lecture halls and tutors' sitting rooms undergraduates invariably found life delightful. The line drawn between undergraduate and don was less of a barrier than that between boy and master in Public Schools. At Oxford, undergraduates and dons drink together and dine together out of college. They often form lifelong friendships.[12] Americans in the university frequently remark on an unfamiliar congeniality between faculty and students. This does not impair respect or breed the proverbial contempt that is supposed to stem from too close a relationship between superiors and subordinates. It is simply that friendships grow out of interests held in common and are not affected by differences in university status. For colonial administration the don-student relationship is important as a forerunner of official ones to follow. The writer has seen private secretaries in their early twenties enjoying an intimate, unaffected social and intellectual comradeship with governors old enough to be their fathers. The fact of common social background, as noted above, is relevant. The easy assurance that comes from membership in the same class obviates a highly formalized official ranking.

Although female students ("undergraduettes" in Hobhouse's contemptuous phrase) had arrived to stay by the 1920's, Oxford, like Public Schools, was nonetheless male-dominated. Women undergraduates could be ignored almost completely. More than female students at Radcliffe or Cornell, the Oxford woman undergraduate was kept apart from most of what passed as normal undergraduate life for men students in the 1920's and 1930's. She was segregated in her own exclusively female college and subjected to stricter social regulations than was her counterpart in American universities. Often, older dons barely tolerated her. Still, the girls were at least present, and they offered the future colonial official his first chance to associate with the opposite sex on a fairly regular and comparatively unselfconscious basis. During "Eights Week," on "May Morning," or on any autumn afternoon in a Cherwell punt, the presence of women of one's own age added to the delights of a new-found freedom. With innumerable sherry parties, "Commem Balls," meetings of exclusive drinking and shooting clubs, and athletic events, the formal and informal gatherings to which women were invited combined to broaden and enrich an already exotic social horizon. It is no wonder that so many Oxonians hated to leave the shadow of the dreaming spires. Nor is it surprising that Furse had no trouble finding C.S. officials on leave in England who would be willing to spend a wifeless week or two in their old colleges on C.O. business. The memory of carefree college days was strong.

Oxford life was far more of an aberration from the national norm than is college life in America vis-à-vis the mainstream of American living. To the average Englishman any university was a never-never land. As late as 1959 an Oxford undergraduate returning to the University was pleasantly surprised when the driver of the truck in which he had got a ride turned into the main street of Oxford rather than using the bypass around the city. Asked why he did not save time by using the ring road the driver replied, "What, and miss all those funny people!" The sense of belonging to a social-educational elite was not lost on future colonial administrators any more than the sense of being on the outside was lost on those, like the driver, who saw Oxford as being so far removed from reality that they were not even envious of it. Aloofness from the general populace, which was characteristic of Public School boys and which was later continued at Oxford, was thus a condition of life that followed the future probationer from preadolescence through to his early twenties. By that time it was too late for most of them to begin learning how the vast majority of English people lived and what they thought. Four years in the hothouse of Oxford were bound to produce an attitude of mind making psychological communication with other classes almost impossible. Furse assumed that the handful of recruits who came from relatively humble beginnings would be so affected by the Oxford experience that they too would eventually display the desired upper-class qualities.[13] The future relationship between officials and colonial leaders and people was also certain to be affected by the quality of aloofness experienced by future officials during their formative years at home.

The bias in favor of Oxford and Cambridge men antedates the C.S. itself. Joseph Chamberlain's private secretaries were in touch with appointments committees at the two universities well before Furse's time. After he returned to the C.O. in 1919, however, Furse gradually built up channels of communication with individual dons and administrators in various Oxford and Cambridge colleges. He preferred these to the pre-filtered systems of formal placement offices.[14] Furse valued the advice of Public School masters and Oxbridge dons over any systematic statements by men he did not know personally. Only *"certain* tutors at Oxford and Cambridge," he writes, could be relied on to identify in their undergraduates the qualities Furse wanted.[15] At the end of his career he told a parliamentary committee that the rationale of his "snowball system" of recruitment at Oxford and Cambridge was that colonial officials would pass the word back to their old schools and colleges that the C.S. was a worthwhile career objective.[16] The long-term effect of this was to assure a continuous supply of interested and appropriate candidates.

Fortunately for Furse the civil service class still maintained enough of its bias against "trade" in the 1920's and 1930's.[17] Ample numbers of attractive candidates were available because, in the first place, they did not wish to take positions in commerce. The declining prestige of the I.C.S. also helped. Knowledgeable Oxford dons could see the handwriting on the wall, as could serving I.C.S. officers. Many of the latter advised undergraduates not to go into a career which the coming self-rule of India was sure to render a *cul de sac*. The Foreign Service and the Sudan Service took so few recruits annually that many good aspirants for overseas positions were discouraged from applying to them. The result of all these factors was that Furse could avail himself of a group of candidates as good, man for man, as that available to any other recruitment agency, and better than some.[18] The generalization that the C.S. got the pick of the crop in the interwar years refers to the administrative services only, however. It remained difficult to interest Oxford and Cambridge men in the professional and technical ranks of the C.S.[19]

Furse's system is best seen in a description of his dealings with three of his closest confidants at Oxford, two of whom were still there at the time of writing. The latter were P. A. Landon, Fellow of Trinity College, and Sir John Masterman, Provost of Worcester College. The third, Dr. Stallybrass, former Principal of Brasenose College, died in 1948.

"It was so easy to work with the Colonial Office when Furse was there," Landon recalls.[20] He agreed enthusiastically with the assertion of Sir Maurice Bowra, Warden of Wadham College, that the essential quality underlying all of Furse's relations with his Oxford "talent scouts" was complete tacit understanding of the criteria which he had in mind.[21] Furse did not have to explain what kind of man he wanted for the C.S., and Landon, for example, did not need to go into great detail about an undergraduate he was recommending. As the son and grandson of I.C.S. officers, Landon knew by instinct what attributes Furse was seeking. Knowing this, Furse accepted Landon's judgment without anything more elaborate than a brief note of recommendation.

Undergraduates interested in the C.S. sometimes took the initiative in speaking to Landon. Just as often Landon first broached the subject himself, occasionally with a young man who had not even considered the possibility. The first talk could take place in Landon's spacious rooms overlooking Trinity's gardens, perhaps at the end of a tutorial. A sherry party did just as well, or a "Bump Supper" when the pick of the college crew was gathered. Landon was always hospitable to undergraduates, allowing them the use of his bachelor quarters for academic and extracurricular meetings. Over the three-year period of a student's stay in Oxford Landon thus had many and various opportunities to observe the behavior of individual undergraduates under a variety of social, academic, and athletic circumstances. From bursary records or discussion at High Table he knew all that was necessary about their backgrounds. A wide acquaintance among Public School masters could satisfy any particular inquiry not otherwise answerable in Oxford. Generally speaking, the amount of intimate knowledge of their undergraduates gathered by Oxford dons in the prewar era exceeded that of American professors, even those in the smaller colleges. "I couldn't help noticing the cut of a man's jib, you know," remarked Landon.[22]

On request or on his own initiative, Landon would pen a short note to Furse, giving the name of a good pos-

sibility and perhaps setting out one or two noteworthy
qualifications. The man had to be of good family. "Philip
Landon cared about that sort of thing," remembers one
of his former students.[23] Ideally the candidates would
have gone to one of the better Public Schools, although
exceptions could be made in cases where a brilliant athletic
or social record at Oxford made up for the shortcomings
of mediocre schooling. Adequate mental equipment was
insisted upon, but "the spectacled chap," in Landon's
phrase, was not suitable. His own First Class Honors
Degree would seem to clear Landon of any charge of
anti-intellectualism in this. He felt that the rigors of tropical living and the peculiar needs of dealing with primitive
peoples called for physical stamina, an ability to get on
with people, and a knack for leadership more than outstanding intellectual capacity. Evidence that the C.O.
felt the same way is provided in a letter written on the
subject by Sir Charles Jeffries, who remarks, "In the
1920's the emphasis was on personal character, leadership
and so forth [and only later did] the good honours degree
criterion . . . come to be established." [24] If a candidate
was captain of the college rugger side, Landon wanted
to know what the other chaps on the side thought of him.
Was he followed because he was respected and liked or
only because he was a good athlete? Had he shown good
judgment and good sportsmanship? Was he at ease at tea
parties, or gauche and ill-mannered? Did he look dons in
the eye and talk in a respectful but unaffected manner
on occasions when great personages were about? [25] "We
talked about character," mused Landon. "And it was
surely essential. But we tried to look at everything about
the chap." [26] More than once he returned to the importance of selecting men who had proved beyond question
that they had the moral fibre to be trusted as guardians
of primitive peoples. For the charge sometimes heard that

only dim-witted athletes went into the C.S. Landon reserves a special scorn. He admits that the average probationer had taken a second class degree. But he argues that this was at best an inadequate gauge of intellectual ability. Many highly intelligent undergraduates were interested in other things than books. They turned the power of their wits to the full scope of Oxford life rather than directing it exclusively towards attaining high grades on examinations.

After a trip to South Africa in the 1930's Landon developed an interest in undergraduates from that country. He tried to help some of them enter the C.S. and was occasionally successful.[27] But he was essentially a believer in the uncanny capacity of Englishmen of a certain class to rule the world. His great regret over the diminution of the Empire is that fewer positions are now open "to our excellent chaps." [28]

Sir John Masterman, a Student (don) at Christ Church in the interwar years and later Provost of Worcester College performed at his college a function similar to Landon's at Trinity. In addition to being one of Furse's "talent scouts" Masterman helped to find men for the Sudan Office. He refutes the commonly held assumption that the Sudan got better men than the C.S., and points out that he sometimes advised enterprising undergraduates to apply for the C.S. because chances for quick advancement were better there than in the Sudan. This was especially true in the 1920's when the university stream was just getting started in some of the more backward colonies.[29] Sir John enlarged on Landon's point about the intelligence of probationers. As he is himself a blue and the possessor of a First Class Honors Degree, he is well protected from suspicion on either academic or athletic grounds. Discussing degrees in relation to intelligence, Sir John felt that Furse was right not to concentrate on the brilliant

student. He pointed out that exceptionally bright undergraduates sometimes failed to get Firsts for reasons other
than inferior intellectual ability, and held that C.S. probationers in the late 1920's and 1930's were an unusually
competent group on all counts. Masterman once advised
a student of his who later became colonial secretary in
one of the Macmillan cabinets not to allow his work for
a First to prevent him from competing for the presidency
of the Oxford Union. In former days this position was
thought at least as important to later careers in London
as a First Class Degree. "He could easily have got a First,"
remarked Sir John.[30] Another cabinet member, when at
Oxford, had changed his major field in midstream; lack
of time to study his new subject ruled out the possibility of a First. When interviewed, Sir John was engaged in correpondence with the civil service commis-
sioners in London, protesting their recent ruling that
no one will be admitted to the Home Civil Service without at least a Second Class Honors Degree. He felt that
entrance to civil service positions, home and overseas,
ought to depend on appraisal of all qualifications, including personal as well as academic ones. This was all
the more necessary, he observed, with candidates for
the C.S. before the war. Their duties were not such as to
allow the relevant personal qualities to be revealed in
written examinations.

Landon and Masterman did yeoman service for Furse.
But undoubtedly the Oxford official who registered the
most significant performance of all was Dr. W. T. S.
Stallybrass, or "Sonners" as his friends called him. Like
Amery, Milner, Lord Cherwell, Lord Haldane, Sir Wolf-
gang Just, and the Duke of Edinburgh, Stallybrass came
from an immigrant family rather than from ancient English stock.[31] His devotion to English aristocratic concepts
in politics was due at least in part to his being a convert

to the cause. Stallybrass was a famous diner-out, one of those college heads who gets around the whole university and has friends in many colleges besides his own. A former civil servant in London, he also had a wide acquaintance there and hewed to definite ideas on the kinds of men needed in the various domestic and overseas services. His interest in the C.S. dated from at least as far back as 1922, when he and John Buchan joined the Oxford University Appointments Committee.[32] He was responsible for many C.S. appointments from other colleges than his own.[33] But Brasenose College, of which Stallybrass was principal, contributed the largest number of probationers from any Oxford college in the interwar period.[34] For this record Stallybrass was alone responsible.

The principal was not content to propagandize for the C.S. at Oxford only. "He was our leading missionary in the Public Schools," remembers his former secretary.[35] At the height of the cricket and rugger seasons "Sonners" was a familiar figure on the playing grounds of many a school. His penchant for sport was complemented by an almost religious zeal to reverse the decline of classics in British education, and to this end he was forever journeying to Public Schools to present prizes for excellence in classics. Another interest of his was the problem to which Furse had referred in the 1927 Governors' Conference: the financial straits of many upper-class families after the 1914 War. Believing with Furse that the proper government of the Empire demanded that colonial administrators have class-bred attitudes of responsibility, Stallybrass directed his attention to ways of assuring the continued entry of sons of the right families to Oxford. Although privilege still played a prominent part in the entrance process at Oxford colleges in the interwar years, the financial obstacle was almost insuperable for the sons of many impoverished gentlefolk. In an age when national scholarships and objective entrance examinations were still not the threat to such boys that they have become since 1945, poverty alone was a sufficient barrier.

Stallybrass's solution was to obtain scholarship funds which Brasenose could control in such a way as to serve the ends of all three of his passions—aristocracy, athletics and classics—but especially the first. A Southampton shipping magnate who had been at Brasenose, Mr. (later Sir Heath) Harrison, had left 5,000 pounds to the college in 1908.[36] He added a duplicate bequest in 1925. The terms of these were, first, that candidates ". . . must be in pecuniary circumstances which justify some financial help." [37] Sir Heath had in mind, however, a particular class of needy boys. They must be members of the Church of England and must have attended one of the following Public Schools: Eton, Harrow, Winchester, Westminster, Rugby, Charterhouse, Shrewsbury, Cheltenham, Clifton, Haileybury, Malvern, Marlborough, Tonbridge, Uppingham or Wellington. Heath Harrison Exhibitioners might receive their awards with or without examination, as the college should determine. Brasenose should satisfy itself that each boy was of impeccable character and that his conduct had been vouched for by reputable school masters. None was required to read for a degree unless he wished.

Later other scholarships were established for the same type of boy whom Stallybrass wished to bring to Brasenose on Heath Harrison Exhibitions. The Arthur Jupp Scholarships and, later still, the Stallybrass Memorial Exhibitions were of this type. The principal did not believe that only impecunious aristocrats should enter the C.S. But among upper-class boys as a group the type was considered ideal. Monied boys could take care of their own careers. Poorer ones who were not helped into some branch of the civil service might slide backwards on the social scale, giving place to others who might not be capable of truly responsible governing attitudes. Penniless boys, moreover, would be glad to accept the difficult living conditions of colonial service life. The profession was an honorable one, if not the most glittering in England's gift. Typical of the undergraduates whom Stallybrass introduced to the C.S. was J. C. Morgan, who went out from Brasenose to Tanganyika in 1934 and later became head of the Central African and Aden Department in the C.O. Two others, both of them Heath Harrison Exhibitioners, became governors, one of British Honduras and the other of the Leeward Islands. Bruce Greatbatch, a Brasenose man of the late 1930's, entered the C.S. in 1940 and is at the time of writing private secretary to the premier of the Northern Region Government in independent Nigeria. "The Principal was always telling me to write to Sir Ralph Furse about one of our Brasenose men," recalls Stallybrass's secretary.[38] He adds with satisfaction that they were invariably accepted.

The ideas of social class and political attitudes held in common by Furse, Stallybrass, Masterman, and Landon are underscored by a Brasenose product, D. A. Fyfe, who entered the Malayan Civil Service late in the 1930's. "It was Sonners who originally suggested that [I] enter the Colonial Service," he writes.[39] "Malaya gave me the opportunity for responsibility beyond my years, [an] . . . experience of fascinating problems and a cross-section of the whole world's population to meet both at work and socially." [40] The social qualifications which the former head of the Oxford University Appointments Committee remembers as being so important to Furse were accepted as right even by some who have commented frivolously on them.[41] After many a scathing remark on C.S. men he has known, a retired Sudan official observed that the best test of the criteria on which Furse insisted was the attitude of British administrators towards native peoples as compared with those of French and Belgian officials.[42] The latter were selected by objective written examinations, and social qualifications were unimportant. "I can't understand why the French never got to like their natives," he remarked.[43] In England and the colonies the writer has often encountered this impression, *i.e.,* that many French and Belgian administrators viewed their charges as barbaric nuisances, whereas the British D.O. would be more likely to see his as attractive children. Belgian administrators with whom the writer has stayed were, on the average, more severe with natives than their British counterparts across the border. Officials in French territories were more interested in the latest news from Paris than in talking about their work, whereas British officials are more often than not so taken up with what they are doing that they do not even know what is going on in the colonial capital, much less in London. It is not possible to prove that the respective attitudes are class-derived. The writer is nevertheless left with that impression.

In any case there can be no doubt that class-identified political attitudes were assumed to be relevant by Furse and that this is why he enforced class criteria in selection. The files of the Brasenose Bursary reveal a high degree of similarity in the "father's occupation" statistics on men entering the C.S. Sixteen listed the standard professions—8 in teaching, law, medicine, and architecture, and 8 in military and overseas service. Three were the sons of clergymen. One each listed "gentleman," international business, and banking. Nineteen left the space blank. All of these, however, had been to a good Public School, and it is fair to assume that the majority, if not all, were from families similar in status to the previous 24. The remaining two were the sons of a station master and a cotton spinner. Even this small degree of deviation from the class rule is mitigated by the fact that three years at Brasenose and one in the C.A.S. course had overlaid the humble origins of even those recruits, an insignificant fraction of the total, whose backgrounds were untypical.[44]

The criterion of athletic prowess, "a by no means unimportant feature," is subject to even less doubt.[45] Analysis of an entire year's "submissions" in C.O. files shows that not a single successful candidate was unable to list both Public School and university participation in sports in his *curriculum vitae*. A large majority not only participated but excelled. "Captain of Rugby Football" or of "The School Shooting VIII" appears again and again. As the Sudan was " a country of blacks ruled by blues," so also were the territories in Furse's purview. "A good Second and a blue," in the words of a colonial governor, summed up the academic and athletic requirements. The second of these has received more than its share of attention. Oxford still smirks at stories of probationers who had nothing to recommend them, so it seems, except athletic qualifications. Nearly everyone can recall an example. As has been indicated, Sir John Masterman considered this kind of criticism to be meaningless at worst and shallow at best. In any case the brilliant student was deliberately avoided and the athlete sought after. Pointing to the grueling conditions of colonial administration, Furse is content to rest his case.

Strangely, the literature of colonialism is less enlightening on the most important selection criterion of all—inner resourcefulness—than on criteria which are easier to define. Furse himself disclaims ability to put the quality into words. Oxford dons and C.O. interviewers depended on admittedly unscientific impressions and in some cases on performance of one kind or another which was thought to have demonstrated the desired attribute. Some felt that family traditions of service were a sure guarantee. "The

Bourdillons," commented the president of an Oxford College, "naturally had no trouble at all getting in." But for the most part the C.O. depended on the judgment of dons who had observed their students' self-reliance in a wide variety of circumstances. "I just knew that that chap would do well," Landon explains.[46] "We made mistakes," muses Furse, "but on the whole I don't think we did badly." [47]

Throughout the academic year Furse received word from his friends in Oxford and Cambridge, and from a few other universiites such as Trinity College, Dublin, and busied himself with checking on the undergraduates recommended. C.S. officials on leave visited their old colleges to meet with prospective candidates and their tutors. Furse himself went occasionally to each of the two major universities and "had an agreeable evening" with his principal contacts. It was these informal talks which laid the groundwork for more formal later stages in the recruitment process. As an Oxford administrator who served in the Sudan explains, there was considerable overlapping in the work of Furse's friends and that of dons who were helping the Sudan Office to do its recruiting.[48] Horsetrading was inevitable. The main difference was that Furse was seeking sometimes a hundred men a year and the Sudan Office only an average of eight.

The best of the candidates were invited to the C.O. for interviews. These were completed and the results announced by letter towards the end of the summer. Successful applicants were told that they would be required to enroll in the C.A.S. course the following semester, that is, in the autumn after they had taken their degrees. Exceptions were made if colonies were pressed for staff or for other *ad hoc* reasons. As part of the background of the average recruit of the interwar years, therefore, the C.A.S. course has a certain significance in the total picture of colonial administration. It is only by comparison with courses given to colonial administrations on the continent that the British training effort appears insignificant. Contrasted with the curriculum of the *Ecole Coloniale* in Paris the Oxford and Cambridge courses seem half-hearted and incidental.

Course enrollment was composed almost entirely of recent graduates. Occasionally an Oxford man would take his course at Cambridge or vice versa. Ordinary curiosity about the other university sometimes explained this.[49] In other instances probationers wanted to study with a particular don. In either case outsiders were taken into Oxford colleges so that they would stand *in statu pupilari* while on the course. The other main category of outsiders was made up of men entering the administrative services from other branches of the C.S. Thus R. A. Nicholson, who had been in the public works department in Malaya, joined the Oxford course in 1931. He rose to be financial secretary in Northern Rhodesia.[50] If they were not university men, such officers were considered to be in need of exposure to the academic atmosphere before attaining to the senior service. They were normally transferred to another colony altogether where their non-university and non-administrative background would not count against them.

The numbers of men on the course varied according to colonial needs and budgets and ranged from 59 in 1930 to 11 in the worst depression year, 1932. The average was in the 30's. The curriculum left ample time for leisure. There was language study, and probationers tended to apply themselves seriously to this in the knowledge that oral examinations by superior officers awaited them at their posts. There were lectures and reading in English law and in the law of particular colonies. Cadets destined for Northern Nigeria read "Mahummedan" law for example.[51] Lectures in anthropology, "British Rule in Africa," tropical forestry, and agriculture completed the list. The Imperial Forestry Institute in Oxford arranged lectures for those assigned to colonies where knowledge of what forestry officers were up to would be useful. Gradually a start was made in the direction of an interdisciplinary approach to the incipient "subject" of colonial studies. Informal seminars were instituted in which administrative and technical probationers could meet, this being the forerunner of what Furse was later to call "liaison training." Had they been inclined and able to take full advantage of this opportunity, administrative students would have gained more from the combined seminar work than would technical officers, for the level of sophistication of technical courses was generally higher than that of those given to administrative probationers.[52]

Prewar course curricula depended on which dons happened to be in residence and what lectures they happened to be offering. Dons may or may not have done recent research in colonies. There was thus a consistently haphazard quality to the course. As late as 1959 its supervisor was able to remark that training was something which began on the job; the course was merely a collection of lectures following the normal undergraduate curriculum, and it "did the men no special harm." [53] Referring to the course, a retired secretary of the Oxford University Appointments Committee put the word "training" in quotes.[54] Professor Sir Alexander Carr-Saunders of London University, an Oxford man, described it as little more than a lure which, due to the notorious pleasantness of Oxford life, was sure to attract good men to the C.S.[55] An additional year in the Eden of English education was certainly not a repellent thought, especially if it was at government expense. Indeed, Furse makes no secret of his primary reason for having the course at Oxford and

Cambridge. As a recruitment aid it was invaluable. Generally, governors in the field cast a skeptical eye on the course. Even those who considered it worthwhile had to face legislatures in which natives were becoming annually more numerous and which understandably questioned expenditures out of taxes for the training of foreign rulers.[56] For, under the decentralized British colonial system, the governments of the various dependencies began to pay for new recruits the moment they were appointed, although the latter would not embark for overseas posts for another year.

The educational spirit imbibed by the prewar generation of colonial administrators, therefore, was the same liberal arts spirit absorbed by other classes of leaders in home and overseas services. The C.O. preferred the semi-trained generalist over the uncivilized specialist.[57] Furse made this specific during the early years of the Second World War in advising C.S. aspirants to take humanities courses in good universities plus incidental officer's training rather than a special military course.[58] He sympathized with the view of the Oxford registrar that education was becoming too specialized and that students were beginning "to think the world is smaller than it is [and] problems simpler than they are." [59] The course provided no specific image of imperialism and no particular rationalization for Britain's presence in the colonies. Portugal's articulated policy of *assimilado* and the more or less intellectualized rationales of colonialism put forward by France, Belgium, and the Netherlands in their training programs stood in marked contrast to Oxford's suave disdain for the whole subject. Britain was never as self-conscious about her overseas possessions as were the other major colonial powers. A reading of Kipling or a lecture on the sacred mission of building a black England across the seas would have been greeted with hoots of laughter in Oxford. The most that the prewar course did was to provide a bare outline of the historical facts whereby Britain had acquired the colonies. Lecturers and their hearers knew each other well enough to let it go at that.

Nevertheless the course did gradually acquire a status of sorts in the university. It was, after all, the only thing of its kind in England. Probationers of other British overseas services took advantage of the T.A.S. course and its successor from the 1920's onwards. A group of Sudan cadets joined the course in 1929, for example.[60] I.C.S. recruits attended specific lectures considered appropriate to their future work, such as those given in 1932 on criminal law and evidence.[61] Although the C.O. had no responsibility for Sarawak until after the Second World War, its (British) Rajah asked and received permission from his Oxford-recruited cadets to join the course from time to time.[62] A small number of C.S. recruits from universities in the Dominions got a taste of England before going to colonies, but a truly imperial administrative corps never materialized.[63] Junior officials from the French, Portuguese, and Japanese colonial services also appeared in Oxford during the 1930's. However, the C.O. and Oxford were sufficiently blasé about this kind of international exchange, soon to become so fashionable, that the Foreign Office had to use persuasive and reassuring language in its dealings with the university. "This is not merely the thin edge of the wedge," wrote a Foreign Office official to the vice chancellor, "and we do not wish to swamp the Colonial Course [sic] with foreigners." [64] Oxford was assured that numbers of such students would be kept small, and there was a vague reference to the "advantage [of having] foreign colonial administrators trained . . . in this country." [65]

By comparison with postwar courses in fact almost

everything about the C.A.S. course had a patchwork and temporary flavor to it. Oxford's reluctance to innovate and to establish precedents gave a hand-to-mouth character to course administration. It was administered as a minor sideline by secretaries of the Oxford University Appointments Committee. The first Colonial Service Club was merely a room in the Oxford shopping district, a place too small and unpleasant to compete with the junior common rooms of probationers' own colleges. It did serve as a meeting room where retired or serving officials could speak to and with new recruits. But as a physical aid to initiating an *esprit de corps* it was not comparable to the present club, with its reading, television, and billiards rooms, bar, dining room, library, and living quarters for transients.

Still, a beginning had been made. It was a typically English beginning, a cautious, half-new, half-old use of existing materials in the service of an idea that was itself not totally new. Members of the course committee, some of them dons, others C.O. representatives, did the best they could with an infinitesimal budget. Together with the talent scouts, they created in Oxford an attitude towards the theoretical study of colonial subjects which was later to serve their country well. When the time came to lay down a more adequate institutional base for serious interdisciplinary approaches to colonial studies another generation of innovators could draw on the abstract and the practical lessons learned by the experimenters of 1926 and their successors.

CHAPTER VI

For a New Age

In Chapter II it was seen that Furse considered the transfer of the C.S. courses to Oxford and Cambridge to be a matter of the first importance. The establishment in both universities of Tropical African Services courses and committees ("Colonial Administrative Service" after 1933) was felt to be an invaluable aid to recruitment as well as a guarantee of more thorough and efficient training. The close working relationship between the C.O. and Oxbridge, long an informal reality on the English scene, was thus institutionalized and strengthened. To the average Englishman in public life there was nothing startling about this. The affairs of the two ancient universities have always been of great interest in Whitehall and Westminster. Oxford and Cambridge retain to the present a fascination for the national consciousness that has no parallel in the United States. Impassioned discussion of university rights and university developments in Parliament and the press is commonplace. It would be unthinkable on the other hand for the U.S. Senate to become much exercised over a proposed road through a beautiful portion of Harvard's athletic grounds or a projected power line which would pass too near the outskirts of Berkeley.[1]

Where sustained contact between the city and the universities is concerned Oxford has normally taken precedence over Cambridge. One reason is the plausible fact of Oxford's greater age. Like the Monarchy, the oldest British university is essentially unique in prestige. The loyalty of its graduates and the interest taken in practical politics by Oxford's administrators and faculties, as compared to Cambridge's, give meaning to the expression "Oxford dreams while Cambridge sleeps." Cambridge graduates do not deny this. When asked about it the former secretary-general of faculties at Cambridge remarked laconically, "Cambridge just doesn't care, you know. It has always been that way." [2] With Furse's understandable preference for his own university added to this traditional state of affairs, the greater importance of the C.O.-Oxford collaboration appears only natural. Furthermore, in imperial matters specifically, Oxford had by the 1930's built up a considerable lead over all competitors. Significantly Cecil Rhodes chose Oxford, not Cambridge, as the proper conditioning ground for his scholars. [3]

Two considerations justify the almost exclusive emphasis of the present chapter on Oxford rather than Cambridge: Oxford's connection with the C.O. was consistently closer than that of Cambridge during Furse's hegemony in recruitment and training work; and the bureaucratic arrangements to be discussed were duplicated with respect to Cambridge.

No one on the Oxford side from 1930 onwards was more important in the development of relations with the C.O. than Mr. (later Sir Douglas) Veale, the Oxford registrar. From Corpus Christi College Veale had entered the civil service, eventually becoming a private secretary in the Ministry of Health. The fact that Veale was willing to give up a most promising civil service career

to come to Oxford as registrar is important in two respects. It indicated the university's awareness of its growing dependence on Whitehall and the need therefore to
have university-London relations in the hands of someone who understood the ways of H.M. Government.
And it showed that the office of registrar had incomparably more prestige at Oxford than at other universities,
even in England. With regard to the C.S. specifically,
the Veale appointment was a godsend. He and Furse
had met before 1930 when Veale took up his duties in
Oxford. Veale formed the perfect bridge between the
separate worlds of scholarship and government. He understood and respected both worlds; his function as inter-
preter and mollifier was to prove invaluable as the time
approached for intensive cooperation in reappraising and
planning for the postwar years.

It has been shown how C.O.-Oxford interdependence
and cooperation manifested themselves in the C.A.S.
course and in joint interest in colonial affairs generally.
The existence of the course at Oxford stimulated recruitment and improved the quality of training syllabi. To
cope with increased numbers of students—the average
class of probationers numbered over 30—Oxford engaged more instructors who pursued more research. Because of its obvious value to the C.S. such research became
increasingly valid in C.O. eyes as an object of financial
support. The exchange of information and the theoretical
contexts for it on the part of C.S. officials on leave and
Oxford faculty members respectively was a self-perpetuating and habitual phenomenon considered valuable by
all concerned. The twin subjects of the development of
colonial studies at Oxford and training for the C.S. were
thereby made inextricable. The social sciences, as they
related to colonial affairs, were seldom given to wholly
theoretical research, since in colonial administration and

its problems a rich field for empirical research was always readily at hand. In the C.S. itself younger officers were less and less ignorant of the anthropological, economic, and historical significance of their work. The traditional contempt for academic training as such became increasingly anachronistic in the eyes of practitioners.

Nevertheless, tradition and precedent were an almost irresistible force in Britain between the wars. The C.A.S. course given in 1939, though extended and improved, was still very much like the original in 1926. Conditions in the colonies had changed. Social science research was gradually beginning to reflect these changes. The areas in which developments had not kept pace enough to suit forward-thinking people in both the C.O. and the universities were those involving provision of funds and institutional facilities for colonial studies and academic course content for C.S. training.

Probationers continued to arrive in Oxford in the 1939–40 and 1940–41 academic years.[4] But even before the start of Anglo-Japanese hostilities, defections to the armed forces had pointed to the inevitable suspension of courses, and of recruitment itself, for the duration of the war.[5] Even if Furse had not been much given to reflection on the need for constant improvement of methods, the enforced wartime moratorium on his work would have made such reflection unavoidable. As it was, he knew from visits to colonies and from experience after the First World War that immense changes would follow the far more disruptive 1939 conflict.[6] In March 1941 the C.O. had received from an Oxford source a memorandum outlining an ambitious program of research in colonial studies.[7] In the subsequent year projects had been mounted, with the aid of Rhodes trust funds, in the Gold Coast and Nigeria. Towards the end of 1941 the Japanese delivered their expected blows at

British dependencies in Southeast Asia, but with unexpectedly disastrous results. Already, well before the postwar rush to self-government, questions were being asked in academic and government circles as to whether the C.S. in Malaya should not have been more alive to the danger of its position. Was the neutral and in some cases hostile attitude of the Malayan population towards the British during the Japanese advance reflective of inadequacies in the prewar administration of that country? [8] The Germans did not invade any British colonies. But in Africa, too, it was obvious that the war was having an unsettling influence which could not fail to call into question traditional assumptions on colonial administration when peace came if not before.

The stage was set therefore for detailed reconsideration of C.S. training and its relation to academic work in the colonial field. Changing colonial conditions demanded it; Furse and his staff at long last had time to undertake it; and Oxford's administration and faculties contained specialists both willing and able to cooperate. This is not to say that a large corps of colonial studies specialists was available. As the most knowledgeable of Oxford dons in the field admitted to Furse, "Colonial experts at present hardly exist." [9] But there did exist a basis for the drawing together of facilities and staff. The spirit was there, and colonial studies did have a history at Oxford, if a modest one.

That history was the work of Miss Margery Perham more than of any other person. Now the senior fellow of Nuffield College and nearing retirement, Miss Perham had maintained a continuous interest in colonial administration since her first visit to a colony (Somaliland) in 1923. Having become a don at Oxford in 1924, and having remained in the university ever since, Miss Perham was by 1940 the recognized academic authority on colonial problems. Her almost annual visits to colonies, mainly in Africa, and a heavy correspondence with personal friends in the C.O. and the C.S. kept her knowledge of colonial affairs up to date. Most important for Oxford at this juncture in the development of the C.S. was Miss Perham's personal collection of literature, published and unpublished, official and private, on colonial administration. This, in addition to the Rhodes House library on imperial affairs, gave Oxford a favored position compared to other universities in this respect. People were working in the colonial field elsewhere. Cambridge, the acknowledged leader in agricultural studies and a competitor in imperial history, would certainly have challenged any Oxford claim to predominance in these areas. In languages, education, anthropology, and the sciences, London University too had considerable achievements to its credit. But in practical collaboration with the C.O. over the past decade and a half, especially in matters concerning the C.S., Oxford's claim to the first place took precedence over that of any other university.

In January 1942, with the British Empire in the Far East collapsing in ruins and a powerful German army threatening Egypt, Sir Ralph Furse met with Miss Perham in Oxford to talk about the future of the colonies. Although Furse's main interest was the C.S. and Miss Perham's the furthering of colonial studies, the value of cooperation between them towards the common goal of a better governed colonial empire was not lost on either. Furse came armed with specific proposals. He had in mind a training scheme far exceeding the prewar course in depth and scope.[10] The old course for probationers, strengthened in anthropology, economics, law, and history, would be retained. To this would be added the innovation of a second course for picked men with several years of service behind them. These, said Furse, in a favorite phrase, would be mainly the "rising rockets," the future governors and top officials in secretariat and provincial posts. The second course would be a refresher, a sort of sabbatical year, in which practical experience could be brought to bear on recent academic advances and means considered for taking advantage of lessons learned by both theorists and practitioners.

With perhaps 80 probationers and 70 "general course" officers to place, Furse thought London University and possibly Edinburgh and some of the provincial universities could be brought into the scheme. The inclusion of London would have advantages politically, he remarked, in an oblique reference to prewar protests that the C.O. had been biased in favor of Oxford and Cambridge. The remark reflected Furse's assumption that the Second World War would be followed, like the first, by social and political upheavals extending beyond the bounds of education. Faculty for such a program, he admitted, would be a serious problem, and perhaps the C.O. would have to supply some of the instructors from C.S. ranks, in both administration and technical services. Manifesting his awareness of quickening impulses to self-rule in the colonies, he voiced a preference for dons who had done recent research there. Such subjects as the relationship between English law and native societies badly wanted objective examination.

Miss Perham promptly wrote to the registrar outlining her suggestions for attacking problems raised by the Furse proposals.[11] A long-standing desire of hers for a center of colonial studies at Oxford now appeared to be a *sine qua non* of the C.O.'s postwar needs as well. "What can Oxford do immediately?" she asked rhetorically.[12] She replied, in an answer that had been on her mind for years, that lectureships in a variety of colonial subjects could be established and research begun. This would provide "value to the Empire as a whole as well as to the training centers." [13] Attaching great importance to the proposed general courses, Miss Perham noted that they would fit in excellently with Oxford's tutorial system and that essays written by experienced officers would be an invaluable addition to the literature of colonialism. Oxford should take responsibility for political courses and London, for example, might manage education and languages. No one university could possibly handle all the necessary subjects. In addition to requirements listed by Furse, there was a desperate need for statistics in economics and sociology. Lack of these was inhibiting C.O. planning now that the Commonwealth Development and Welfare Act had been passed. Colonial administration should be approached comparatively, analysis being made of Dutch, American, Russian, and other methods.

In correspondence with Furse and Veale during the spring of 1942 Miss Perham expanded on the theme of changing colonial conditions in relation to world politics and scholarly research. The bland assumption of many that the Colonial Empire would go on forever, that Britain had unlimited time to develop and improve administrative techniques, was shown to conflict not only with aspirations of native intellectuals but in a less immediate if equally ominous way with anti-colonial prejudices in the United States, Russia and elsewhere.[14] The old, somewhat disdainful attitude towards other colonial powers gave way increasingly to a realization that if colonialism was to be put on trial after the war it might well be necessary for the European powers to draw together.[15] Detailed knowledge of each other's methods and policies would be an indispensable prerequisite to cooperation in so improving colonial administration that protests by natives and foreigners alike could be met with

a defensible assertion that colonialism was both morally
sound and practically necessary.

Miss Perham maintained that previous neglect of colonial studies had hurt the Empire.[16] She observed that
Parliament and the C.O. were at last coming to their
senses and cited as evidence a recent grant of 500,000
pounds annually for colonial research and the establishment of a committee under Lord Hailey to advise the
C.O. on its allocation. The 1930's, she went on, had seen
a steady improvement in the quality of C.S. recruits. But
rationalization of training was overdue. Referring to the
growing complexity of administrative work, especially
as regarding the economics of underdevelopment, she
wrote that officials still did not sufficiently understand
the work of technical officers. "Problems of colonial administration have reached a stage where they require
more expert handling than hitherto," she pointed out.[17]

The collaborators often felt that their discussions were
cut off from reality in a time of preoccupation with military disasters. In May 1942 they were heartened, therefore, when the House of Lords undertook a full-scale
debate on the C.S.[18] Debates on colonial subjects in both
houses had been notoriously underattended in the past,
although the record of the Lords was better than that
of the Commons.[19] Marshall of the R.A.F. Lord Trenchard led off the debate with a strong speech recommending accelerated localization (Africanization) of the
C.S. His military service in Nigeria and South Africa
and his experience as a director of the United Africa
Company had persuaded Trenchard that the C.S. needed
a staff college comparable to those in Paris and Lisbon
and not unlike the military colleges in Britain. He felt
that a new selection board ought to be constituted, containing members from the staff college, business, and
the C.S. Training should consist of one intensive year

in the new college, followed by another in a colony. He agreed with Lord Moyne, who had been secretary of state up until two months before the debate, that dead wood should be weeded out of the service and new blood brought into governorships and other senior posts. Both paid tribute to the C.S. as a whole, and neither was thinking of the dissolution of the Colonial Empire. Their criticism was entirely constructive.

Lord Hailey, with Lugard one of the best known and most respected colonial experts in the chamber, agreed that Africanization should proceed and recommended the consolidation of many of the smaller colonial territories into more viable federations, drawn together by a united and interchangeable colonial service. Lord Hailey maintained also that C.S. probationers needed wider social and economic conditioning and training in keeping with changing colonial conditions. To the remarks of his three colleagues Lord Cranborne, then secretary of state, replied with a strong defense of the C.S. More unity was necessary, he agreed, but Lord Trenchard's proposals on selection were redundant. Selection should be based on character, and the then constituted appointments board was quite capable of identifying that. As for training, both the question of institutions and that of course content were at that moment being examined, he said, within a wide context of world politics, colonial advance, and Empire economics.

Such debates were rare. The colonies were given more knowledgeable and attentive consideration in the Lords than in the Commons due to the presence in the former house of a comparatively large number of men who had had service in either the C.O. or the C.S. Also the less powerful house could devote more time to colonial questions than could the Commons, where all the affairs of an empire at war had to be dealt with and constituencies satisfied. Even so, such esoteric topics as C.S. quality seldom drew the attention of either Parliament or the press before 1945. The general public knew almost nothing of the subject. When the parliamentary under-secretary of state for the colonies, Harold Macmillan, presented the colonial estimates in 1942, fewer than 20 members of the Commons were present.

Accustomed to public and parliamentary indifference, Furse found it all the more justifiable to make his plans and take action quite outside the normal framework of democratic government. The staff college question was one which he had discussed with any specialist who would listen, among others with the former chief of the Imperial General Staff. He knew of course that highly specialized training was given to French and other continental recruits. In his talk with Miss Perham in January 1942 he had sounded out the idea of founding a special administrative school. This met with closely reasoned and determined opposition from both Miss Perham and Veale. "Colonial subjects," said a memorandum on which both had worked, "are more likely to flourish when they are not isolated but are specialized branches growing from some main tree of knowledge. Further, it is to be hoped that Colonial students [*i.e.,* probationers] will not concentrate exclusively upon colonial subjects but will take advantage of the best the University has to offer in other directions." [20] This was a solid affirmation of the liberal arts faith and a rejection of the narrow specialization which many at Oxford believed to lie at the roots of much social malaise in the world. With specific reference to the C.S., they felt that what was needed in administrative work among primitive peoples was a broadly educated and well-rounded man with a topping of special course work at the end of his normal university course. The narrowly trained specialist might know more about office management and finance. But would he be able to deal effectively with human beings and human problems?

Embellishing on the theme of more specialization on a liberal arts base Miss Perham wrote to the registrar that, in the past, suspicion of specialist courses had been grounded in traditional English distrust of theory. "This attitude," she thought, "probably reaches its height in the colonial field." [21] D.O.'s had always worked in remote areas unknown to most academic people in Britain. Tasks were highly empirical. But this isolation from the world of ideas was precisely why the university had much to give the administrator. It was not uncommon for D.O.'s to ponder the wider meaning of their work and to welcome observations from objective outsiders. Left to himself, the lonely D.O. was too often thrown back on the shallow and out-of-date reflections of his colleagues. All were too much taken up with the press of daily chores to be able to raise their eyes to wider horizons and perspectives. The modern university with its commitments to empirical research could offer officials a change of scene, a respite from the merciless demands of routine, and an opportunity to reflect on the general implications of colonial administration. This they could enjoy in the congenial company of working scholars as well as their own colleagues from all over the Colonial Empire.

Miss Perham referred to the sketchy prewar training courses and discussed her views of what should be included in more systematic courses after the war. Administrators needed first of all an understanding of the true historical background of British colonialism, the derivation of policy, the strands of development in each colony, economic interests, humanitarianism, racial relations, and the juxtaposition of conditions in the United Kingdom and colonial policy. Comparative colonial background was vital, due to the parochial character of the average civil servant's career. As foreign interest in and criticism of colonial rule increased, administrators must know not only about other British colonies but about the dependencies of foreign powers as well. Economic theory was a crying need, especially for secretariat-bound officials in the age of state planning. Correspondingly there was a need for study of municipal and county government in the United Kingdom by administrators assigned to the more primitive colonies where existing institutions were so plainly inadequate that models would have to be imported from the metropolitan country.

Miss Perham then reviewed the age-old cliché that administration cannot be taught but must be learned on the job. The C.S. need not fear the corrupting influence of theorists, she felt. The C.O. and the University acting together would carefully single out for C.S. courses only those faculty members with recent research experience in colonies. Such research, she reminded her C.O. readers in a gentle prod, was quite beyond the capacities of colonial governments. They had neither the trained staff nor the funds to undertake it. University people on the other hand devoted their full time to this kind of work. The university atmosphere, for all its ivory-tower faults, was more conducive to following truth than a rough-hewn district headquarters where only one aspect of truth clamped its iron grip on officials in every waking moment and effectively excluded all else. Dons could advise administrators on further reading in their fields of special interest and could, in research visits to colonies, stimulate fresh-minded discussion and relieve the boredom of isolation. Moreover, it was the colonial studies specialist in British universities who more than anyone else had the capacity to address massive popular ignorance of colonial matters in the United Kingdom. Capping her argument with a thrust at both the traditional antitraining line and overspecialization, Miss Perham held that Oxford was the ideal place for future special courses; nowhere else in the world would students be safer from the stultifying effects of narrow vocationalism than in the wide-lawned residential colleges where generations of Milners and Amerys had supped and talked with dons.

Assured that the university was fast putting its house in order, Veale shepherded through the Hebdomadal Council an official application to the Colonial Development Fund for a grant to found a comprehensive colonial studies program at Oxford.[22] Always the diplomat, he followed up an inconclusive first meeting of the tri-university curriculum committee with a proposal that he discuss another approach with Furse before trying again.[23] To Furse he proposed that Oxford and Cambridge should manage everything except languages, leaving these to London and thus avoiding separate, identical courses at all three places.[24] London would thereby have an opportunity of receiving and influencing all probationers, not just those in technical fields.

The nagging and all-important question of money was never far from the planners' minds. Veale applied first to the university's own social studies board and was told that prewar decisions on spending precluded an allocation to such an upstart as colonial studies.[25] It was this rebuff that prompted the registrar's decision to approach the C.O. An application for an initial grant of 2,250 pounds was acknowledged by Sir Charles Jeffries with the comment that the Hailey Committee would deal with it in due course.[26] The university, as opposed to the social studies board, however, did agree to give Miss Perham an assistant, and Corpus Christi, Veale's college, was cajoled into a promise of help. Feelers were put out to the United Africa Company, to Lever Brothers, and to the Rockefeller Fund. The U.A.C. subsequently agreed to support a faculty appointment. It was noted by the Hebdomadal Council that some African students at Oxford were helped by the Carnegie Foundation, but apparently no move was considered in that direction. When Sir William Goodenough of Barclay's Bank Overseas wrote to Veale on an extraneous matter, the registrar was quick to seize on the possibility of help from that opulent source.[27] Finally, after more than 18 months of silence broken by an occasional evasion from the C.O., Veale resorted to the ultimate tactic. He had Lord Simon, the lord chancellor and an Oxford graduate, write directly to the secretary of state pointing to the connection between C.S. and university needs.[28] Support for the total Oxford effort was eventually secured. But not without agonies familiar to educational fund-raisers everywhere.

The machinations of Veale, Miss Perham, and their colleagues had coincided with and aided the development of modern social science scholarship at Oxford and in those branches of the C.O. which were responsible for advising the secretary of state on research. It is not possible to single out any one person or institution as having been primarily responsible for the development, which, after all, had been manifesting itself gradually throughout the interwar period. For the C.S., as has been noted, increased reliance on social science research was a function of the growing complexity of administration. In this process, both the relationships between British officials and colonial peoples and between administrative and technical personnel stood out as being appropriate objects of academic inquiry. Miss Perham and others at Oxford were convinced that colonial studies demanded an interdisciplinary approach and that colonial administration was now too important and complex to allow a continuation of former reliance on in-service training alone. The rise of social science and the C.O.'s manifest belief in it forecast, during the war years, a pronounced vocational bent in postwar training. Thus far, however, the C.O.-Oxford collaboration had been confined almost exclusively to the inspirational realm. Continental countries had sometimes been over the same ground, most of them earlier than the British, though in differing circumstances and with differing policy aims. France, Belgium, the Netherlands and even Portugal had translated their intellectual convictions into academic courses and thence into administrative practice.[29] For the British, however, the conceptualizing talent resulted more slowly in intrusions into the inter-racial sphere of day-to-day administration. It is a moot question whether they despised theory as much as some believe. But the British devotion to empiricism and precedent was a reality which the Oxford theorizers had to face in their abstract discussions of the relative merits of *a priori* and in-service training for colonial officials.

Academic development in the colonies themselves also promised to affect C.S. training in these years. In 1943 the secretary of state wrote to the Oxford vice chancellor seeking the university's help in furthering higher education in the colonies towards the aim of self-government.[30] Late as it seems from the vantage point of the 1960's, the policy again contrasts with those of the continental powers. The latter were still thinking in terms of bringing promising natives to their own European capitals for education. The C.O. proposed setting up a commission on higher education in the colonies which would contribute, as always, to a pace and type of development to be determined by the capacity of each territory. The commission, headed by a noted jurist, Mr. Justice (later Sir Cyril) Asquith, was composed of distinguished scholars and members of the C.S. Included were Miss Perham and Sir Donald Cameron, one of Lugard's successors as governor of Nigeria, and before that the most famous of Tanganyika's governors.[31] It is clear from the correspondence that the C.O. and the university regarded C.S. training, colonial studies in the United Kingdom, and the nurturing of colonial universities as all part of a unified approach to postwar development in the overseas dependencies. "We must build up a comprehensive structure," wrote the secretary of state to Lord Simon.[32] Not only must existing institutions such as Makerere, Fourah Bay, and the University of Hongkong be strengthened but new colleges must be founded and their ties with British universities improved. The major problem of teaching staff was recognized. It was seen that luring dons to the colonies, still today a difficult task, would not be easily arranged.[33]

Lord Hailey's committee faced the need, in Oxford and elsewhere, for funds in aid of research and looked to the early establishment of a colonial social science research council. Miss Perham and two other members of the Asquith Commission visited Africa and the West Indies to investigate development possibilities. Riots in the Caribbean colonies in the 1930's were a prime cause of inquiries leading to passage of the Commonwealth Development and Welfare Act in 1940. The will to do something about long-neglected colonial economies was there; Parliament was at last agreeing to appropriate funds; but the whole intricate question of planning and training staff to carry the plans forward required exhaustive exploration before the end of the war would make action possible. By the end of 1943 Oxford and Cambridge had founded a joint committee to consult on means of releasing staff for temporary teaching work in colonial universities. The committee was also to keep in touch with the C.O. on all matters of common interest. Miss Perham, the leading light of Oxford's own committee on colonial studies,

was also the university's main spokesman on the joint committee, and she and Veale were Furse's principal contacts
where C.S. training was concerned. Veale, although not
a member of the exclusively academic committees, was
always the university's voice in negotiations with other
universities and the C.O. Thus, governmental-academic
cooperation in the three related fields of effort vis-à-vis
the colonies was based not only on affinity of interest
but on the long-standing personal experience of consultation. The spirit of cooperation in the Oxford-Cambridge-
London group, organized to distribute postwar courses
for the C.S., was not as warm as that of bodies from which
London was excluded. But by the beginning of 1944 it
too had benefited from the advantage of past effort to
agree as well as the experience of exchanging views.

Tri-university discussion prior to January 1944 had
taken place mainly through correspondence and occasional meetings of individuals. A conspicuous lack of
progress convinced Furse that a full-dress official committee, meeting at the C.O., was the only solution. This
group would be charged with reviewing past C.S. training
in the light of contemporary conditions, recommending
new courses, and dividing subjects among the three institutions. The under-secretary of state, the Duke of Devonshire, agreed to chair the committee. Each university
was to send four representatives, and the C.O. would
have a like number of its specialists present. After the
Fisher Committee, the Devonshire Committee was the
most important consultative body figuring in the interwar history of the C.S.

For Furse the most significant condition demanding
review by the Devonshire Committee was the continuing
and harmful lag between training for technicians, which
was fairly well advanced by the outbreak of war, and
training for administrators. While he rejected vocational

courses for administrators, Furse was impressed by the value of such courses to officers in the other services. In forestry for example, one of Furse's first loves, an "apprentice tour" scheme had been discussed as early as 1936.[34] Members of the forestry service were soon taking a one-year course at Oxford, followed by an apprentice year in colonies and then more courses in the university. By the time they embarked for their colonial posts as fully accredited officers they had had a "sandwich" of two training years interspersed with a year of practical experience. The scheme enhanced quality and also gave the Forestry Service an *esprit de corps* and a sense of unity.

An aspect of the forestry program which especially appealed to Furse was the availability of senior officers from the colonies as lecturers in the Oxford courses. Previous to this Lugard and other retired officials had lectured at Oxford and Cambridge to probationers taking the old courses. Occasionally an academically inclined official had been able to obtain leave to do special research in a field related to his career duties. K. A. Busia, an African D.O. from the Gold Coast, for example, studied social anthropology at Oxford on a Carnegie grant during the war.[35] Rare as they were, all such study experiences were straws in the wind.

In the middle of the war Veale wrote to the Colonial Higher Education Commission in London that the increase in colonial studies at Oxford clearly foretold a different kind of training for C.S. recruits.[36] He corresponded also with Furse, and their letters groped towards a new rationale and method for postwar courses. "You want your people . . . to believe," wrote Veale, "in the value of what they are doing . . . that on the whole the British Empire has been a beneficent Institution, and that its aim has been to improve the lot of the subject races by making them share in the progress of the civilized world and contribute to it." [37] It would be intolerable, he went on, if those who taught colonial history believed "that the British Empire was acquired by piracy and brigandage, and that we cling to it now to satisfy the selfish greed of a few capitalists." [38] Oxford, he maintained, chose its faculty for scholarly eminence, not missionary fervor. Placing the courses there would assure probationers of exposure to academic objectivity, whereas a staff college would result in an undesirable aura of doctrinal uniformity. Drawing the two ideas together, the registrar spoke of the needs of C.S. beginners. "In their professional careers your people will have to listen with open (but not unstable) minds to criticisms with which they must be able to deal." [39] At Oxford they would meet anti-imperialist talk, he thought, but would be exposed also to a sophisticated and informed case for responsible imperialism. Veale closed with a swipe at staff college lecturers: "Public opinion in the University will be some protection against any school being governed by mandarins." [40]

Replying, Furse wrote that he "never wanted an organization which would, so to speak, impregnate the minds of our younger officers with a particular attitude towards the Colonial Empire and its history." [41] "But I suspect," he continued, ". . . they have been exposed to a lot of rather defeatist ideas . . . and have not been given a chance of obtaining a balanced idea of the facts. This I want to correct in order that they may go out with some real knowledge of the true position, and with facts and arguments in their minds which they can fall back on when they are exposed to misleading views or criticisms." [42] This was a far cry from the spirit of French colonial training courses. In Paris beginners were given to understand in highly specific terms that their mission was no less than the complete Frenchification of native populations and that in following her destiny in Africa France was doing both a Christian and a civilizing task.[43]

The registrar expanded on his defense of liberal arts institutions as against staff colleges. Academic training for all kinds of work was on the increase, he said, and this was good.[44] Lawyers and soldiers obviously needed specialist courses, and the professions as well as businesses were wise to encourage junior executives to take courses in spare time. But education was becoming *over*-specialized. As a result, students tended to think that things were simpler than they really were. Famous Oxford graduates had proved by their success in life, he held, that a broad education was advantageous regardless of later specialization. The best antidote to the "seditious" teaching of staff colleges was getting professionals of all kinds back to Oxford from time to time to bask in the unspecialized atmosphere of the liberal arts and humanities.

Furse professed ignorance of academic matters, but he agreed with Veale's general views and saw an additional advantage in having administrative probationers at Oxford. Like their prewar colleagues, they would be able to mingle with technical and professional recruits at the training stage and thus lay the groundwork for future collaboration in the colonies. He thought Miss Perham was right to insist on more thorough general training for administrators after the war and especially on more liaison training for both administrators and technical officers.[45] Another advantage of Oxford was its superior ties with colonial universities. The future leaders of the colonial territories would be graduates of these institutions. British officials working with these leaders would have to know in the future not only what traditional local rulers thought and planned but also, increasingly, the state of mind of the rising urban intellectual.

As to the division of subjects for postwar training, the three major universities had shown little inclination to agree during the two-year period before the Devonshire Committee met. In unguarded moments the Oxford side could admit that their preeminence was confined mainly to Miss Perham's colonial administration and that in imperial history the laurels were shared with Cambridge. In anthropology London was superior. The metropolitan university also showed signs of determination to overtake Oxford in colonial studies. In the fields of language and education London's stature was such as to inspire no pretensions at all in Oxford or Cambridge.

Representatives of the three universities had met in London in 1942. The tone of the meeting was set by an opening proposal by the Oxford vice chancellor that postwar C.S. trainees be allowed to choose the university where they would pursue their courses.[46] If accepted by London this would have left the field to Oxford and Cambridge. Most recruits would be recent graduates of the two older universities or, if not, would naturally prefer a year at one of them to a course in London. The remainder of the meeting was devoted to claims and counterclaims. Furse was sufficiently discouraged to suggest that continued failure to agree would compel the C.O. to reopen the question of founding a staff college. The registrar then offered, with a generosity not calculated to impress London, that the latter have all probationers for the second (language) half of the first course, leaving all of the second course and the first half of the beginning course to Oxford and Cambridge.[47] No one at Oxford seriously thought that London would accept this. The proposal was in fact meant to impress upon slow-moving

Oxford college administrators that they would have to put their houses in order in the field of colonial studies. Then followed an Oxford-Cambridge meeting where it was agreed that, small as their love for each other was, they should present a unified front to London.[48] Oxford would concentrate on law and government and Cambridge on history and agriculture. Oxford was so concerned about the general London threat by this time (1943) that its partisans were even willing to see the despised Barnett House, a center for social work, included in their list of resources.[49]

As time for the first Devonshire meeting approached, Furse tried desperately to keep a trickle of recruits flowing to the understaffed colonial governments. Recruitment for the technical services kept up fairly well during the war. But the armed forces quickly snatched up men released by the universities for appointment to colonial administrative posts.[50] Universities had the power to recommend deferment, and Furse made frequent trips to Oxford to see members of the Appointments Board. "After the last war," he told Veale, "there was something like a breakdown in Colonial Administration, although the problems at that time were nothing like so difficult or extensive as they are likely to be after this war." [51] Oxford could help by deferring a few probationers long enough for them to take their (accelerated wartime) degrees. The university responded by allowing men to count colonial service as war service and giving credit for the latter.[52] From the start of the war no probationers were sent to Cambridge, although a small number did continue to arrive in Oxford during 1939 and 1940. A member of Furse's staff induced the War Office to permit a scheme whereby appointees, although going immediately into uniform, had their C.S. appointments confirmed and dated from the time of appointment rather than from the time of actually taking up their duties in colonial posts.[53] This was of no immediate use to harassed colonial governments. But it assured them a supply of recruits the moment peace came.

The reappraisal preceding the actual meetings of the Devonshire Committee had not produced a thorough evaluation of prewar recruitment and training methods. It did air these methods in a way that would have been impossible under normal peacetime conditions. The political maturity of colonial peoples, everywhere advancing throughout the interwar period, was furthered by the war, which weakened the hands of colonial regimes. Changing conditions in the colonies would have called for reassessment of governmental precepts and techniques in any case. Britain was forced, during the Second World War, to focus attention on governments beset by popular unrest from below and by war-induced political weakness above. It was fortunate for both Britain and the colonies that academic interest in colonial problems had increased during the 1920's and 1930's. With the coming of war and the moratorium in recruitment and training which it necessitated, the development of colonial universities was a live issue. Social science research into colonial problems, both in the new colonial universities and in Britain, had produced, by 1944, an unprecedented knowledgeability in both London and the major universities. The C.O., always in close touch with university dons and administrators, was in an incomparable position to make use of the new knowledge. This was especially true by comparison with most continental powers, whose colonial offices and universities were under alien military occupation at the time. Britain's opportunity to think out her position relative to the sprawling Colonial Empire and to plan a comprehensive program of postwar development was unique.

The instrument of whatever changes Britain would try to effect in the colonies after the war was the C.S. and especially the senior service, the administrative corps. In 1943 Furse produced a long memorandum on postwar training for administrative officials.[54] The memorandum, an outgrowth of Furse's own observations in the colonies and his talks with scholars, was the working paper on which the Devonshire Committee was asked to base its deliberations. It was both a comment on the past and a blueprint for the future. Analysis of the work of the Devonshire Committee must therefore be prefaced by discussion of the Furse memorandum, the influences which shaped it, and its meaning in terms of social, economic, and political change in both Britain and the colonies.

CHAPTER VII

A New Service

IN February 1944 Sir George Gater of the C.O. wrote to the Oxford vice chancellor reminding him that Furse had just presented the university with a memorandum on postwar training for the C.S.[1] The Asquith Commission on higher education in the colonies had also been advised of the Furse memorandum, he said, since the subject of the postwar C.S. was intimately connected with that on which the commission was working. Oxford, Cambridge, and London would now be asked to participate together on a committee to review the Furse proposals, which would then be submitted to the Asquith Commission and finally to the secretary of state for his approval. It was the C.O.'s understanding that Oxford would be represented by its vice chancellor, the registrar, and two heads of colleges, Sir Richard Livingstone, president of Corpus Christi, and Dr. Stallybrass, principal of Brasenose. The first meeting of the Devonshire Committee was scheduled for the following month, in the C.O.

Furse's memorandum began with a rather turgidly phrased prediction of sweeping postwar changes throughout the world and especially in the colonies. "The pioneer era of colonial development has passed," he wrote.[2] There was a time in the late nineteenth and early twentieth centuries when the aims of colonialism and the tasks of administrators were straightforward and humanitarian; they were clearly perceptible to the British home population and were almost universally approved.[3] Now, however, there was hesitation and questioning, both at home and in the colonies themselves. Some colonial legislatures, notably in Ceylon, Jamaica, and the Gold Coast, contained native majorities or would do so in the near future. These were "vocal, often critical, sometimes abusive," whereas formerly native populations had been overwhelmingly apathetic or favorably disposed to the ruling power. At home political attitudes of indifference to colonial questions were giving way to genuine interest in colonial welfare and to assumptions, often more enlightened than knowledgeable, that independence was simply a matter of Britain handing over authority and leaving the dependencies to themselves. World opinion, particularly in the United States, was increasingly critical of colonialism without being much informed about social and political realities in the colonies.

As for the C.S., the time was already past when its task was mainly to deal with traditional chiefs in the spirit of indirect rule. The educated native, or "intellectual," was now the most important phenomenon on many colonial scenes. Civil servants would have to understand and sympathize with him and work cooperatively with him in preparing for self-rule. In a prophetic passage Furse remarked that economic planning had now replaced the static task of administering justice and that American money might conceivably flow into Africa and Asia in such quantities that the whole face of societies would be changed overnight. This was written in 1942! To meet the challenges of these unprecedented changes a new C.S. would have to be created. It was the C.S. and its sister service in the C.O. which would bear the burden of interpreting colonial questions to the British people. The main object of a new recruitment and training program would be to prevent too great a rift developing between colonial policy and public opinion in the United Kingdom.

Up until this time Furse had not been openly critical of training courses. He now pointed to defects which would have to be remedied if the C.S. was to meet postwar requirements. Before 1939 a cadet's theoretical training ended when he left the Oxford or Cambridge course. A handful of administrators had received grants from the Carnegie Corporation for study leaves in the 1930's, but the rich practical experience of most was never communicated to the world outside the colonies.[4] There was insufficient connection between training as given before the war and research, although the two should have formed natural counterparts. Lastly, and most seriously from the standpoint of everyday administration, the lack of rapport between administrative and technical personnel in secretariat and provincial offices continued to plague efficiency. It will be remembered that Furse had addressed this problem by proposing that the two kinds of officials should take certain courses together in England before leaving for the colonies. But the "senior service" complex died hard in remote areas.[5] It could not be shaken once officers had been assigned to their posts. Changes would have to be attempted at the training stage and with more determined effort than before the war.

In listing new training objectives Furse provided both an evaluation of the old system and an indication of changing conditions in the colonies and Britain's responses to them. Improved contact between the C.S. and public opinion at home would be furthered by increased use of senior and middle rank administrators as lecturers. "Public opinion" to Furse meant *informed* public opinion. The universities, Whitehall, Parliament, and the press were as far as his hopes reached. Postwar training courses should aim at a high degree of sophistication regarding foreign colonial empires. Prewar probationers went out to their posts with little knowledge of the British Colonial Empire as a whole and almost none of the dependencies of other nations. Comparative colonialism was to be a key subject in the new syllabus. The widest implications of the work of technical departments must be brought home to administrative probationers so that past vocational parochialism might be broken down. Poor morale, a feeling of being cut off from reality and unappreciated by the public in England, was a problem that could best be faced by giving cadets a sense of mission early in their careers. The Empire had been too Roman in the past, had concentrated too much on material things and on dispensing justice and keeping order. "In Africa and the Pacific, as well as in Asia, we are dealing," wrote Furse, "with people to whom spiritual and esthetic values are often more important than they have come to be for the average modern European." [6] Britain must learn from the Greeks and the French and teach her administrators something of the spiritual and artistic background of colonial peoples. A properly designed training course would fuse a pride in Britain's record with an awareness of the indigenous cultural base on which the structure of self-government was to be built.

Furse felt that the French and the Dutch had been more successful in establishing a relationship of trust and understanding with native intellectuals than had the British. The latter on the other hand were superior in dealing with traditional authorities. Could training equip the new British official for better relations with "the new type of colored man"? [7] Furse did not give a definite answer. He confined himself to noting that British society was changing, too, and that probably these changes at home and in the colonies would result in a broadening of the recruitment base. He looked forward in fact to "the probable selection of more men who had climbed the social and educational ladder by means of state scholarships." [8] Having won their positions through hardship and struggle, they would, Furse thought, be naturally sympathetic to native leaders who had risen by similar means.[9]

In this way Furse specified his conviction that the C.S. had always been and would remain truly representative of British society. This view was amplified by a senior member of the C.S. in Tanganyika in 1960.[10] Representativeness, he said, is not to be gauged by the number of social categories from which recruits are drawn. They may be, and indeed should be, all taken from the top class. There is no social injustice as long as access to that class is reasonably open. The measure of injustice is social discontent resulting, in extreme cases, in organized protest and realignment. The view is that of the classical liberal aristocrat.

Furse then outlined specific suggestions for reform of the training syllabus. All administrative probationers would take a three-stage course. First there would be a preliminary course similar to the prewar C.A.S. course but suitably improved. Upon graduation from this cadets would proceed to their colonies for an apprentice year. They would then return for a second and more advanced course whose value would be enhanced by the practical experience just completed. In addition to this procedure, which was for new recruits only, there would be a totally new course, or sabbatical year, for selected numbers of the most promising officers. From the vantage point of the 1960's these proposals do not appear especially unusual. But when the training attitudes of the 1920's and earlier are recalled they appear as a radical departure which Furse would only be able to put across to traditionalists in the C.O. and the C.S. by means of the most persuasive arguments. Running through the memorandum in fact was an apologetic tone reflecting the expectation that serving governors would view the new syllabus as the brainchild of a madman.

Developing his suggestions, Furse took up the stages of the proposed courses. The preliminary year would stress the mission of the Empire and would include an introduction to unusual subjects not covered previously. It was vital that cadets be placed under sympathetic superiors once they reached their apprenticeship posts and not under men unqualified to teach or impatient with beginners. During this time the cadet would meet the educated native, "before he has had time to acquire prejudices." [11] On return for the second course year probationers would be given deeper exposure to the social sciences and would participate in seminars led by dons sophisticated enough to counteract the expected "bolshevist" tendencies of young men with a little learning and a little experience. Furse well remembered one such cadet who had gone out to Nigeria in the 1930's and had soon resigned to write an angry book. Basking in the glow of years and worldly achievements, this same cadet, when he had become Australian Ambassador in the Hague, explained that the book "was the work of a young man disappointed to find the system functioning with defects which were damaging and unnecessary, and that some of the officers were letting the team down; but it was the work, too, no doubt, of an immature young man." [12] Furse did not deprecate such men. In fact, he tended to prefer them to subservient, unquestioning types. But he wanted their rebelliousness to have a constructive outlet and a chance to cool in the English winter. Rebels could then return to their colonies refreshed, matured, and perhaps less positive. For the special course, reserved to "rising rockets," men who would some day become governors or chief secretaries, Furse proposed renewed stress on comparative colonialism and a maximum of free time for private research. Miss Perham's hopes for a stream of essays, possibly publishable, on a variety of colonial subjects, obviously lay behind this suggestion.

Finally Furse touched on the question of where the courses should be placed. He noted Lord Trenchard's proposal of Liverpool University.[13] Trenchard had felt that the older universities would be too preoccupied with established courses to pay enough attention to colonial studies and that a lesser institution could be depended on to try to build its reputation by taking exclusive responsibility for a new field of scholarship. A red brick university if chosen would also protect the C.O. from the charge of class bias which would surely be made if Oxford and Cambridge were chosen again. Furse had no difficulty rejecting the Liverpool idea. It would, he said, destroy at a blow the system so painfully built up in cooperation with Oxford and Cambridge whereby the C.O. had maximum control of its courses although they were actually housed outside London. Moreover the incomparable academic advantages of Oxford, Cambridge, and London were a big price to pay for the doubtful gain of a special department in a second-rate university. Such a department might develop a staff college atmosphere, cut off as it would be from not only London but the softening effects of residential colleges as well. A far better solution would be to keep and develop the connection with Oxford and Cambridge and spike the social bias charge by including London.

But the clinching argument in favor of the three universities in Furse's opinion was their superior equipment for offering courses in subjects needed by both administrative and technical probationers. London had its School of Oriental and African Studies as well as an unexcelled education faculty and impressive resources in economics and tropical medicine. Oxford and Cambridge were strong in colonial history. Both had good law faculties and established specialists in anthropology and geography. Oxford was preeminent in forestry and Cambridge in agriculture. Certainly, Furse reasoned, a program which included all three of these universities would be the best the C.O. could hope for. Admittedly biased in favor of the older universities, he had the weight of logic on his side.

The Furse memorandum reflected official thinking in the C.O. and the C.S. and the opinions of leading scholars. It is fair to say that it embodied a microcosm of knowledgeable British views on the position of the Colonial Empire in the early 1940's, a critique of colonial policy and administration in the interwar era, and a projection of the place the colonies would have in the postwar world. As a stock-taking and a *caveat* the memorandum and the report of which it became a part overreached in importance any comparable document issued since the end of the First World War.

In retrospect the meetings of the Devonshire Committee appear to have been hardly more than occasions for embellishing on the Furse memorandum. The committee was purely advisory. From the start it was highly unlikely that any of its recommendations would be immediately or comprehensively enacted. It is appropriate then that the deliberations of the committee be examined and evaluated more as reflections on the interwar years than as a forecast of new arrangements. The latter must be included from time to time, if only to set prewar phenomena in relief. The comments of committee members and witnesses are valuable chiefly, however, as additional perspectives on events and policies of the 1920's and 1930's. The war brought such great change that the post-war colonial empire was almost unrecognizably different from its predecessor. In the words of a former colonial administrator, commenting on the historical integrity of the interwar era, "the ethos of that particular past [was by 1945] dead and done with." [14]

In the C.O. itself, as opposed to the C.S., there was real, though somewhat abstract, comprehension of changes in colonial society. A memorandum prepared for the secretary of state the year before the Devonshire Committee assembled summarized recent developments in the dependencies and described the changing roles of administrators.[15] Technical and professional services were becoming Africanized, the memorandum pointed out. Although this process was slower in administration, there was also a gradual devolution of power from British to native officers in secretariat and provincial posts in some colonies. Urban and (mainly traditional) local councils were being strengthened in accordance with long-established policy in West Africa, Southeast Asia, and the Caribbean. By the outbreak of the Second World War considerable progress had been made in this area of institution-building. Major cities such as Accra, Lagos, Freetown, Columbo, Dar es Salaam, and Kampala had long since been governed by municipal councils on which natives were represented and in some cases had majorities. Colonial constitutions, beginning with those of Ceylon and Jamaica, were undergoing constant revision, as often as not accompanied by native protest that revisions were "mere window-dressing" rather than genuine democratic reforms.[16] Nevertheless revisions increased native representation in legislative councils at a time when natives of Belgian colonies had no political rights at all and when representation in French and Portuguese colonies meant sending deputies to metropolitan parliaments.

The rise of the educated native caught the C.S. somewhat off balance. Unlike civil servants in Britain, the memorandum continued, colonial officials were accustomed to accepting full responsibility for governing, especially in provincial administrations. They not only implemented policy, as did their colleagues in England, but *made* it as well. "In most colonies the Civil Servant *is* the Government, and not the servant of the Government." [17] Members of professional services such as educationists maintained contact with events in Britain. They were not only sympathetic to but were positively and consciously aiding native advance.[18] Administrators, on the other hand, the memorandum said, were more rigid and devoted to precedent. The seniority system left policy in the hands of officials whose ideas were rooted in the years when their careers began. By the early war years when native intellectuals "were beginning to make conscious demands and criticisms," too many administrators nurtured in Lugardian principles of respect for native chiefs saw the urban African as a threat to order.[19] "What these people need," remarked a D.O., "is not education, but the stick." [20] Younger administrators who did not share this reactionary attitude wrote to Miss Perham for advice on how to deal with unfamiliar urban authorities, whereas in former times she had received inquiries mainly concerned with traditional chiefs.[21] Such officers saw it as their duty to help natives prepare for managing a modern welfare state. But they felt keenly their own deficiencies as teachers. Most knew little or nothing of local government in England, as indeed they could not have been expected to do in view of prewar selection criteria which favored the rural gentry. Younger sons of squires and parsons would be adept at dispensing justice in the time-honored manner. They would be the last to know much about the development of state-supported social services in Britain and the techniques of county welfare organizations. Their attitudes to visiting scholars varied according to the individual degree of receptivity and adaptability each had in relation to the new role of government in the colonies. Some looked on academic people with almost pathetic gratitude, seeing them as leaders in a normally hopeless battle to awaken public opinion at home to colonial realities.[22] Others were disgusted by the presumption and conceit of scholars in holding, as one did for example, that "the study of the African is a scientific subject." [23]

Administrators in the interwar period were not generally given to corresponding with scholars and members of the C.O. staff. But as colonial studies developed at Oxford and communications improved, specialists in both Whitehall and the universities came into increasingly direct contact with administrators in even the remotest districts. Visits and exchanges of letters became more frequent in the 1940's. Out of these came a picture of the C.S. at work which was invaluable to the Devonshire Committee and which would not have been available a generation earlier.

For many D.O.'s their work and life was still the infinitely rewarding experience which had made permanent expatriates of overseas Englishmen for centuries. This breed of D.O. could be found in Arabia, Africa, the West Indies, the Pacific, and Southeast Asia from the 1940's to the 1960's, and their ethos has survived in India, Burma, and the Sudan. Their governing attitudes everywhere outlived the rise of urbanization and industrialization in the colonies. As long as there remained primitive, thinly populated areas, away from the Europeanizing coasts, old-style D.O.'s ruled on as always. The poor morale of colonial civil servants, about which so much has been heard in recent years, relates more to officials who were not content with the lonely life of the bush. Even in the 1930's, when C.S. morale generally was at its height, complaints arose which indicated that, if conditions had not changed up-country, the mentality and outlook of officials had.

From committee members and witnesses the Devonshire Committee heard extensive evidence that a variety of morale factors were affecting C.S. performance. Loneliness and a sense of abandonment were fairly common. In a letter to Veale a D.O. in Nigeria expressed amazement that an official in "such a center of the universe as Oxford" would be interested in the problems of a lowly colonial administrator slogging along in his remote district headquarters.[24] Irritation with the amount of paperwork he had to do and which made it impossible for him to see as much of his people as he wished was voiced by another D.O.[25] Interestingly, this particular lament was put in the same terms as one raised over a decade before in the same colony.[26] The "real work," complained another, ". . . of seeing and teaching the Sultan and Company, setting going a lot of rural projects on which villages have asked for their communal savings to be spent, thinking about the coming District Heads (native) Conference, and the like" must give way too often to the drudgery of writing reports to the Secretariat.[27] So great was the aversion of some senior officials to report writing that they saddled subordinates with such tasks and spent their time happily trekking through the bush to visit and consult with native chiefs. A young administrator who had been promoted to be private secretary to the African prime minister in his colony remarked nostalgically that the promotion, although an honor and a compliment to him from leaders who were guiding the country to independence, was also a bitter pill, since it ended his contacts with the people of his former district.[28]

Withering blasts at all higher officialdom, the secretariat, the governor, and the C.O., were common. "For my sins," a D.O. in West Africa complained, "I have been posted to the Secretariat, to half-sexed work for which I have no inclination or training." [29] The C.O. and the secretariats were blamed as of old for destroying continuity by transferring officials so often that they lacked enough time to come to know their districts.[30] The C.O., it was felt, did not appreciate the effect on local administration of the chessboard moves which they sometimes made from London. That the criticism was justified was brought home recently by a C.O. official responsible for postings. He spoke of the combinations of talent which he was able to make due to his intimate knowledge of the C.S. It apparently did not cross his mind that the abrupt promotion of a chief secretary to a governorship and the transfer of the colony's most able provincial commissioner to replace the former would necessitate a whole series of other moves with great disruptive effect throughout the colony. This "game of musical chairs" went on throughout the interwar period and continued to the 1960's.[31] C.O. planners concentrated on the advantages of having a particular official in a particular job and not on aftereffects.

Members of the Devonshire Committee, both during and after their hearings, heard enough from colonial administrators to convince them that traditional attitudes to training had lost their attraction for a majority in the C.S. "I wish I had had before embarking on my career the benefit of the courses suggested," wrote a provincial official from his post in Africa.[32] Miss Perham remarked on the eagerness with which D.O.'s would respond to theoretical discussion when she visited them in their posts.

Many felt the narrowness of their horizons and welcomed any chance to lift their gaze from mundane daily chores. The most imaginative of them knew that they lacked perspective. A young official lucky enough to be in England on leave when the Devonshire Committee was meeting testified that the service was precedent-ridden and badly needed to have its "joints loosened." [33] He agreed with Lord Hailey, also testifying that day, that the new emphasis on economic development demanded formal academic training going well beyond prewar courses. He agreed too that it would be wrong to restrict advanced courses to the select few who were destined for secretariat work. "Bush D.O.'s" needed training every bit as much as secretariat specialists, perhaps more. One serving official went so far as to send a note on training direct to Furse. [34]

The help desired by progressive officials was not confined to economics and finance, much as their days were filled with economic development problems. Many now realized that they were destined, in the words of a noted anthropologist, "to be . . . primary agents in transforming (colonial) societies." [35] Britain had made a sincere and well-meaning effort to build up native political institutions. The attempt had failed because natives had preferred to copy the Europeans. It was not for Britain to resist the trend but to channel it so that rising native administrators would be ready when the time came for full self-government. This was easier said than done. The most enlightened administrators knew that natives would demand and doubtless get independence whether they were ready or not. Would native officials and politicians accept anything in the way of inspiration and guidance from European administrators as anti-colonialist sentiment grew in volume and intensity? What was the prevailing image of the British colonial civil servant in native eyes? [36] Miss Perham herself disclaimed ability to gauge it. Commenting on Veale's analogy between D.O.'s and English country squires, she remarked skeptically, "No one can really know what the African thinks, but I . . . doubt if he regards any D.O. in anything comparable with this position." [37] The Devonshire planners and C.S. practitioners alike had to reckon with inadequate financial resources available for colonial development in any case. In view of this, did it really make any difference what Britain, through an improved C.S., tried to do in the colonies?

Such were some of the more notable realities and attitudes of mind in the C.S. and in the colonies generally as the Devonshire Committee undertook its review. In the committee meetings themselves an effort was made to identify specific criticisms of prewar training, its philosophy and content and the views of colonial governments as voiced by testifying officials. The classic view of training held by Lord Milner in South Africa, Lord Lugard in Nigeria, and before their times by many proconsuls in India was that experience was the only real teacher. Training was "being given a job and being told to get on with it." [38] In the Devonshire meetings and in attendant correspondence this view was overwhelmingly rejected. It might be held that this was not surprising, since the C.S. had had, after all, a formal training scheme since 1926. But prewar courses had lasted barely nine months; they were part of the normal Oxford and Cambridge scenes and were subject to all the usual distractions which that implied; they preceded and were apart from career practice; colonial governments looked on them with ill-disguised contempt, while honoring them in principle; and probationers usually saw them mainly as a means of tasting the delights of university life for an additional year rather than as a preparation for service.

Professor Engledow, the Cambridge agriculturalist, stigmatized the old courses as dull and inadequate.[39] An exciting innovation in the 1920's, they had quickly settled into the established pace of life at the two imperturbable residential universities. Dons regarded the courses too often as necessary nuisances rather than as opportunities for breaking new ground. Lectures tended to be uninspired and by-the-way. Undergraduates fresh from a classics or PPE (politics, philosophy and economics) program could not but regard the course as a comedown.[40] Paradoxically the old C.A.S. course was criticized for being at once too much seduced by Oxbridge life and too much apart from it. When the registrar protested to Furse that prewar probationers had not taken full enough advantage of the university's rich academic offerings, Stallybrass answered that they had involved themselves too much in its extracurricular life.[41] The barb went to the heart of Furse's favorite conception of the value of residential colleges. He rated informal, intimate discussion, running "into the wee hours of the night" over set lectures where the give-and-take of productive discussion was impossible.[42] Stallybrass, the last to retire in hundreds of such encounters, did not underrate their value. But he felt that C.S. trainees had neglected the tougher realm of social science inquiry. Postwar probationers could still be members of a service club—indeed, this would contribute to a necessary *esprit de corps*—but it must be a more serious club.

Professors Engledow and Carr-Saunders carried forward the attack on the old courses' lack of pre-experience theorizing. They agreed with Saunders of Cambridge that if theory was useless then universities might as well close their doors.[43] Both the I.C.S. and the Sudan Service, said Engledow, were convinced of the value of vocational courses for administrators, especially as their countries advanced into the era of native participation in government.[44] Now that the initiative lay with dynamic native progressives throughout the Colonial Empire, the static justice of a ruling class was no longer enough. If this was so, then the role of guide, familiar to colonial officials even during the 1930's, called for high sophistication in political theory, anthropology, and economics. The university's task was no less than to "build a mental bridge" over which the C.S. could lead colonial populations from primitive trusteeship to the modern welfare state.[45] To advance this staggering responsibility, both the universities and the C.O. knew, ambitious new research programs would have to be mounted. This would have to be done in the remaining war years while there was still time and before the end of hostilities demanded the immediate dispatch of large numbers of untrained recruits to understaffed colonial governments. In a letter to the registrar Furse pointed out that even if the C.O. had been in favor of more scientifically designed courses in the 1930's the universities would not have been able to offer them.[46] Nevertheless, not only the academic members of the Devonshire Committee but Furse himself feared the reaction of the tradition-dominated C.O. to training proposals based on a rejection of the established in-service training ethic.[47]

It was not only the blind and the reactionary, however, who defended the old system and its rationale. Sir George Tomlinson and Sir Christopher Cox were neither inexperienced nor narrow-minded. Tomlinson wrote to Veale urging that the Devonshire Committee not go so far in its devotion to theory that it ignored practical realities on the ground.[48] Having sounded some colonial administrators and consulted his own experience, he reported that at least some of the past courses—surveying, for example —had been a positive waste. Cadets could get enough bush engineering and basic surveying from their public works officers on arrival in their posts. In the past many had had to unlearn inappropriate principles acquired in the C.A.S. course as these had aimed too high and had resulted in confusion during early career service. Agreeing, Sir Christopher Cox cautioned against filling empty heads before a solid basis of experience existed for theories to be grounded in.[49] Cox, a career academic and, as such, no enemy of abstract conceptualizing, was a strong proponent of mixing theory and practice.[50] His testimony before the Devonshire Committee immediately followed his return from a tour of the colonies. His talks with officials persuaded him of the value of Furse's three-stage training plan, with theory reserved mainly for officers who had had both the preliminary course and a tour of duty behind them.[51] Cox also seconded Engledow's criticism of the old course as having induced boredom in probationers accustomed to the rich fare of a liberal arts curriculum. His views were based on an assumption that the human mind, especially that of a young man selected for ability to do hard work under trying conditions, would normally resist or ignore abstractions in the absence of previous experience. Without the latter there would be little or nothing on which to base evaluation. The same abstractions introduced to the same mind at a later stage would find a fertile field in which to work their powers of suggestion and guidance.

Developing his views, Cox vigorously opposed dividing the C.S. into an elite and "the others" for purposes of the proposed third or special course. This he compared with the "eleven plus" examination given to English school children. On the basis of this, decisions are made whether or not pupils, at the age of eleven, have the ability to pursue higher education. Colonial officials who appear to be somewhat dull by comparison with their fellows, said Cox, are exactly the ones who tend to become dogmatizers. For this reason they need further exposure to theory and to the merciless atmosphere of advanced seminars. Had prewar generations of probationers been given the advantage of the proposed sabbatical year much of the hidebound quality of colonial government could have been mitigated.

The friends of formal course work prior to experience did not believe that books were a panacea or substitute for in-service training. They did not think or recommend that academic institutions and faculties could provide all that was necessary to make a good administrator. Professor Engledow favored not only theoretical courses but also a Socratic "time for idling" in which probationers could think for themselves before being subjected to the all-consuming demands of career work.[52] If planning was of increasing importance, planners needed leisure in which to think calmly as much as they needed a philosophical framework to guide and nurture their thoughts. Engledow thus put his finger on a lack from which colonial administrators have always suffered. A provincial commissioner in Tanganyika, who had recently spent ten days recovering from fever, remarked that, although this was hardly pleasant, at least his periodic bouts of fever gave him precious time in which to think out his next moves. In normal work days the pressure of routine made such thought impossible.[53]

There was awareness too among committee members that the old courses had lacked breadth. The subject of colonial government had been treated too much as though it was a separate, watertight discipline. A governor in West Africa who had taken the Cambridge course in the 1920's said that he had felt, all during his career, a gnawing suspicion that his preparation had been too parochial and that he knew far too little of the great world outside his colony.[54] Even in the prewar years the colonies, in Miss Perham's words, were "becoming part of the world." [55] Could there not be a new conception of C.S. training to provide for the administrator's new role? Were not the position and morale of administrator-teachers implicitly different from those of their predecessors who had more actual power and fewer guidance duties? [56] The C.O. had been able to say, in so many words, to prewar recruits that C.S. careers offered immediate assumption of more real power than did less exotic and better-paid careers at home.[57]

Furse's assumption all during the interwar period had been that administrators must be, first and foremost, generalists. At the secretariat level specialist work was better left to a generalist than to a highly intelligent specialist who might lack the particular attributes of character and leadership which Furse considered essential. Specialists could be depended on to have mastered their own fields. But did they have enough imagination and perspective to serve in planning positions? Would the average "rising rocket" in the administrative service, on the other hand, be able to cope with increasingly sophisticated problems of colonial development? The dilemma, as the committee knew, was already being addressed in colonial capitals by encouraging promising administrators to specialize in such fields as finance and economic planning, labor relations, social welfare, and land use.

Committee members were agreed that prewar training had been almost totally inadequate in this regard. But could specialized subjects be usefully offered to probationers? Or were they better left to a later stage by which time experienced officers would have demonstrated aptitudes which could be usefully built upon a university course? What was the "liaison training" Furse had in

mind? The Devonshire Committee minutes indicate that
no one quite knew. Long after the secretary of state had
approved the committee's report, Oxford members were
still uncertain and had got no guidance from the C.O.[58]
All concerned in Whitehall and Oxford accepted the
principle of academic training. Yet the C.S.'s empirical
tradition lingered on in practice. Academic planners were
unable to evolve a workable training solution in the still
relatively unexplored field of colonial government. As
of 1960, there appeared to be no official in Africa or
Southeast Asia who pretended to know of a syllabus for
this most subtle of training problems.

Other aspects of the old syllabus were more susceptible
of straightforward analysis and planning. Furse knew
what he wanted in the field of colonial policy. Lectures
were required which would be on a high level of sophistication and which would emphasize comparisons with
other colonial systems, but which would not give new
recruits an overcritical view of colonialism before they
had gained practical experience. Stress was to be put on
Britain's honorable record and achievements and on the
difficulties of ruling a vast colonial empire with limited
resources. Faults must of course be admitted. But postwar cadets would have to withstand more criticism of the
very phenomenon of colonialism than had their predecessors. To do so they would need a ready stock of hard
facts about the past. Prewar probationers had been sent
out to govern a relatively confident empire. They had
been concerned not with whether colonialism was justifiable but with how administration should proceed. Where
colonial policy was concerned, the new training assumptions reflected the mood of an empire at bay. The easy
assurance of the 1930's seemed remote now. Although
the Devonshire discussions were taking place only a few
years after the most confident era in C.S. history, the tone

of the meetings seemed to presage a totally new colonial atmosphere, requiring a wholesale reappraisal of aims on the part of the metropolitan power.

Miss Perham raised the question of the relative merits of classics and social science. In a letter to the registrar after the Devonshire Committee had concluded its sessions, she inquired, "Has it not always been the idea that [administration] derives . . . from higher education . . . especially Greats—intuition and experience? Should we now revise our views?" [59] Furse and other believers in "character training" and the liberal arts stood firmly on a traditional base while recommending appropriate additions to traditional syllabi. But a majority on the Devonshire Committee and among its advisors felt that Greats were no longer enough. Perhaps, some suggested, they were totally inappropriate. Was it not positively harmful to clutter the minds of colonial administrators with ideas tied to situations in the time of Pericles? Courses were needed, it was argued, which emphasized real conditions in the territories to which trainees would be going. Nevertheless a good half of the committee members felt that classics still had a place, if not the prominent one it had occupied previously. It was the basis on which specialist training should be built. To proceed without it was to make the mistake that Dartmouth, Sandhurst, and Woolwich made—the mistake of narrowness. Prewar courses had erred on the side of overgeneralization. This was fair enough in times when colonial administrators' first task was to give an example of strong character, honesty, and orderly management of minimal government. In times of deepening complexity and broadening scope of government, however, administrators would be hindered if they did not have at least basic familiarity with the techniques of office management, accountancy, legal case work, social welfare methods, and a practical introduction to town planning and road building. But did they not need also, and perhaps most of all, what one district commissioner called "human understanding?" [60] Could this be taught? If so, was there any other method except long, painful, and costly exposure, from early school years onwards, to the great thinking of the ages?

Throughout the years of the present century colonial governments themselves had little influence in recruitment and training processes. As governments they have accepted the lead of the C.O. and of other authorities— those, for example, in Westminster, Whitehall, and the academic world—who have made their views and wishes known through the established channels of communication and policy. The Devonshire Committee made a determined effort, as the Fisher Committee had done, to elicit the opinions of individual members of the C.S. and also those of colonial governments. Out of the written and oral testimony emerged a picture of C.S. attitudes on the brink of the independence era. If somewhat fragmentary, the picture is nonetheless unique as a measure of opinion from a usually silent civil service body.

Senior members of the service, including a number of eminent governors, not surprisingly defended the traditional rationale of in-service training. The senior governor of the service, Sir Arthur Richards (afterwards Lord Milverton) of Nigeria, put forward the classic argument that experience is the only possible teacher.[61] That this was a reflexive position with him, however, and not a rational conviction based on open-minded weighing of alternatives, came out in subsequent questioning by committee members. Sir Arthur completely reversed himself and ended by not only agreeing with the new rationale of academic course work but loudly lamenting his own lack of training. Other governors stuck to their guns. Even

Richards' reversal must be taken with a grain of salt in view of the circumstances of the Devonshire inquiry. The meetings were, after all, in the C.O., not in colonial capitals where governors are gods. The chairman was not only the under-secretary of state, but a duke and one of the premier peers of a most class-conscious realm. Committee members were men of prominence in their respective fields, highly intelligent and not likely to be awed by a mere colonial governor. It is not to be wondered at that Richards and one or two others backtracked somewhat from positions to which they were committed emotionally and by career experience. But it is doubtful that their basic beliefs were much shaken in the process. Veale found that Sir Arthur was a different man altogether when they met again in the splendor of Government House at Lagos a year later.[62]

In the working atmosphere of rural and urban offices a widespread suspicion of academic training persists to the present day. In the spring of 1961 the governor of North Borneo made the statement that he did not set much store by university courses for his junior administrators but attached the greatest importance to placing them immediately under the supervision of experienced officials.[63] This view was echoed in African and Pacific colonies by administrators of all ranks during surveys in 1960 and 1962. In the Devonshire meetings C.S. officials tended to generalize from their own experience. Those who had entered the C.S. straight from military service were especially vehement in condemning academic preparation and theorizers generally. "Beachcombers"—C.S. men on temporary duty in the C.O.—testified that course work might be useful after a preliminary tour of duty but certainly not before.[64] Furse's plan for a three-stage training-experience "sandwich" lasting four years in all was viewed with horror by several governors who pointed out that such length was outlandish in view of the fact that the average C.S. career covered only 26 years.[65] One governor gave the committee pause by reminding them that native members of legislative councils were already up in arms over the cost of training, which fell, after all, on colonial budgets. Even those who favored course work urged that the preliminary course be as short as possible, certainly no longer than two academic terms, so that the first group of postwar cadets could reach the understaffed colonies without delay.

The latter pleas gave evidence of the real attitude of most senior officials towards the ambitious Devonshire scheme. Many hoped that preliminary courses would be postponed altogether during the immediate postwar years and that advanced courses would be taken by selected men only, specifically those slated for rapid promotion through secretariat ranks to governorships.[66] If accepted, this plan would have solved the problem of designing courses for both the still-primitive rural districts and the more specialized and modern posts in urban secretariats. It would also have driven the wedge still deeper between the D.O. and his bureaucratic colleague in the capital. Sir Arthur Richards' advice showed that he considered C.S. needs to be unchanged. What was needed was still the tough practical man. It was the C.O., and not field staffs, which required men of high intellectual capacity.

There was less than complete unanimity among the governors, however. Sir Arthur Benson, soon to become governor of Northern Rhodesia, deplored the deepening split between D.O.'s and secretariat officials.[67] Even Sir Alan Burns, not the most progressive governor, agreed that fully 95 per cent of new recruits badly needed preliminary training before they could be of any real use in colonial posts.[68] Sir Philip Mitchell, then governor of Kenya, replied to a questionnaire on the training proposals that he favored the scheme strongly and that he especially agreed with Furse on the need to educate the British public to colonial realities.[69] He also seconded the committee's stress on the value of courses in comparative colonialism.

The matter of control of public service members by colonial governments rather than by the C.O. received much attention. The atmosphere of mutual distrust and suspicion still lingered on. Echoing Lugard's words of a half-century before, Richards complained that the C.O., through its control of postings, was hampering continuity of administration.[70] He argued, as Sir Hugh Clifford had done in 1927, for autonomous administrations in each colony, based on differing local conditions.[71] The perennial unity aim was thus shown to be as stubbornly resisted by senior members of the C.S. in the 1940's as it was in Joseph Chamberlain's time. Improved intercontinental communications and the rise of nationalism drew the colonies together; tradition-minded natives and colonial civil servants kept them apart.

Regarding in-service training for recruits, Richards insisted that only the governors in each colony were fit to say which administrators had the ability to act as instructors. Veale, however, found on arrival in Sir Arthur's colony that this was largely a false issue, since no officers had time to teach beginners. Preliminary course work was thus the alternative to no training at all. In observations in some twenty British colonies from 1948 to 1962 this situation has been found to be as difficult, if not more so, as it was in immediate postwar years. The most that experienced D.O.'s have been able to do is to allow recruits to accompany them on their rounds. The best men have developed a knack of explanation-on-the-run. Others are more or less irritated with having to put up with ignorant and useless subordinates, who are therefore left to discover for themselves how administration proceeds.

A generalization that can be made about the attitudes of governors at the time of the Devonshire meetings is that most were somewhat out of touch with contemporary conditions of in-service training in their own colonies. Sir Arthur Richards was favoring a type of training that had worked well enough in his own cadet days but was less workable in 1945 when colonial regimes were pressed to the wall for lack of staff. The pace of government was faster in the latter time and the scope of effort greater. Ironically the C.O., although much farther removed from rural districts than were the governors in their capitals, was often in a better position to measure their requirements. Beachcombers in the C.O. expressed themselves freely. Visits by C.O. personnel to colonies were more frequent. It was therefore natural for the C.O. to consider governors uncooperative and for governors to look on the C.O. as a nuisance and a tyrant. It was so in Amery's day and in Lugard's. It is still so today, generally speaking, when there are fewer colonies every year and when communications with London are at peak efficiency. "See if you can't stir them up a bit out there," said an assistant under-secretary of state to a visitor leaving London for Africa in 1960. "The C.O. never tells me anything and never listens to what I tell them," a governor complained some weeks later.

In their testimony two governors agreed with the Devonshire Committee that rapport between administrative and technical officers was deplorable.[72] Sir Bede Clifford, governor of Trinidad, urged that administrators be given an understanding of not only the technical officer's work but of that of the business community as well.[73] An exclusively civil service attitude, he felt, was a relic of the past when business was considered demeaning. In a business-dominated modern colonial world its continuation would be disastrous. Yet there seemed to be no specific proposals of how relations between the various services and communities could be improved. The registrar believed that a local government course, taught in such a way as to include all types of technical problems, would help. The governors thought on the other hand that bad relations were largely, if not wholly, "a matter of personality." [74] This, too, was a reflection of prewar selection criteria and of the inability of senior officers to appreciate the complexity of contemporary local government problems.

Generally the responses of governors had not given an impression of progressive-mindedness at the highest level in the C.S. The most tangible evidence of an awareness that the age of independence was dawning was a request from Sir Bede Clifford that the C.O. issue a statement to reassure British officers on their tenure.[75] The statement should put London on record, he felt, as contemplating the indefinite retention of white officers in the colonies. The governors and other senior officers who testified or sent their views to the C.O. confined themselves to pious hopes, for the most part, that the new training scheme would strengthen the service and to platitudinous comments on individual aspects of Furse's proposals. A compilation by the C.O. of cabled responses from thirty governors makes dull reading.[76] Those who did more than signify approval scarcely went beyond a terse comment on the value of one or two paragraphs in Furse's memorandum. In return for a lengthy report by Veale on his visit to Nigeria, that colony's governor sent perfunctory thanks but no comments.[77] The kindest remark the registrar could make a few years later was that Their Excellencies had had no training themselves and doubtless could not really imagine what the C.O. was talking about.[78]

As for more junior officers in the colonies, the Oxford-Cambridge-London delegation which visited Nigeria in 1945–46 came back with the firm impression that they lacked faith in their superiors. Nothing short of a wholesale reform of the service, Veale was told, could bring about needed changes. Without these the postwar era would find the C.S. unable to give the colonies strong, inspired leadership. Some of this, no doubt, can be ascribed to normal discontent, an attitude of mind that is characteristic of juniors. In this case, discouragement was understandably greater than ever as a result of overwork by a war-thinned corps of exhausted men. The registrar tempered his judgment with the comment that the first postwar arrivals of recruits had given heart to the whole service. Morale improved everywhere. But the seniority system had done its demoralizing work. A precedent-ridden service was facing not only the usual effects of its own disgruntlement but a newer and far more serious challenge in the form of native unrest in an anticolonial world.

Thus far selection criteria had been mentioned only in passing. While the Devonshire Committee was concerned primarily with training, it was demonstrated again, as with the Fisher Committee, that the subjects of selection and training were essentially inseparable. The Devonshire meetings and attendant correspondence did not produce anything like a comprehensive review of C.S. quality. But there was a large number of highly suggestive and noteworthy sidelights. Many of these were normal, in that any service of comparable size would be liable to similar criticisms. Without actually alleging that prewar recruits had been on the whole unimpressive, the governor of Northern Rhodesia called for a probationary term covering both of the first two courses and the intervening year of practical experience.[79] At the end of such a probationary period the C.O. would be able to "weed out the duds," using evaluative comment from academic supervisors in England as well as from officials in the colonies. A young D.O. testified that the retention and promotion of mediocrities had had a stultifying effect on efficiency and morale. Veale, on returning from his visit to West Africa, submitted a text of his report that included the remark that "the Service has failed to adjust itself fully to . . . changes . . . [and] if that were not the case, there would be no particular point in changing the courses." [80] Furse disagreed with the logic of this. It was changing *conditions* which required new training methods, and this did not reflect in any way on the quality of the service. The published version of Veale's report omitted the objectionable reference.[81]

A former member of the C.S. who has written extensively on the subject would have it both ways. Furse was right in holding that conditions had changed and that the established selection criteria were still appropriate.[82] Referring to "the excellent system of selection," he maintained that the men of the C.S. were "in general quality as good . . . as anything England can produce." [83] It was not selection criteria which were wrong but the posting and promotion systems. Veale was therefore right to criticize these and also the old training courses. The former D.O. did admit, however, that Furse had not always succeeded in recruiting as good a type, within the context of the traditional selection criteria, as he (Furse) wished.[84] But the authentic article, an all-round man from a good Public School, armed with modern training, was the best that could be hoped for.

With this Sir Christopher Cox disagreed. The Public

School prefect, whose rationale both at home and in the colonies emphasized "the justice of a ruling class," was inappropriate to the age of independence.[85] Sir Alexander Carr-Saunders went further. He wrote to the Oxford vice chancellor that there was running through Furse's whole memorandum "a feeling of dissatisfaction about the Service as it is." [86] The men are "rather empty-headed, though . . . conscientious and honorable officials." [87] The fault lay in selection criteria, the London professor continued, which were themselves tied to the English educational system with its undemocratic bias in favor of certain groups.[88] In a blistering reply the vice chancellor singled out Carr-Saunders' suggestion that placing the courses at London would go far towards correcting the alleged abuses. But he did agree that the universities should "draw more and more on the intelligence of all sections of the population." [89] Were the vice chancellor and the former head of the London School of Economics then condemning elitism? Yes and no. Each felt that inequality was endemic, and they agreed that, everything considered, the C.S. had got the best men Britain could produce. But educational reform must aim at giving access to higher learning to young people then denied it. A truly democratic system of access would not result in equality; it would allow for the development of latent talent in large numbers of people otherwise lost to society. Such reform would not come overnight. In the meantime the C.O. was right to insist on quality as evolved by the existing system, however narrow it might be. All three men, Sir David Rose (the vice chancellor), Sir Christopher Cox (himself a Public School man, dean of an Oxford college and the secretary of state's advisor on education), and Sir Alexander Carr-Saunders (an Etonian and Oxford man who had defected to the City) may seem to have been taking highly inconsistent positions. To seek a spiritual reform without an accompanying structural one may strike egalitarians in that light. In England, the land of the well-born radical and the climbing conservative, such inconsistency, if that is what it is, was not thought unusual.

Lord Hailey drew on his own I.C.S. experience to favor a set of selection criteria that would be broader geographically as well as socially.[90] The Scotch and the Irish, he maintained, were less hidebound than the English and would better understand and cooperate with native intellectuals. Sir Arthur Richards, a governor never well known for the radicalism of his social views, spoke out against developing an elite corps.[91] He meant by this, however, that the prewar selection system, together with intercolonial transfers, had severed the C.S. from local peoples. At least, senior officers had been so severed. The British imperial system must not follow the French in evolving a horizontal administrative and social structure. Rather, each colony must develop according to its own cultural lights. A service capable of contributing to such development would have to avoid too much mixing of staff among the separate colonies. Each colony's civil servants would better serve out their careers in their own colony, thus becoming experts on its character and needs.

Carr-Saunders did point to characteristics of individual colonial civil servants which he felt were damaging to the service's over-all effectiveness. If the institutions from which the men came could not be changed, at least the overly shy, neurotic type could be avoided.[92] With a Liverpool University professor who had made an analysis of the C.S. in the West Indies he agreed that such types abounded in Public Schools and in many Oxford and Cambridge colleges.[93] A selection system tied to these institutions, unreformed, was exactly what the postwar Colonial Empire could not afford.

Should selection criteria change with colonial conditions? Carr-Saunders put this question to Furse in the fifth Devonshire meeting. The answer was an unequivocal "no." Professor Engledow observed that "heart as well as head" was still needed, especially in rural districts.[94] "It is superfluous to observe," said a C.O. memorandum, "that the Colonial Civil Servant must not be a crook, a lunatic or a drunkard." [95] He must be free of racial snobbery and must be able to accept the rising, educated native. He must not be the sort who harbors a grievance. Particularly, and this must have been reassuring to Furse, he must not be a person "who can find satisfaction in life only by gratifying intellectual or aesthetic tastes." [96] With unanswerable logic the memorandum remarked that colonial posts, even urban ones, simply did not provide sustenance for such tastes. "Reasonable intellectual ability" was taken for granted. Beyond that the recruit had to have genuine interest in people, for people were his daily stint. The introvert, even if intellectually gifted, would be a certain failure. Finally, moral and physical toughness were required. No one who knows the colonies would disagree with this. The former is defined partly as a belief that "there is some positive good in the British way of life and that the ideal of the British Commonwealth is a worthy one." [97] Basic spiritual values form the natural counterpart to this moral patriotism, a rejection of any purely or primarily materialistic outlook on life. This last, so dear to Furse and to everyone in the Devonshire Committee who preferred an underpaid post in civil service or a university to a richer but less rewarding commercial position, was echoed by Veale in a letter to a D.O. in Nigeria. He was glad, the registrar wrote, that the young man had survived wartime disillusionment with the service, ". . . had not yielded to the blandishments of the trades but had decided to stay in the Government service." [98]

The traditional selection criteria, then, were still valid. Perhaps more so than ever. The endless effort to get competent men would continue; mistakes would doubtless continue to be made. But the changing colonial conditions, of which all were aware, prompted alterations in the *preparation* of probationers rather than in their selection. Holding that postwar recruitment must have a broader social base than before, Furse nevertheless came down on the same definition of the right personal attributes that he had used in the 1920's. His reason for still preferring the upper-class recruit had not changed. The seasoning effects of belonging to a secure ruling class rather than to the ambitious, insecure ranks of the *nouveaux* would usually assure that candidates would have the acceptably responsible governing attitudes.

Did the committee, or a significant number of its members, go along with Furse's view of the public service ethic in relation to British class structure? The answer is that the issue was not one on which an official position was taken in the committee's report. Members or witnesses did express themselves, notably Sir Alexander Carr-Saunders and Sir Christopher Cox. Both have since elaborated their views. [99] In brief they felt that any natural ordering of society would result in stratification due to innate inequalities. It was pointless to attack the idea of privilege as such.

This much was theoretical. As for the reality of C.S. recruitment within the wider framework of British class structure and spirit, Carr-Saunders and Cox passed favorable judgments on the results actually attained by Furse. Their judgments were favorable not in relation to some arbitrary, hypothetical standard but to the stubborn facts of social organization at the time and to the needs of colonial administration as evaluated by Furse. Time alone would tell whether or not the system was right. Both men retain the belief that the C.O. could hardly have operated its selection mechanism in any way other than it did, in view of the class system within which it had to function. Whether that structure needed reform and whether colonial administration was better or worse as a result of the structure's impact on civil service ideas and techniques are of course completely separate questions. They will be examined in the following chapter.

The Devonshire meetings also provided a view of the mechanism and content of colonial policy in the interwar years. Never in the previous history of British imperialism was change coming so quickly or running so deep. At the first meeting the Duke of Devonshire remarked that interest in the colonies was growing considerably in both houses of Parliament. The duke as a member of the Lords and the secretary himself in the House had both noted the change.[100] One manifestation was an increased willingness to spend on colonial development. Treasury control had not relaxed, as every Oxford administrator and colonial researcher knew.[101] Although more money was available it was harder than ever to procure it. Oxford's plea for larger block grants met with the explanation that each application for individual projects would have to be dealt with *ad hoc* after detailed C.O. examination of rationale and proposals.[102] Colonial secretariats learned the same agonizing lesson. Nevertheless the new emphasis was on development and on approaching independence, not just on the maintenance of law and order as in the past.

As has been seen, Amery and many C.O. officials through the decades had denied that the swing to more positive government in the colonies was more self-interested than enlightened. Imperialists had long denied that there was a conflict between London's interests and those of colonial peoples. We may note that there were two sides to London's growing concern for colonial development during the early years of the Second World War. First, the impending "loss" of India made it clear to civil servants, members of Parliament, and scholars that Britain's future claim to great power status would rest on retention of a considerable colonial empire. The population, land area, and industrial-military capacity of the Home Islands alone were plainly insufficient. "Our relationship with the colonies," Miss Perham wrote to Veale, "is one that is going to demand much more of this country than it has hitherto. They have become relatively of immensely greater importance to our national well-being, just at the time when they are beginning to make conscious demands and criticisms." [103] An assistant under-secretary of state wrote to Oxford at the same time that development was candidly based on the need for a stronger imperial economy.[104]

The question of colonial development aside, secondly, wartime Britain was immeasurably more self-conscious about her overseas possessions than at any previous time. Demands at Oxford for more and better books on colonial subjects were not new. What was new was the rising volume and urgency of the demands and their general import. The colonial story must be told, not merely to inform that small group in Britain which maintained a professional or amateur interest in the empire, but to arouse public opinion at home and abroad and to win converts to Britain's cause.[105] Uninformed criticism must be answered with facts and ideas.[106] The Oxford registrar and governing body would barely condescend to take notice of the new Tropical African Services committee in

1926. During its prewar life the committee had been a neglected stepchild. In 1944, however, Veale wrote to the secretary of the faculties to prepare for making the successor committee a statutory body of the university.[107] The reason frankly given was a "quickening interest in the Empire" throughout England. In the sixth meeting of the Devonshire Committee Sir Charles Jeffries suggested dropping the word "native" in references to colonial peoples and secured the committee's agreement in principle that the new training courses would be open to colonial as well as British officers.[108]

Other colonial empires, once the objects of jealousy, derision, or fear in Britain, suddenly became worthy of serious study. The Devonshire Committee heard references to the need for examining Dutch, French, and American practices particularly.[109] Exchanges of students with the colonial staff college in Paris would be resumed on the prewar basis. It was even proposed that exchanges take place with the American equivalent of the C.S., although the suggested project, which Miss Perham hoped might be financed by the Pilgrim Trust, was eventually set aside. The subcommittee on economics of the new colonial studies committee at Oxford announced that the primary emphasis in its new syllabus would be on comparative colonialism.[110] The British ambassadors in Paris and Brussels found at this time that the French and Belgian governments were not only willing but eager to cooperate with Britain in presenting a united colonial front in world diplomacy.[111] What the rise of the Italian and German dictatorships could not do in the 1930's was now accomplished by the disapproval of one's allies, the protests of colonial peoples, and by moral stirrings in Britain itself. Britain's diplomatic defensiveness and the haste with which she was pressing for colonial development did not always produce instantaneous results in the colonies. There were reports of a wide divergence between theory and practice. But attitudes in London and Oxford at the end of the Second World War bore scant resemblance to those of the 1930's and earlier.

It has sometimes been alleged that the new attitudes were a function of the Labour party victory in the General Election of 1945.[112] The views of individual Conservative and Labour party members have certainly differed, although the programs of all cabinets since 1945, or for that matter since 1919, have been virtually identical in the realm of colonial advance. In practice, negotiations conducted by the C.O., colonial governments, and native leaders have proceeded uniformly and steadily towards the goal of self-rule no matter which party held power. The only change which Sir Charles Jeffries, a career civil servant, noticed after the Labour victory in 1945 was that the desperate urgency of administrative appointments was made worse. Submissions were held up and each candidate's personal history investigated in an effort to block those whose qualifications were merely social.[113] The matter was finally turned back to the civil servants with an apology for causing useless delay.

If party politics did not affect colonial policy materially, the C.O. was nevertheless in a changed position in late war years vis-à-vis its master, the House of Commons, not to mention public opinion and the colonial governments which it existed to serve. Gone were the days when public and parliamentary apathy was the bane of the C.O.'s existence and when colonial governors ignored it with impunity. Thousands of British servicemen had seen the colonies during the war. Their interest continued afterwards. Business contacts expanded greatly as soon as the war ended. Faced with a desperate economic prospect, the Labour government embarked on a series of development schemes which brought the colonies more and more to the attention of press and public. Telephonic, cable, and personal communications between the C.O. and colonial capitals grew to such an extent that many governors despaired of ever having enough time to devote to the daily routine of government.

These and other changes exerted a powerful effect on the C.S. itself. Sir Bede Clifford's request for a policy statement that the tenure of British officers would be guaranteed by the C.O. had no chance of acceptance. Before the war it would not have been necessary even to make such a request. Governors who had successfully bullied both the C.O. and their own staffs, or whose competence was sometimes questioned, now faced a public gaze not completely unlike that which kept members of Parliament in line. Yet throughout the C.S. generally the changed situation brought about a deterioration of relations with the C.O., which, if not always cordial, had at least been satisfactory. Junior officers as well as governors had to suffer the annoyance of frequent interruption of work by visitors from Parliament and elsewhere. The volume of written reports demanded by the C.O. and reflecting mounting public interest in the colonies grew steadily. The burden of preparing these fell mainly on junior staff. There were other and more important causes of bad feeling which will be referred to below. In short, the Second World War drew a heavy line between two distinct phases in C.S. history. After 1945 virtually nothing was the same. There were changes in the colonial milieu, notably in native attitudes and in patterns of work. A different sort of recruit was being sent out from Britain. Everyone was less sure of the future and even of the present. Strangest of all, colonial policy, which had been formerly made, or nearly so, by oneself, was now the plaything of a chain of offices and office-holders stretching all the way from the British public to scores of local districts throughout the empire. Administrators were becoming civil servants in the domestic sense, something they had never been before. They were becoming implementers upon whose positions and work there played a galaxy of foreign and local pressures.

Furse had favored residential universities for the postwar courses for the same reasons which had prompted him to establish the 1926 courses at Oxford and Cambridge. Recruitment of the types of men he wanted would be facilitated; continuity in the Oxbridge traditions of the service would be assured; a particular C.S. *esprit de corps* would continue to find its origins in the intimacy of college life and that of C.S. clubs. The Devonshire Committee soon agreed that the first or preliminary course would start at Oxford and Cambridge, all probationers going in their third terms to London for language training and special lectures on the colonies to which each was assigned.[114] There proved to be a marked improvement in the quality of the courses, especially in anthropology, comparative law, local government, and colonial economics. The already high level of courses in history and administration was also raised. Generally speaking, improvements stemmed from long-term developments in colonial studies in the three great English universities, including most prominently an increase in empirical research in all major colonies. In practice the forward stride seemingly made by London University was not after all to be in courses for administrators but in predominance in the affairs of the new Colonial Social Science Research Council.[115] Some London University people felt that Oxford had gone back on its agreements. The feeling was understandable; the underlying cause of differences between plans and programs was, as so often in C.S. history, the lack of funds and the pressing needs of colonial governments for staff.[116]

After the thinkers and the planners departed, the C.O., and more especially Furse, resumed day-to-day control of training courses. All the brave talk about integrating the C.S. course with Oxford life was to prove largely illusory. The main difference was that enterprising postwar probationers could avail themselves of a better menu of social science material than could their predecessors. In retrospect it is more than ever clear that the Devonshire Committee was intrinsically advisory and consultative in nature. It had contributed much. But the initiative and the continuing responsibility was, as always, Furse's.

The postwar atmosphere at the Commonwealth (formerly Colonial) Services Club was indicative of the changes that had taken place in Britain and in the colonies. Buying his pint at the bar, the new probationer was as likely as not to find an African, West Indian, or Malay officer at his elbow. The library down the hall contained fewer volumes of reminiscences by former governors and eccentric D.O.'s and more social science tomes, some of them not even published in England. At Blackwell's, in lecture halls, and in the junior common rooms of the new graduate colleges, if he chanced to go there, he would find an astonishingly large number of people who spoke his language with queer accents. "Before the war," Miss Perham observed to her seminar, "there was a bare trickle of students from America and other foreign countries. Now they come in battalions!" In the 1930's D.O.'s in East Africa and Trans-Jordan were amused but not unduly bothered by the arrival occasionally of delegations from that mysterious League of Nations in Geneva. "How funny to be asked questions about my work by a little man from South America," remarked a senior officer in Tanganyika.[117] Now there was a new organization based in New York. Its questions seemed less funny and more irritating. The world of backwaters and byways was no longer Britain's to manage by herself.

"Our great virtue was not having an idea."
—A British Officer [1]
"I cannot hear what you are saying, for
what you are is thundering in my ears."
—African Proverb [2]

CHAPTER VIII

Retrospect

THE underlying assumption, implicit more than spoken, of the Devonshire planners had been that the peoples of her dependencies would continue to require Britain's guidance and management for many years to come. Had this not been so, the emphasis in the meetings would have been on designing a training program for a service whose only function was to hand over authority to indigenous people. Yet the plans were ambitious and in the main optimistic. To the extent that they looked back, the committee members were critical; looking forward, they were confident and determined. The C.S. was seen to be facing a time of unprecedented challenge and trial.

Although the brilliant future foreseen by some of the planners appears illusory in retrospect, the time and effort of the Devonshire Committee were not wasted. Their nine meetings had given them a retrospective view of colonial policy and administration over the two decades since Furse's course had begun at Oxford and Cambridge. Many who knew the colonies best had been able, through direct or indirect participation in the Devonshire deliberations, to join in a collective searching of the national conscience. The wartime moratorium on Furse's normal

196

work allowed for an appraisal of colonialist experience, an introspective interlude without a precedent in the half-century since Britain had embarked on her last phase of imperial expansion. By 1945 she had not only regained all areas lost to the Japanese but had assumed the administration of Italy's former African empire, as well as large areas in Europe, the Middle East, and the Pacific. These responsibilities strained her resources to the breaking point. They gave additional evidence, if such was needed, that Britain's experience in governing other peoples was historically and geographically unequaled.

Although the ambitious plans for a three-stage training program for all recruits and sabbatical leaves for experienced officers became an immediate casualty, due to desperate staff needs in the colonies, part of the Devonshire program was implemented. The beginning course was strengthened. Within two years of Potsdam, colonial needs had been met sufficiently to allow recruitment and training to resume on a normal basis. All new recruits took the one-year "A" course. This was a considerably improved program by comparison with its predecessor. The influence of new research, especially in anthropology, economics, law, and colonial administration, was reflected in the quality of lectures and in their practical value to probationers. The idea of a second training year, following a year of experience, did not survive the planning stage, however. Inadequate funds ended its chances, along with those of a large-scale study leave program for experienced officers. A trickle of such officers began to arrive in Oxford and Cambridge for this "B" course in the late 1940's. The course roughly approximated the Devonshire plan. Officers took seminar work for a few hours each week and otherwise pursued special research under the informal guidance of dons chosen by themselves. The B course has become a sought-after plum among many C.S. officers in mid-career. A glance at C.O. lists of late years will show evidence that officers have taken advantage of the experience to write and publish essays on subjects of which they have special knowledge. Enrollment has never been large. In effect the B course has remained an expensive frill, involving only a small percentage of the C.S. Many B-course officers view the program as an additional qualification which might be helpful in getting jobs when their colonies become independent. Few have had any prospect of rising to a governorship.

Nevertheless the contributions of the Devonshire program to colonial development have been considerable. Not least among these has been the provision of courses in England for native officers. The existence of the program has made it easier for social science techniques and information to be brought to bear on the difficult problems of the transition era. All three of the leading universities have become important centers of Commonwealth studies and have improved their links with colonial universities. With C.O. bodies responsible for development coordination and with the Colonial Social Science Research Council they have played a part in easing the birth pangs of new nations. They have continued to offer support in the even more difficult early years of independence. The two years of preparation and the 18 months of meetings were not spent in vain, even though the service for which planning was carried out was not the principal beneficiary.

During the interwar period the old C.S. rose to the first place among Britain's overseas administrative corps. Furse's long struggle, aided occasionally by outstanding statesmen such as Amery and Milner, and supported by the quiet efficiency of his own staff, had by 1939 brought the service to a peak of prestige, unity, and experience. As a *ruling* rather than a teaching, guiding, and supporting service it little resembled its post-1945 successor. During the 1930's it had begun to inspire an *esprit de corps* comparing favorably with that of the I.C.S. in its great days. This was evidenced in the popularity of the C.S. in Oxford, Cambridge, and the Public Schools. After 1945, by contrast, a cynicism towards the Empire reminiscent of 1919 made the work of the talent scouts difficult.[3] The right people, as Furse defined them, were no longer as interested. The government in Westminster was not their government; the England of austerity was not their England. The C.S. suffered coincident blows from above and below: as native pressure for more participation in government increased, so did the disinclination of Furse's class to enter the service.

The new C.S., which seemed to have been born just in time to die, has developed its own character. It has a proud record, though a very different one from that of its predecessor. Its personality, described by one of the secretary of state's advisors as "the transition personality," has been marked by a willingness to serve under native superiors.[4] A new type has emerged, one not entirely dissimilar to the international civil servants of the League of Nations and the United Nations. As far back as the 1930's some members of the C.S. showed their capacity for flexibility and tolerance and their lack of racial bias by serving native ministers, notably in Ceylon. Some remarked that the new work was preferable to the old.[5] Corruption and injustice were more noticeable, but at least things were beginning to move.[6] Many a British official in new African states feels the same way today. The type is not unknown in Southeast Asia. The successful psychological transition made by these disinterested civil servants gives rise to the hope that the knowledge and experience of the C.S. will not be totally wasted. Might there not be an international underdeveloped areas service, in which retired C.S. officials could enlist, which would be available for administrative, professional, and technical work on a contract basis?

If a few of the old types have found the new conditions of government to their liking, the vast majority has not. The head prefect wanted to rule. That is what he understood, what he felt in his bones and enjoyed doing. The era of independence has destroyed his ethos. He is irreconcilable precisely because that ethos—paternalism—is the one interracial psyche of politics that is totally impossible under contemporary world conditions. The Cotswold hills in the west of England are full of retired colonial officials who bear this stamp. They make no pretense at being able to adjust to the idea of self-rule by people whom they saw as children only a decade or so ago. Their suspicion of the new scheme of things is made stronger by the conviction that most natives do not accept it any more than they themselves do. Self-government appears to be nothing but a selfish power grab by unscrupulous, half-educated opportunists, the least attractive and most dishonest element in an otherwise pleasant and admirable population. This feeling is fed by reports of disorder and corruption in newly independent states and by letters from old employees who paint a black picture of modern conditions. "Today," writes an Asian to his old boss, now retired in a Kentish village, "nobody cares. . . . There is much distrust and very little cooperation. . . . The clerks are concerned with trade union activities and politics. . . . Rabble-rousers resort to the game of placing the present-day ills on the foreign domination. However, there are level-headed people even among the so-called ignorant classes who are grateful for the benefits of the British. . . . It is common talk . . . that they would prefer to see the

British Government taking over again." [7] In the Philippines as well as in British colonies, such sentiments are by no means rare.[8] But they are the voice of a doomed spirit. Time has passed it by. As in the day of colonialism, the majority in new countries today is either apathetic towards government as such or generally content. Among the educated, of course, an overwhelming majority is passionately committed to the new status of independence, and these are the people in whose hands their countries' destinies lie.

Nearly a full generation has passed since the heyday of the old C.S. Its great times are definitely and clearly marked off as a historical period with an integrity of its own. Its characteristics, like those of a museum piece, may be examined almost without reference to the present. The traditional selection and training system are seen in this light as a key determinant of British colonial policy between the wars. Sir Ralph Furse, the father of the colonial service, influenced that policy in a vital way, for he embodied, exemplified, and enforced the criteria of selection and the complexion and rationale of training. His system was elitist and intuitive. It was reactionary more than conservative because Furse's values were those of an elite which had already begun to lose influence when he returned to resume his duties at the C.O. in 1919. Yet Furse's system was allowed free rein all during the interwar period. The men he sent out to rule the colonies lived by a code which had steadily eroded in England during their fathers' youth. It was the code of paternalism. A body such as the Fisher Committee, looking into the selection system for the home services in 1930, would not have dared sanction an elitist and paternalistic spirit, as that committee in fact did.[9] The colonies received paternalistic government, even after the

Second World War, because Furse's system was not sufficiently challenged in Britain or in the colonies until after his retirement in 1948.

The character of British colonial administration depended on the personalities and talents of individual administrators in the governments of various dependencies in Africa, Southeast Asia, and the West Indies. The spirit of the men in charge accented *noblesse oblige*. For all its authoritarianism, and it was essentially authoritarian, its aim was *service*. Its motivation was duty to the governed. The gift of Britain to her former dependencies was a mixture of authoritarian spirit and machinery plus democratic ideals—not, as is sometimes imagined, a set of democratic ideals and institutions. The latter would have been almost totally inappropriate to the political capacities of countries whose populations were illiterate and socially primitive. Democracy of a sort is, of course, possible in primitive societies, but not the kind which evolves gradually over a period of centuries into a highly sophisticated pattern of socio-political assumptions and methods in an urban-industrial milieu.

The men of the old C.S. conducted themselves and therefore the government in a way that set them off from the peoples they ruled. They stood by their own, *i.e.,* British, standards. If colonial peoples, or some among them, became to an extent "black Englishmen," it was not because the C.S. consciously or deliberately furthered such a process but because individuals chose to copy their overlords. Cultural imperialism *à la française* was foreign to the British official. An English gentleman, he was not inclined to proselytize or indeed even to care what others thought or did. In England he considered himself apart and above. Abroad he became even more culturally rigid. In a non-English atmosphere his standards solidified because they were yet more distinct and noticeable than in England, where at least they were recognized as normal. It is meaningless to say, as one author has recently done, that Britain's standards were too high in Africa.[10] Height is a subjective quality as applied to one system in comparison with another. The degree of adherence to a given standard is a more valid comparative device, and in this, as a Belgian once put it to the writer, the British were "plus strict que le bon Dieu lui-même." E. M. Forster tells us that this was because the character of the British, especially of the upper classes, was undeveloped.[11] With a retarded character, according to Forster, the Britisher has been persistently inhibited and unable to share himself and his world with outsiders. Be that as it may, the colonial official was aloof from his people more than were his opposite numbers in the dependencies of other powers.[12] Cultural assimilation did not take place in British colonies on anywhere nearly the same scale as in those of Portugal and France. The explanation lies to a significant degree in the character of the men Furse selected.

While members of Parliament talked about democratization and guidance towards self-government in the colonies, dignifying these concepts with the name of "policy," Furse's D.O.'s ruled on in the old way. Though standing apart from his people spiritually and socially, the average D.O. was on easy terms with them and was genuinely concerned for their welfare within their own cultural context. Officials were sometimes told by their superiors that they must cease doing all the work and begin training natives to run their own political apparatus. This happened when a new governor arrived in the Sudan in 1927, bringing with him subversive ideas from service in India. It happened when Cameron came to Tanganyika in 1925 with the notion that indirect rule was not enough and that the Africans must be guided to a polity in which they managed their own affairs. Many officers of all ranks agreed. But in fact the British official remained an autocrat. His discretion, his judgment, his personality remained the essential ingredients of policy.[13] There is less distance today between policy as voiced in London and policy as exercised in the colonies. During the interwar period the hiatus was wide.

The impracticability of an over-all policy, imposed from the imperial center, meant also that each colony had to advance or not advance according to its own capacity. A measure of Britain's inability to control this process from the Home Islands is again found in Furse's system. If London's ideal had been a Marxist "to each according to his need," instead of a Leninist "to each according to his work," a colony's backwardness would have necessitated and produced more, not less, aid from the center. But Furse's posting guides were grounded in his reading of each colony's personality and his knowledge of its ability to pay. Not only did the Gold Coast get more schools because she had a larger revenue than Sierra Leone had. She also got a more able administration, generally speaking.[14]

The dilemma of whether to lead the colonies away from their own cultural precepts in preparing them for self-rule or whether to respect their existing institutions and govern them in an authoritarian way was not resolved by 1945. It was talked about, mainly in England. But in the meantime the D.O. went through his daily round of government in the old way, acting on instinct and precedent rather than on London's policy, whatever that might be. The Devonshire planners came closer to resolving the dilemma. They opted clearly and strongly for a Westernized future in the colonies. Yet the first trainees, observing English local government institutions in action, showed themselves to be more than somewhat mystified.[15] How were British models to be transferred to the colonies if the instructors did not understand and sympathize with the models? The reaction of the typical D.O. selected in the interwar years was one of opposition to the whole idea of teaching natives anything that seemed to run counter to indigenous civilizations or that had developed without reference to such civilizations. This attitude, complemented by the factors of poor communications and modest funds, left the field to Furse's English gentleman. And of course to the natives themselves. By the time Britain had resolved her policy dilemma it was the latter who held the initiative.

The new stress on social sciences recommended by the Devonshire Committee came too late. By the time the first cadets trained in the new spirit arrived in their posts, Kwame Nkrumah had already raised his revolt against officials trained, or untrained, in the old. The handwriting of independence was on every wall. Paternalism had done its work and reaped its reward. While Furse's head prefect had his back turned up-country, the educated natives of the coastal towns had seized the initiative and were setting their own pace of advance. Ironically, this proved the rightness of the classical D.O.'s view that training by example is the only effective kind. Natives, ran this view, will take what they like from imported models and ignore the rest. The march to self-rule, in the words of a noted student of colonialism, "is not an invented but an inherent thing, which they [the natives] . . . must learn to measure and manage." [16] And so they did. The colonies passed from the stage of civil service government to the transition stage of cooperative government not because London had decreed it after a full-scale Parliamentary debate but because indigenous leaders had taken matters into their own hands.

Prewar courses, though serious in intent and doubtless effective in giving probationers a general idea of what they could expect on the job, were no match for in-service training. Cadets left the classroom behind and were bound from then on by precedent and the example of experienced superiors. From his first D.C. the cadet imbibed a preoccupation with existing native culture and method. While his French opposite number across the border was busily selecting talented natives for Frenchi-fication in Paris, the British junior official became a student and often an amateur of things as he found them. It would be perhaps too much of a tribute to say that he understood his charges. But he learned at very least what could and could not be done to, with, and by the natives. Already a conservative in England, he naturally became a conservative in policy affecting native life. If anybody made concessions in this intercultural confrontation between ruler and ruled, it was more often the ruler.

An American anthropologist has called the relationship between British and Africans "organized misunderstanding." [17] Accepting this, a former member of the Ceylon Service remarks that the alternative to this minimal and efficient relationship is the complete acceptance of one man's culture by the other.[18] For a British civil servant to "go native" was not unheard-of. It usually meant an immediate lessening of his influence among his own kind. In extreme cases it brought about resignation or dismissal. Unlike Portuguese administrators, the average British D.O. never thought of "descending" in this way. He could be charmed by native custom or become a student of some aspect of native lore. He did not expect natives to come over to his way of thinking. He held to his own personal code of conduct and did what he could to uphold law and order in the traditional British fashion. Breaches of justice were dealt with as sternly as offenses demanded in the eyes of colonial law. This was the situation as long as the British had the power to keep it so. Once colonial governments entered the transition stage and native officials obtained power, the ability of the British to set standards was increasingly diluted.[19] Between the wars most colonial governments had not reached this stage, however. The question of conflicting interests, when they arose, were settled according to British standards because it was the British who held the power. But it was a matter of great professional pride with experienced D.O.'s that they had attained such a level of rapport with native peoples that conflict could in most cases be avoided. As long as the great majority of the natives preferred to follow their own traditional ways the system of organized misunderstanding operated smoothly. It was only later, when educated, untraditional natives began to agitate, that the system became inappropriate and an impediment to progress.

The major drawback of in-service training, one which its staunchest proponents cannot dismiss, was the static nature of government which it supported. Precedent was king. Even in 1960 the first thing a newly arrived cadet in Sierra Leone did, for example, was to sit down at a desk in his bush headquarters and address himself to a mountain of files. These contained, among other things, minutes, memoranda, and instructions written by his predecessors, often as far back as the early years of the century and before. The weight of the past sat heavy on beginners. When he went on his first trek, the new cadet did so not as a free agent but as an assistant to a senior man. Any open-mindedness or penchant for improvisation he may have possessed was at once subjected to the weighty challenge of example. Native chiefs were accustomed to the old D.C. and he to them. On their mutual regard and cooperation rested the order of the district. The system may be open to all sorts of criticism, but it worked.

Against this, what was an eight-month session with dons and books at Oxford? Even when the D.C. departed and the young D.O. was on his own, he was no less a prisoner of the system. His sub-district was only one of many. The sheer magnitude of conventionality overwhelmed him. The past, the pressing demands of immediate tasks, and the glaring fact of his inexperience all worked to the advantage of precedent. "Our new D.O. was a bit bumptious when he arrived six months ago," remarked the wife of a provincial commissioner recently.[20] "But he seems more settled and happy now."

It was native progressives who benefited most from the precedent-ridden character of the training system. Native leaders did not see it that way, and in fact they reserved some of their most biting criticism of the British for this aspect of colonialism.[21] Nor did the British plan to leave the field to native leaders in this way. But the result of many generations of leading young officials to the font of the past and at the same time allowing native leaders to choose their own future paths was no less inevitable for being unplanned. "I can regret," writes Miss Perham, "that the white man has not been allowed another fifty years at least in which to build his civilization in Africa."[22] It was the static nature of the white man's government which made this impossible. Some native leaders have made polite gestures of gratitude for what is described as a deliberate British effort to promote self-rule.[23] But these should not be taken too seriously. In the first place, "gratitude," in the words of a retired colonial official, "is not a normal virtue of human beings."[24] And in the second place, there would be no point in expecting gratitude for an unintentional gift. In any case it was the educated native who took advantage of a system that was at once fossilated and tolerant. The experience and capacity of leaders in former British colonies is an outgrowth of this combination, itself a product of the traditional British belief in in-service training.

Why did Britain react so slowly to the need for more vocational and systematic training? Part of the answer is in the time lag between training and the effects of training. Reforms instituted in 1945 had no chance of being effective for at least a decade. Even by that time all senior positions in colonial governments were still held by men trained in the old way. Secondly, Furse's selection criteria made for a service whose spirit and motivation were cut off substantially from domestic British socio-political developments. The Devonshire criticism of officials as being rather empty-headed was imprecise. The D.O.'s head was far from empty, but the things it was full of were not appropriate to colonial needs after 1945. His preoccupation was with leaving native institutions alone as much as would be conducive to justice and order; [25] beyond that he wished to interfere only enough to support indigenous forms and to keep them operating so as to prevent unfair treatment of any element in society. Scientific training would have accented development, the dynamic rather than the stable. Yet, just as the selection process contributed inadvertently to the rise of native elites, so the training system allowed by default for the evolution of native business groups, civil service bodies and politicians interested in development and experienced in its primary processes.

The reports of both the Fisher and the Devonshire committees held that the *theories* of the recruitment and training systems respectively were indefensible. What is the standard against which such systems should be judged? The previous chapters have not attempted a systematic comparison of British and other colonial methods. But a brief comparative statement will be the most valid way of supporting final generalizations on the practical effects of Furse's system. It may identify or illuminate dimensions of that system as contrasted with others operating at the same time and in comparable geographical and cultural settings. The hiatus between policy statements in London and actual practices in the colonies had its counterpart in other colonial empires. In their case, too, the civil service approach to policy, impact, and legacy is instructive.[26]

The French, for example, were by no means unsuccessful in their policy of cultural overlay.[27] Despite the abruptness or violence involved in their departure from Indo-China and Guinea, French culture has left indelible marks in Africa and Asia. But the nature of French rule has resulted in a transition stage markedly different from the British. The disintegration of *France d'Outre-Mer* has been less graceful than the breakup of the Colonial Empire, and its political offspring have been in many places less capable than the leaders of new Commonwealth countries. Selection for the French overseas service was by examination, and candidates were not interviewed.[28] Neither the old aristocracy nor the *haute bourgeoisie* were interested in service outside France, except in military and semi-military positions. Most colonial posts were filled by ambitious *monteurs*. Professor Crocker found, for example, on a tour of French West Africa in 1943 that fully a quarter of the officials, including four governors, were Corsicans.[29] Others were from the West Indies and Breton. They had the conceit of French culture and the determination to implant it, without the easy comfort of secure social backgrounds. Their motivation was not service to natives but personal promotion and cultural proselytizing. The Senegalese noncommissioned officer assigned by the *commandant du cercle* at Timbuktu to act as guide to an American on safari in the Sudan some years ago spoke of his French superior as "Monsieur Baton." The severity of the French up-country is notorious. Moreover, French officials mixed with the natives quite freely and were not above haggling in the marketplace. It would be absurd to hold that there were no humanitarians in the French service and no brutes in the British. But, generally speaking, the French officer came from a lower social class and was guided by a spirit other than *noblesse oblige.*

The French officer's training took place in a special staff school, the *Ecole Coloniale,* where the clear aim of cultural permeation was stressed and which was divorced from French liberal arts education. The phrase *France d'Outre-Mer* sums up Paris' attitude to its dependencies. There is no British equivalent. In the words of Ghana's ambassador to the United Nations, "The French set out to assimilate their subject peoples by sharing with them the highest known form of civilization . . . the French. The British made no such effort with theirs, but left them free to pick up such Anglo-Saxon attributes as they saw fit to embellish the African personality." [30] Political representation was provided, as in the case of British colonialism, but in early years it consisted of sending Francophile natives to the Assembly in Paris, not to local legislatures as in British colonies. Officers of the French colonial service were interchangeable among the various territories, and care was taken not to send men back to the same post a second time for fear they might become enough fascinated with local custom to forget the Frenchification aim. The service was thus more of a *corps d'élite* than the C.S. It ruled a more centralized empire whose individual units did not develop in the autochthonous way that was characteristic of British colonies.

In the case of the Portuguese, in many ways the strangest and least known colonial system, it is too early to judge the results. Even more than the French, and for a longer time, the Portuguese have followed a policy of assimilation.[31] Dr. Salazar has stoutly insisted that any discussion by the United Nations of Portugal's overseas provinces is a violation of the Charter.[32] Goa resisted pressures similar to those which removed Britain and France from India and was ultimately joined to India by outside forces, not domestic revolt. The tiny colonies of Macao and Timor have thus far outridden the noisy nationalism of China and Indonesia. When asked what he thought of the arrival of a powerful Communist army on the Macanese border in 1949, my full-blooded Cantonese agent replied, "We Portuguese are not concerned with what the Chinese do about their internal affairs." Until recently, when revolt broke out in Angola, assimilation seemed to be working well. Like the French before 1945, the Portuguese considered their colonial service to be an imperial elite corps open to residents of all territories.[33] Entry to the service was by examination, and there was a staff school in Lisbon to train recruits roughly as the French trained them, *i.e.,* in a spirit of cultural overlay. Nothing could be farther from the British model.

The Netherlands during the interwar period had a colonial service comparable to that of France where recruitment and training were concerned.[34] Furse noted in one of the Devonshire meetings that the Dutch took their recruits at a younger age than did the British and gave them highly specialized training courses.[35] Although this was not considered appropriate to British colonial policy at the time, there were those in the C.O. and the C.S. who looked with respect on the efficiency and orderliness of Dutch administration in the East Indies and even suggested that Britain might well emulate it in part.[36] What impressed the British about the Dutch was their tight control over dependent peoples and the efficiency of their technical services. Belgium's colonial service also epitomized these qualities.[37] It, too, was recruited and trained in the French manner and with similar aims, except that the Belgians were slower to train native elites. Yet for all their efficiency and careful economic planning in the East Indies and the Congo, Holland and Belgium have left behind a legacy of disorder and bitterness towards colonialism that has no equal in former British territories. Their civil servants were strict and efficient but were unable to communicate to native peoples a sense of being concerned for their welfare. They concentrated on conferring an alien culture rather than on nurturing an indigenous one.

Leaving aside the Portuguese, we may make one or two generalizations about European colonial systems in comparison with the British. All produced native elites devoted, even fanatically so, to the imported culture. All looked on the British system disapprovingly, some with scorn for its weaknesses, others with fear lest its easygoing ways infect their own colonies nearby. Still others looked on the British with anger, resentment, or exasperation. Many French, Belgian, and Dutch colonial civil servants, serving or retired, have spoken of the fallacy of Britain's thinking in comparison with their own. At the bottom of all such comparisons lay a set of practical assumptions as to what the colonial power was doing in her dependencies and why.

Continental officials had clear, definite, and rational conceptions in mind, complete with formulas for implementation and comprehensive answers to any possible disagreement by natives or foreigners. If the local people failed to go along with any given program or policy aim it was because they came from an inferior culture and had not yet advanced enough to see the light.

Similar discussions with British officials have yielded entirely different results. Getting a D.O. to talk philo-

sophically about his work is, in the first place, often difficult if not impossible.[38] If a rationalization of colonialism
is forthcoming at all, it will as likely as not be disguised
as a euphemism. This could indicate nothing more than
shyness or reticence of talking about fundamentals. Or
it might mean that the man has not thought of his work
in such terms. Most D.O.'s, for example, talk about their
sense of obligation to the natives in inverse proportion to
the depths of their feelings on the subject.

The attitudes of officials in the various colonial services,
in a word, provide perspectives on the practical meaning
of policies and on the nature of colonial legacies worldwide. In Europe the most able and influential elements
in society avoided overseas service, leaving the field to the
ambitious and the clever. In France, traditional attitudes
towards the idea of authority and towards the prestige
of public service were carried abroad; French colonial
governments inevitably suffered from the low esteem in
which Frenchmen hold government as such. Objective
civil service examinations without interviews put a premium on the kind of intelligence which manifests itself
in written answers to specialized questions. They ignored
other qualifications such as personality, mental and spiritual stability, and racial attitudes. Staff school training
bred a rulebook mentality in recruits which often lasted
throughout their careers. The administrations of continental powers therefore tended to be rigid, doctrinaire,
efficient, and inspired by cultural conceit. In Britain, by
comparison, recruits were drawn from the most secure
and relaxed element in the population, the one having
the most profound sense of obligation to the governed.
If this attitude was ludicrous, misguided, outdated, hypo-
critical, arrogant, or maddening to many British social
critics, it was nonetheless genuine to those who possessed
it and acted on it. It inspired such confidence in oneself

and in one's way of life that the question of transferring
that way of life to others scarcely arose. The D.O. had
a loose hand on the reins. He did not try to implant his
own mores in native populations, and he was surprised
or amused to find people voluntarily emulating him. When
at last the natives, having developed on their own, demanded self-government, the demand appealed to his
sense of justice and fair play. He may have thought it
premature. But as a matter of implicit right, it struck him
as quite reasonable.

Both kinds of systems, continental and British, lacked
imagination and foresight. Each was doomed to give way
to other political arrangements once the nationalist infection took hold. The final question which history will
ask of the various colonialisms, therefore, will be the
question of legacies. In a short time these are all that will
remain of the phenomena. Appraising the totality of Britain's impact on primitive areas and equally on ancient
civilizations in Asia and Africa, one is struck with the
absent-mindedness with which she went about her tasks.
Preconceived notions were not confined to the Continent.
Britain indulged them too. But the European powers at
least tried to forge logical, consistent, and continuous
links between policy and implementation. Inspiration
often set sail from the United Kingdom, but somehow
seldom reached the colonies. When it did so, it arrived
a mere vestige of its original form. Policy was most often
a locally evolved product, hand-tailored in each separate
dependency. It derived from existing on-the-spot facts
of life. If it was more or less permanently behind in its
attempts to keep abreast of change, at least its outdated
conceptions related to local reality and not to alien abstractions. Step by empirical step it compromised with
each new progressive impulse. In this gradual process
native leaders educated themselves to the practical mean-

ing of self-rule. Experience taught them. Their hard-fought battles for the right to gain that experience were waged against prejudice in the minds of colonial officials that no one could govern as responsibly and well as themselves. The respect of native leaders for the integrity of government as such was an inevitable outgrowth of their struggle against that prejudice.

In the French sense of the word Britain lacked a policy. She did have officials, and they exercised authority. The administrators of the colonial service were the actual executors of such policy as there was. A retired member of the Cyprus and Gold Coast services comments, "My only thought was to see that my department was efficiently run. If in moments of introspection one realized that this meant that one had to set an example of diligence, care and above all integrity, that was something very rarely present in the conscious mind. . . . The best administrative officers were not those who had high-falutin' ideas about [policy] but who gave their whole minds to their daily chores—restraining here, encouraging there, advancing everywhere, with never a thought of the wider implications of their efforts." [39] The statement, at once a denial and an affirmation, goes to the heart of the matter. The meaning of British colonialism cannot be understood through the "windy generalizations" of policy statements in Parliament or the C.O. Real policy was what the men in authority made it. Its indispensable ingredients were their personal attributes and the example they gave. If it was unconscious policy it was none the less effective.

Essentially the legacy of British colonialism is the residual impression made by a few thousand individuals in some fifty territories around the world. Institutions such as legislatures and ideas such as free speech are not transferable in any measurable sense. There may be superficial similarities in the way these are used by metropolitan and colonial peoples respectively. The acceptance of imported notions is determined by the aptitude and inclination of the importing native, not by colonial policy, conscious or unconscious.

In the future there may be signs of other legacies. The political cooperation of member states in the Commonwealth is an example. Administrators of national and international technical assistance programs might also benefit from the experience of the colonial service. The elitist bias is inimical to American social traditions and is therefore not likely to be copied in the United States. But perhaps Furse's emphasis on character as demonstrated in personal interviews could be given more serious attention than it has received hitherto. In a country where "scientific" evaluation is so much in vogue, from grade school onwards, such attention could have a most wholesome effect.

The legacy that will endure longest is the personal one. The unbending integrity of individual administrators has been stamped on the consciousness of native leaders in countries now independent or soon to become independent. Their governments, so different from colonial regimes in other respects, have in common with them the high prestige of governmental careers among the most able elements of the young male population. In some ex-colonies it is the lingering aura of public service authority left from British times that serves as virtually the only unifying force in an otherwise factious social and political atmosphere. More than the characteristics of colonial rule, the personal achievements and services of individual officials are remembered. In up-country villages, one still hears that this road or that bridge was built in Mr. ——'s time or that the village well was dedicated by the wife of H. E. Sir ——.

Even this sort of memory will fade. It will go the way of

particular institutions, ideas, and methods of the colonial time and will be replaced by native equivalents. In time Ghana and Malaya will be even less able than the United States to distinguish between British and indigenous elements in political traditions that have come down from pre-independence times. Britain's North American possessions were colonies in the literal sense of the word. They were settled by Englishmen who took their political theories and institutions across the ocean with their furniture.[40] As this has not been the case with most African and Asian colonies, the purely British contributions to political forms will be more difficult to isolate as time goes on. Many new nations in Africa and Asia owe their present unity and progress, such as it is, to leaders who have either served in British administrative bodies or have gained self-confidence and a capacity for self-assertion by playing the salamander to such bodies. The latter group is the larger and more important. Bu Bakr, Nkrumah, Margai, Nyerere and even Tunku Abdul Rahman received from the colonial service a challenge, an example, and an opportunity. They watched it, fought it, and learned from it. At times the members of the service ignored them or treated them roughly. All have run afoul of British justice. But never did the handful of foreigners who ran their countries make it impossible for them to gain experience and confidence. Long before independence, they could look forward to designing their countries' destinies in ways of their own choosing.

Shortly after he retired, the last British governor of Cyprus spoke of that country's independence as a triumph for Britain. The contrast between this attitude and that of the Belgians in the Congo, the Dutch in Indonesia and the French in Guinea requires no further emphasis. The retired governor went on to describe the "monuments to our administration" in Cyprus, the last and most important being "the conception of an impartial and dedicated public service." [41] The claim symbolizes what some former members of the colonial service would like to think they accomplished. The record of new governments' actions over the decade of the 1950's would seem to make that hope, if not vain, at least premature. The colonial service has left behind not dedicated and impartial administrations—these are British concepts and therefore inappropriate—but *capable* ones. And capable in their own way. That is the enduring monument to the colonial service.

A Note on Sources

MY primary sources of information have been talks with knowledgeable people and various kinds of printed material, the bulk of it unpublished. Since 1944 I have made fairly regular visits to Britain and to territories then or now associated with Britain and with other colonial powers. These journeys covered some 25 British or ex-British dependencies in the West Indies, the Atlantic and Mediterranean, the Middle East, Africa, Southeast Asia and the Pacific. They provided opportunities to speak with a representative number of administrators of all ranks and with officers of other departments. Talks with non-British officials and with native leaders were fewer in number, although they were helpful in allowing contrasts with British colonialism and occasional perspectives on native attitudes to the British.

In Britain itself, members or former members of the Colonial Office and academics were especially helpful. University dons and administrators and Public School headmasters, some of whom had been involved in the development of the Colonial Service, gave me much invaluable assistance. This related not only to education but also to British society in general and to class stratification.

Printed materials fell into three categories. First, there were Colonial Office papers. Access was provided to a full year's "submissions," or complete files on applicants for posts in the colonies. I was fortunate in being able to see a certain number of memoranda on policy. Members of the C.O. library staff prepared statistics on the educational backgrounds of all successful candidates for the C.A.S. in the years 1931–40 inclusive. Certain papers of the Colonial Civil Servants Association and of the Overseas Service Pensioners' Association have come my way.

At Oxford, secondly, I was given access to registry papers pertaining to the affairs of various university bodies in the interwar period. These included the Devonshire minutes and correspondence, private letters, minutes of T.A.S. and C.A.S. committee meetings, and papers of the Committee on Colonial Studies. I was able to inspect relevant documents and files of the Oxford University Appointments Committee and of Brasenose College. Record books and other papers of the Commonwealth Services Club and of the Institute of Commonwealth Studies were also useful.

Thirdly, I journeyed with the scholarly hosts to Chancery Lane for heavy sessions in the Public Record Office. This was not so much to discover new materials and ideas as to verify old.

Most of the secondary sources which I consulted are familiar to students of colonial history. They consist of published books and articles, newspapers, Parliamentary Debates, and a large number of Command and Colonial papers published by the Stationery Office. Listed here are only a few examples of useful works in a selection of categories.

As regards the personality and character of British leadership groups, especially educational and civil service, I have watched, always with interest and often with amusement, the many flashes of light sent down into the darkness of a very dark subject by various artists. No one is more delightful and convincing than E. M. Forster, especially in *Abinger Harvest* (1953 ed.), although Angus Wilson's *Anglo-Saxon Attitudes* (1956) is also deft and is more complete. In an historical chapter of his *Prospero's Cell* (1945) Lawrence Durrell says some fascinating and, I think, accurate things about the British overseas, as he does in fact in some of his better known works. John Masters, particularly in *Bhowani Junction* (1954), and Alan Moorehead, in *The White Nile* (1960) and elsewhere, give us uncommonly fine sketches of the displaced British, military and other. Robert Graves' *Goodbye To All That* (1929), although dated, cannot really be left out of a list such as this. Nor can G. J. Renier's whimsical but not entirely frivolous *The English: Are They Human?* (1931).

With particular reference to society and education in Britain I have benefited from the works of C. P. Snow, especially the series of novels which so mercilessly lays bare the politics of a Cambridge college, and from the swollen love-hate literature on Oxford. For present purposes it is necessary to go no further back than Max Beerbohm's incomparable *Zuleika Dobson* (1911) and then to come down to the present via such old faithfuls as Christopher Hobhouse's *Oxford* (1939). Leonard Woolf's *Growing* (1961) talks about England, Cambridge, and Ceylon at the turn of the century, but it is astounding how much of what he says still has pertinence. Sir David Kelly's *The Ruling Few* (1952), Lord Tweedsmuir's *Memory Hold the Door* (1940), and Sir Roy Harrod's *The Prof* (1959) illuminate aspects of Oxford life in their very different ways. In *The Long Week-End* (1940) Robert Graves and Alan Hodge use newspaper records to trace, rather systematically, the course of British society between the wars. One or two more specialist works are useful, such as the essays of Lord James. The editors of *The Twentieth Century* (in their issue of October 1957) ask "Who Rules Britain?" as do, more or less regularly, *The Observer* and other periodicals.

On the subject of imperialism-colonialism there are the usual histories, historical essays, philosophical works, and specialist books. One can get hopelessly mired down without even leaving the continent of Africa, not to mention the rest of the ex-colonial world. The late Professor Vincent Harlow's *The Historian and British Colonial History,* 1951, indicates something of the scope involved for those who would do their homework. Miss Perham, in her Reith Lectures, 1961, *The Colonial Reckoning,* and John Plamenatz, in his *On Alien Rule and Self-Government,* 1960, show how to go about it from a landrover and a desk respectively. A rich background can be found in *Africa and the Victorians* by Gallagher and Robinson, 1961. Salt and mustard are added to otherwise bland passages by such masters of the bush and mountain as Joyce Cary (*Mister Johnson,* 1939) and Aubrey Menen (*The Prevalence of Witches,* 1948). Social scientists such as Meek, Macmillan, and Hussey (*Europe and West Africa,* 1940) and Professor Frankel (*The Economic Impact* on *Under-Developed Areas,* 1953) can be most enlightening. Lastly and very importantly, there are the works by or about pro-consuls and the cliff-dwellers of Whitehall. Miss Perham's *Lugard* (1956 and 1961) is justly famous. It should be read in conjunction with personal memoirs of those who did not rise so high, such as C. Temple's *Native Races and Their Rulers* (1918). Harold Ingrams ruled and wrote about islands and jungles and deserts from the Indian Ocean to West Africa by way of Arabia (*Arabia and the Isles,* 1942), and few governors can have seen so much water as Sir Arthur Grimble (*A Pattern of Islands,* 1952). Sir Charles Jeffries and Professor Parkinson give us rather different peeks into the same Colonial Office (*The Colonial Office,* 1956, and *Parkinson's Law,* 1958). No reference shelf would be complete without Lord Hailey's staggering *African Survey* (1956 ed.).

Notes to Chapters

NOTES TO CHAPTER I

1. Mr. Ormsby-Gore (later Lord Harlech) in Melland, F. H., ed., *Lord Hailey's African Survey* (London: Macmillan, 1939), p. 18.

2. Harold Ingrams, "Administration and the Overseas Service," in *New Fabian Colonial Essays,* ed. by A. Creech Jones (New York: Frederick A. Praeger, 1959).

3. Sir Charles Jeffries, *The Colonial Empire and Its Civil Service* (Cambridge: Cambridge University Press, 1938), p. 3. The present chapter draws heavily on this volume.

4. C.O. 429. Vol. I. W. A. Ross to Earl Granville, Dec. 28, 1868.

5. *Ibid.*

6. *Ibid.* F. R. Sandford to T. F. Rice, July 27, 1869.

7. *Ibid.* Mrs. H. C. Southey, Aug. 22, 1868.

8. *Ibid.,* April 26, 1869.

9. *Ibid.*

10. *Ibid.* Unnamed private secretary to Rev. Richardson, Dec. 19, 1870.

11. *Ibid.* Ex-governor of the Bahamas, letter of Aug. 24, 1867; ex-governor of Labuan, letter of June 30, 1867.

12. *Ibid.* George Grover to secretary of state, May 30, 1867.

13. Sir Edward Marsh, *A Number of People* (London: Heinemann, 1939), pp. 123–24. I am indebted to my friend, F. L. Greenland, for calling this passage to my attention.

14. Selbourne Report, C.O. 123, March 1900, C.O. Library.

15. *Historical Notes on the Oxford University Appointments Committee,* 1892–1950 (mimeographed), compiled by F. B. Hunt and C. E. Escritt.

16. *Ibid.,* p. 5.

17. C.O. 430, Vol. II, Feb. 9, 1908.

18. See "The Civil Service Competition of 1908," *Oxford Magazine Supplement,* Oct. 29, 1908.

19. See Sir Ralph's book, *Aucuparius* (London: Oxford University Press, 1962).

20. C.O. 323, Vol. XIII, 1909, Individuals. The minute is dated Dec. 10, 1908.

21. C.O. 430, Patronage Register, 1907–1909, Vol. II, letter of May 26, 1908.

22. *Ibid.* This volume is filled with petitions, complaints, and requests concerning pensions, leave, passage money, etc. Each case is handled *ad hoc,* and there are many references to the shortage of official funds.

23. C.O. 323, Vol. XIII, 1909, Individuals, letter of July 3, 1908.

24. Jeffries, *op. cit.,* p. 20.

25. C.O. 323, Vol. XII, Memo #36808, Nov. 1909. The Patronage Committee dealt with promotions and transfers, not with recruitment.

26. Francis Newbolt, *Appointments Handbook,* Colonial Office, 1942 (1948 ed.), p. 11. The origin of the phrase is discussed in Furse's own book, *op. cit.,* p. 17.

27. Sir Arthur Grimble, *A Pattern of Islands* (London: Murray, 1952), pp. 1–8. This official was a member of the C.O.'s Fiji Department, not of the recruiting staff.

28. Interview with Sir Maurice Dorman, governor of Sierra Leone, at Government House, Fort Thornton, Freetown, Feb. 5, 1960. Interview with Sir John Macpherson, former governor-general of Nigeria, July 27, 1960, London.

29. C.O. 429, Patronage, Vol. I, Individuals, #20433.

30. Furse points out that this query sought to determine what sort of man the father was and what influence he might have had on his son. Letter to me, Dec. 8, 1961.

31. Note 29 *supra,* #1923.

32. *Ibid.,* #39719, W. G. Adams.

33. *Ibid.,* #23634.

34. *Ibid.,* C. C. Brown, no number.

35. *Ibid.,* #39719.

36. *Ibid.*

37. *Ibid.,* #2227.

38. *Ibid.*

39. *Ibid.,* Lt. Blackiston, #36405.

40. *Ibid.*

41. *Ibid.,* #1923.

42. Sir Charles Dundass, *African Crossroads* (London: Macmillan, 1955), pp. 8–9.

43. C.O. 323, 1909, Vol. XIII, Jan. 16, 1909.

44. *Oxford Magazine Supplement,* Nov. 7, 1907.

45. C.O. 323, Vol. XIII, 1909, Individuals.

46. *Ibid.* This does not agree with the information published in the magazine cited above which has Parkinson tutoring with H. Sturt for 6 weeks, *loc. cit.,* p. 3.

47. C.O. 429, Patronage. Vol. I, Individuals, #20453.

48. *Ibid.*

49. *Ibid.*

50. *Ibid.,* #1923.

51. *Ibid.,* #26988.

52. *Ibid.,* Lt. A. Ackland, #20453.

53. *Ibid.,* Lt. J. P. S. Brown, #1923.

54. *Ibid.,* #39719.

55. *Ibid.*

56. *Ibid.,* #29126.

57. Cf. "Former District Commissioner On National Assistance," *The Times* (London), March 5, 1962 (Home News). My attention was called to this article by H. E. Newnham.

NOTES TO CHAPTER II

1. Jeffries, *op. cit.,* p. 40.

2. Amery, *My Political Life* (London: Hutchinson, 1953), Vol. II, Chapter IX.

3. For example, Amery proposed in all seriousness that a solution of the Cyprus problem might be for Greece to join the Empire. See *My Political Life,* Vol. II, pp. 368–69.

4. Cf. J. E. Wrench, *Alfred Lord Milner* (London: Eyre & Spottiswoode, 1958), p. 386.

5. *Op. cit.,* p. 340.

6. This has been the assumption of many critics including Labour Party M.P.'s. The sentiment was conveyed to me by Mr. Wedgwood Benn (Lord Stansgate) in a letter of April 1, 1958, when he was "shadow colonial secretary." It is evident, too, in the writings of anti-British nationalists, e.g., George Padmore, *The Gold Coast Revolution* (London: Dobson, 1953).

7. *Op. cit.,* p. 346.

8. Hansard, Vol. 189, cols. 6–7, Dec. 7, 1925.

9. *Ibid.,* 198, 2407–08, July 29, 1926. Amery also sought to foster better cooperation between London and the colonies by having C.S. men, "beachcombers," assigned temporarily to the C.O. Sir John Nicoll, former governor of Singapore, told me in the fall of 1962 that he did not find that the scheme worked particularly well. Beachcombers were treated rather shabbily by home civil servants.

10. *Ibid.,* 208, 1721–22, July 11, 1927.

11. *Ibid.,* 219, 2702, July 13, 1928.

12. Cf. Cmd. 2744, 1926 and Cmd. 3235, 1928. These command papers are the reports of the under-secretary on his trips to West Africa and Southeast Asia respectively.

13. Wilson was not, however, a career colonial servant. The first of these to be permanent under-secretary was Sir John Macpherson.

14. Cmd. 2884, *Appendices to the Proceedings of the Governors' Conference,* 1927, pp. 11–12.

15. *Ibid.,* p. 13.

16. Cf. Robert Graves and Alan Hodge, *The Long Weekend: A Social History of Great Britain, 1918–1939* (London: Faber, 1940), especially pp. 70, 251.

17. *Loc. cit.,* pp. 13–14.

18. Philip Woodruff (pseud.), *The Men Who Ruled India* (London: Cape, 1954), e.g., Vol. II, p. 71.

19. Quoted in Padmore, *op. cit.,* p. 103.

20. *Op. cit.,* p. 14. Furse and I have engaged in discussion

involving a certain amount of friendly disagreement on this point. Sir Ralph states that it was certain qualities of personality and character he was seeking and that social strata were incidental. He further states that family background and schooling of a certain sort did almost invariably contribute to the desired personal characteristics. For my part I readily concede, as will be indicated in chapters IV and V, that not all successful candidates were from upper social strata and/or certain schools and universities. Given the undeniable and undenied connection between breeding, educational institutions, and personal characteristics, however, and given the statistics on recruitment in the 1920's and 1930's, it would seem that Furse and I are each looking at the same phenomenon, but from slightly different angles, and putting stress on different aspects.

21. *Ibid.*

22. Cf. Graves and Hodge, *op. cit.,* pp. 213, 223.

23. *Ibid.,* p. 14.

24. *Ibid.,* p. 26.

25. Interview, Sir Charles Jeffries, London, June 22, 1960.

26. Letter to me, Aug. 16, 1960, from W. R. Crocker, then Australian High Commissioner to India and former D.O. in Nigeria during the 1930's.

27. *Loc. cit.,* p. 14.

28. Cf. Woodruff, *op. cit.,* Vol. II, Chapter IV.

29. Interview, Peter du Sautoy, Accra, Feb. 9, 1960; cf. Grimble, *op. cit.*

30. Interview, C. N. Lawrence, Lusaka, Feb. 13, 1960.

31. Interview, H. E. Newnham, Oxford, Aug. 6, 1959; Letter, Newnham to me, Aug. 31, 1959.

32. *Ibid.,* letter of Sept. 2, 1959.

33. Col. 198, *Post-war Training for the Colonial Service* HMSO, 1946 (the Devonshire Report), p. 21.

34. Cf. Report on *Staffing of the Agricultural Departments in Colonies* (C.O. Papers), 1920; Cmd. 1166, *Report of the Inter-Departmental Committee on Forestry Education,* 1921; Cmd. 2825, *Report of the Committee on the Colonial Agricultural Services* (the Lovat Committee), 1924; Report of

the Lovat Committee on the Colonial Scientific and Research Services in the 1927 Governors' Conference (in Cmd. 2883, 1927); Cmd. 3049, *Report on the Colonial Agriculture Service,* 1928.

35. Interview, Sir Ralph Furse, London, Oct. 13, 1960.

36. Letter, Feb. 4, 1927, C.O. to Oxford registry; letter, May 1, 1928, under-secretary of state to Oxford registrar.

37. Letter, Sept. 18, 1928, T.A.S. course supervisor (Truslove) to the Oxford registrar.

38. *Loc. cit.,* p. 26.

39. E.g., interviews with J. P. Murray and A. C. Jamieson, Ndola, Northern Rhodesia, Feb. 18, 1960. Both of these officials were selected and trained in the interwar period. Their opinions are typical.

40. Cf. J. D. Fage, *An Introduction to the History of West Africa* (Cambridge: Cambridge University Press, 1955), p. 178.

41. Letter, A. N. Strong to me, July 17, 1960.

42. Letter, H. E. Newnham to me, July 26, 1960.

43. Cf. Georges Hardy, *Histoire de la Colonisation Française* (Paris: Librairie Larose, 1928). The author of this book was the director of the *Ecole Coloniale;* I attended the training course given to new officers in a U.S. Government department in 1952. The final series of lectures was on the subject "The American Thesis."

44. See Cmd. 3554, *Report of a Committee on the System of Appointment in the Colonial Office and the Colonial Services* (the Fisher Report), 1930, pp. 18–19.

45. Figures kindly provided by the C.O.

46. *Loc. cit.,* p. 26.

47. No serving or retired governor I interviewed failed to pay tribute to Furse and his efficiency. Interviews with Sir John Macpherson, London, July 27, 1960, with Sir Maurice Dorman, Freetown, Feb. 5, 1960, with Sir Alexander Waddell, Kuching, March 16, 1960, and with Sir Kenneth Maddocks, Suva, April 14, 1962.

48. It would be impossible to document this universally

agreed-upon assertion without making a survey of all C.O. Lists in the period. A check on Oxford men entering the service in the years 1927–40 reveals that less than half were still in service 10 years after appointment. This was a comparatively low turnover period. Cf. W. R. Crocker, *Nigeria* (London: Allen & Unwin, 1936), p. 240, and his book *On Governing Colonies* (London: Allen & Unwin, 1949), p. 121.

49. Cf. Bishop Ingham, *Sierra Leone After 100 Years* (London: Seeley, 1894), pp. 310–11, and W. R. Crocker, letter of Aug. 16, 1960, to me.

50. Cf. Woodruff, *op. cit.,* Vol. I, p. 36, and interview with K. D. D. Henderson, Oxford, Dec. 8, 1960. Mr. Henderson, formerly of the Sudan Service, is the author of *The Making of the Modern Sudan.*

51. Hansard, 197, 1585–86, July 5, 1926.

52. Cmd. 3235, *Report of the Rt. Hon. W. G. A. Ormsby-Gore on His Visit to Malaya, Ceylon and Java in the Year 1928,* p. 23.

53. *Loc. cit.,* p. 17.

54. Cf. Crocker, *Nigeria,* pp. 111, 239–40, 259. Furse's concern with the problem of continuity is reflected in a contribution he made to the report of one of the early Cambridge conferences. See African No. 1178, Colonial Office, *Summer Conference on African Administration,* 1951, Appendix A, pp. 169–71.

55. Interview, F. J. Pedler, London, July 27, 1960.

56. The diary of a D.O., printed in Crocker's *Nigeria,* is a long and detailed diatribe against the prevailing lack of continuity.

57. Letter, Furse to me, Dec. 8, 1961. Sir John Macpherson observes that officers leaving their parent colonies were apt to be used only in secretariats, because of the language problem. (Letter of June 19, 1962, to me.)

58. Letter, A. N. Strong, July 17, 1960, to me.

59. *Loc. cit.,* p. 28.

60. Cmd. 3235, p. 23.

61. Cmd. 3554, p. 24.

62. Hansard, 219, 2654–55, July 13, 1928.

63. See *My Political Life,* p. 188.

64. Cmd. 3554, p. 2.

NOTES TO CHAPTER III

1. Amery, *op. cit.,* p. 339.

2. Hansard, 227, 1421, April 30, 1929.

3. *Loc. cit.,* p. 20.

4. *Ibid.,* p. 7.

5. *Ibid.*

6. *Ibid.,* p. 19.

7. *Ibid.,* p. 7.

8. Cf. Mark Abrams, "The Elite of Tomorrow," *The Observer* (London), Sept. 4, 1960.

9. Duke of Devonshire, Corona Club speech, 1923.

10. Jeffries, *op. cit.,* p. 132.

11. *Ibid.,* Appendix I.

12. Cf. Cmd. 3628, *Colonial Office Conference 1930 Summary of Proceedings,* 1930, pp. 185–86.

13. Jeffries, *op. cit.,* pp. 131–32.

14. Cf. Joyce Cary, *Mister Johnson* (London: Gollancz, 1939), especially pp. 86–87, 122 ff., 155, 158–59, 165.

15. Cf. Crocker, *Nigeria,* pp. 111–12.

16. See Apter, D. E., *The Gold Coast in Transition* (Princeton: Princeton University Press, 1954), Chapter I.

17. When I maintain that it is not surprising that the committee would approve the sources Furse used in recruiting, I should add that it was *not* a foregone conclusion that the committee would approve the interview system of selection. As Sir Ralph points out to me (his letter of Dec. 8, 1961) it was quite to be expected on the contrary that Fisher, Meiklejohn, and Scott, all of whom had had to pass examinations to enter the civil service, would have favored a similar system for the C.S.

18. Hansard, 222, 1419, Apr. 30, 1929.

19. November 7, 1906, p. 1.

20. *Loc. cit.,* p. 97.

21. Cmd. 3554, 1930, p. 19.

22. Cmd. 3628, 1930, p. 88.

23. Interview, Sir Charles Jeffries, London, June 22, 1960.

24. For the numbers involved in the exchange see Hansard, 227, 1421, April 30, 1929.

25. R. K. Kelsall, "The Social Background of the Higher Civil Service," in William A. Robson, ed., *The Civil Service in Britain and France* (London: Hogarth, 1956), p. 151.

26. *Loc. cit.,* p. 20.

27. *Ibid.,* p. 23.

28. Quoted by Sir Hugh Foot, former governor of Cyprus, at Oxford, Oct. 11, 1960.

29. *Britain and Her Dependencies* (London: Longmans, 1943), p. 41.

30. See Furse, *op. cit.* Some of the following information comes also from interviews and correspondence with Sir Ralph.

31. Letter from H. E. Newnham to me, July 26, 1960.

32. Interview, A. D. Garson, London, July 7, 1960.

33. The Savile Club has reciprocal arrangements with the Cosmos Club in Washington and serves a comparable clientele.

34. *Loc. cit.,* pp. 24–25.

35. The details which follow are drawn partly from interviews with Furse, Garson, and others (as noted) and partly from Francis Newbolt's *Appointments Handbook,* a confidential C.O. document privately supplied to me.

36. A former Oxford University Appointments Committee secretary, E. A. Greswell, wrote to me on Dec. 4, 1960 that "there was never a shortage of candidates and their standard of personality, social qualifications (which were very important) and integrity was high." Mr. Greswell served from 1928 to 1945.

37. Francis Newbolt, *loc. cit.,* p. 3.

38. Furse says that he tried to send "strong reinforcements" to places going through difficult times, such as Kenya has ex-

perienced, and that the poorest colonies got a sprinkling of better men so that even the least popular colonies would always have on their staffs men capable of rising to the senior posts. (His letter of Dec. 8, 1961, to me.)

39. An entire file of submissions during a certain year, which cannot be identified, was made available privately for my inspection. Submissions cited in the text will be identified by an alphabetical and/or numerical designation. This one is taken from Submission J. 1.

40. *Loc. cit.,* p. 3.

41. *Ibid.,* p. 4.

42. This is especially evident in marginal notes in submissions M. and A.

43. Submission A.

44. *Loc. cit.,* p. 13.

45. Submission E.

46. Submission X.

47. Submission Z.

48. Submission B. 1.

49. Submission C. 1.

50. Submission J. 1.

51. Submission D. 1.

52. Interview, A. D. Garson, July 7, 1960. Wilson is a pseudonym.

53. *Loc. cit.,* p. 13.

54. As recounted by Harold Ingrams, in the C.O., Sept. 23, 1960.

55. As Furse points out in his letter to me of Dec. 8, 1961, however, his continued influence depended now on the good will of board members, who "could have clipped [his] wings sharply if they had chosen to."

56. Furse was not in the C.O. during the tenures of Bonar Law and Viscount Long. He served a total of 17 ministers during his career, two of them twice each.

57. Cf. many people's low opinion of Lord Elgin, described by Miss Perham in *Lugard,* Vol. II, pp. 237 ff. and the high opinion of Lord Passfield in Sir Drummond Shiels' "Sidney Webb as a Minister," in Margaret Cole, ed., *The*

Webbs and Their Work (London: Muller, 1949), p. 206.

58. *Ibid.* (Shiels). Passfield is given credit herein for unifying the C.S.

59. Letter, H. E. Newnham to me, Dec. 10, 1959.

60. Interview, Oct. 13, 1960, London.

NOTES TO CHAPTER IV

1. Sir Henry Newbolt, *Poems New and Old* (London: Murray, 1912), p. 94.

2. Letter, Furse to me, Aug. 15, 1960.

3. Furse's introduction to *A Perpetual Memory,* by Sir Henry Newbolt (London: Murray, 1939), p. xvi.

4. House of Commons, Select Committee on Estimates, *Fifth Report,* Sessionals 1947–48, "Colonial Development," June 30, 1948, testimony of Sir Ralph Furse, p. 462.

5. Letter, Furse to me, Aug. 17, 1960.

6. Cf. "Headmasters' Report," *The Observer,* London, Oct. 2, 1960, p. 6.

7. Interview, F. J. Pedler, London, July 27, 1960.

8. House of Commons, *op. cit.* note 4 *supra,* p. 467.

9. Interview, Sir Claude Elliott, Eton, Sept. 23, 1960.

10. House of Commons, *loc. cit.* note 4 *supra,* p. 467; see also *Aucuparius.*

11. Letter, Sir Ralph Furse to Mr. (later Sir Douglas) Veale, Nov. 18, 1941, Oxford University registry.

12. Letter, W. R. Crocker to me, Aug. 16, 1960.

13. C.O., *Appointments Handbook,* p. 12.

14. Board of Education, *The Public Schools and the General Educational System* (The Fleming Report), London, HMSO, 1944, pp. 7, 19, 54.

15. Interview, G. C. Turner, Chichester, Oct. 4, 1960.

16. *Loc. cit.,* pp. 106 ff.

17. Cf. the list in the Fleming Report, pp. 125–26 and in Graves and Hodge, *op. cit.,* p. 212.

18. The Fleming Report contains no figures. But a glance at the list of schools in the Headmasters' Conference in 1944

shows that the total number of students enrolled in its 83 member schools in the interwar period could not have been as many as 75,000 in a population of over 35,000,000.

19. E.g., C. Wright Mills, *The Power Elite* (New York: Oxford University Press, 1959), pp. 63 ff.

20. *Fleming Report,* pp. 6 ff.

21. These terms are used in David Riesman, *The Lonely Crowd* (New Haven: Yale University Press, 1950); cf. also his *Individualism Reconsidered* (Glencoe, Ill.: The Free Press, 1954), p. 14.

22. *Loc. cit.,* p. 29.

23. Brougham Committee, 1830, Clarendon Commission, 1861, Taunton Commission, 1868, Bryce Commission, 1895, Fleming Committee, 1942; and see the articles by the Archbishop of Canterbury, "Origins and Scope of the G.B.A.," *The Times* (London), Dec. 14, 1960, p. 11, Dec. 15, 1960, p. 11.

24. *Fleming Report,* p. 54.

25. *Ibid.;* cf. R. K. Kelsall, *Higher Civil Servants in Britain* (London: Routledge, 1955), Graves and Hodge, *op. cit.,* p. 419.

26. In 1938, for example, 66 out of 96 recruits had been to Public Schools, and 11 of the remaining 30 were from the Dominions (C.O. tables).

27. Cf. *Fleming Report,* p. 113.

28. Cf. H. Grose-Hodge, *Ends and Means of a Public School Education,* Bedford School, June 22, 1960.

29. Interview, G. C. Turner, Chichester, Oct. 4, 1960.

30. Interview, Lady Elliott, Eton, Sept. 23, 1960.

31. The prep school sub-stage may be considered part of the Public School stage and definitely less important due to the extreme youth of boys at that time.

32. Cf. John Vaizey, "The Public Schools," in *The Establishment,* Hugh Thomas, ed. (London: Blond, 1959), pp. 23 ff.

33. Graves and Hodge, *op. cit.,* p. 212; and see Bertrand Russell, *Power* (New York: W. W. Norton, 1938), p. 213.

34. Letter, W. R. Crocker to me, Aug. 16, 1960. Am-

bassador Crocker, in his letter of June 19, 1962, to me, adds: "The Public Schools are primordial. The main reason for the difference between the Colonial Services in French or Dutch or Belgian Colonies on the one hand and the Colonial Service in the British Colonies on the other, is that England had the Institutions of the Public Schools, of Oxford and Cambridge, and of Sandhurst. These gave a very definite set of social and even moral values. They are much more important than any snobberies that went with them. It was a question of what was 'done' and 'not done.' . . . The fake gentleman . . . existed but was not a really significant figure."

35. E.g., the Wolfenden Report; and see "Public School Values," *The Observer,* Sept. 25, 1960, p. 19.

36. D. J. West, *Homosexuality* (London: Penguin, 1955).

37. Cf. Russell, *op. cit.,* and E. M. Forster, *Two Cheers For Democracy* (London: Arnold, 1951).

38. A headmaster recommending one of his boys for the C.S. in 1907 wrote that "he performed his duties in accord with those Public School traditions which combine good discipline with friendly relations between director and directed." Letter of March 1, 1907, on behalf of W. G. Adams, Application #39719, C.O. 429, Vol. 1, "Individuals," Public Record Office, London.

39. Interview, R. W. Young, George Watson's, Edinburgh, Oct. 7, 1960.

40. E.g., interviews with Furse, Oct. 13, 1960, with Sir Maurice Dorman, Feb. 5, 1960, with A. D. Garson, July 27, 1960, with Sir Alexander Waddell, March 16, 1960, and with Sir Charles Jeffries, June 22, 1960.

41. Cf. Lord James, *Education and Leadership* (London: Harrap, 1951), p. 19.

42. Interview, A. L. F. Smith, Edinburgh, Oct. 7, 1960.

43. Cf. Sir Arthur Grimble, *op. cit.,* p. 1.

44. Cf. H. Grose-Hodge, *Notes For the Use of Masters at Bedford School,* p. 33.

45. Interview, I. D. McIntosh, Edinburgh, Oct. 7, 1960.

46. Grose-Hodge, *loc. cit.,* p. 23.

47. Interview, R. W. Young, Edinburgh, Oct. 7, 1960.

48. Cf. letter to *The New Yorker,* July 2, 1960, pp. 58 ff., signed by Malcolm Bradbury and Michael Orsler.

49. See Grose-Hodge, *loc. cit.,* p. 37.

50. Letter, W. R. Crocker to me, Aug. 16, 1960.

51. *Commonwealth Challenge,* A Quarterly Review, Harold Ingrams, ed. See Vol. VII, No. 2 (Jan. 1959), p. 1.

52. Interview with D. Parfit, Head Boy of Eton, Oxford, Aug. 30, 1960.

53. *Ibid.* The Head Boy of Eton was left to do as he liked his final year, 1960–61. He spent part of the year in Paris and part of it in New York.

54. Grose-Hodge, *loc. cit.,* pp. 15–16.

55. Interview, A. L. F. Smith, Edinburgh, Oct. 7, 1960.

56. *Ibid.* Mr. Smith is uniquely qualified to make this observation. He was director of education, Government of Iraq (British), 1921–31 and rector, Edinburgh Academy, 1931–45.

57. The story was told, for example, by Sir Hugh Foot in a talk at Oxford on Oct. 11, 1960. He was formerly in the Nigerian Service and retired from the C.S. as governor of Cyprus in 1960. That the story may be an old standby, claimed by more than one colony, is indicated in the fact that I heard it, almost verbatim, in June, 1962, from A. N. Strong, but applied this time to Ceylon.

58. For example, Col. J. E. H. Boustead, who was in 1961 advisor to the Sultan of Oman. When I stayed with him in 1954 he was British Resident at Mukalla, Eastern Aden Protectorate. He left the British army in 1918 because there was not enough action. He had been wounded three times during World War I. In 1918 he went to Russia on his own and enlisted as a private in the White Forces in the Crimea, eventually being promoted to commissioned rank in the Wrangle armies. When the fighting stopped in Russia he went into the Camel Corps in the Sudan but was bored with the inaction of life there. He was a member of the British expedition which almost reached the top of Mt. Everest in the 1920's. He became a member of the Sudan Political Service after the Everest expedition. During the war against the

Italians in Ethiopia he commanded the Camel Corps force which invaded the country and he was wounded twice. He joined the Aden Service after 1945 and helped organize the Hadhrami Beduin Legion. Forced to retire from the C.S. because of age in 1958, he went to Oman and took service with its ruler.

59. Interview, I. D. McIntosh, Edinburgh, Oct. 7, 1960.

NOTES TO CHAPTER V

1. John Betjeman, *The New Yorker,* Aug. 27, 1960, pp. 31 ff.

2. "Knocking in Vain on College Gates," *The Times,* London, Nov. 15, 1960, p. 13. Discusses the continuing domination of entrance to Oxford and Cambridge by the Public Schools.

3. In the period 1931–39, for example, Oxford and Cambridge provided 426 out of a total 528 entrants to the Colonial Administrative Service, or roughly 80 per cent (C.O. Tables).

4. This is the unvarying judgment of Cambridge sources consulted, notably Sir Kenneth Pickthorne, J. T. Saunders, A. D. Garson of the C.O., Sir Claude Elliott, Sir Maurice Dorman, and Furse himself, who, though not a Cambridge man, was better placed than anyone to judge the comparison. In a talk with Furse on Sept. 5, 1962, I learned that the most important single "talent scout" in England was H. A. Roberts of Cambridge; Oxford's Mr. Sumner gave, on the whole, the most trustworthy judgments of undergraduates in that university. These additional facts do not, in my view, negate or lessen the value of examples of university recruiting given in this chapter. The Brasenose record of successful applications, for instance, speaks for itself.

5. 218 from Oxford; 208 from Cambridge (C.O. Tables).

6. A few of the more interesting and informative sources are: John Buchan, *op. cit.,* Christopher Hobhouse, *Oxford* (London: Batsford, 1939), Dacre Balsdon (pseud.), *Oxford*

Life (London: Eyre & Spottiswoode, 1957), Sir Roy Harrod, *The Prof* (London: Macmillan, 1959), Max Beerbohm, *Zuleika Dobson* (London: Heinemann, 1911), Sir David Kelly, *op. cit.* Most of the colleges have histories which are more or less informative, though many are written with a deliberate mercilessness towards the uninitiated reader.

7. Cf. an address given before the Industrial Welfare Society in London, *The Times,* Sept. 22, 1960, p. 6, blaming the older universities for "their curiously negative . . . almost hostile . . . attitudes to the development of an industrial society."

8. Letter, Furse to me, Aug. 15, 1960.

9. A check on probationers at Oxford in the years 1927, 1931, 1932, 1936, 1939 and 1940 shows: 54 majoring in classics and modern history, 19 in classics and law, 17 in classics, philosophy, and economics, 15 in straight classics, 9 in classics and geography, 8 in classics and literature, 7 in classics and science and 5 in classics and languages (registry files; records of Commonwealth Services Club).

10. The correspondence between Sir Douglas Veale and the D.O.'s he met on his trip to Nigeria in 1945–46 is revealing (registry files). Any number of the letters employ Greek and Latin quotations liberally.

11. H. Grose-Hodge, *Ends and Means of a Public School Education,* Bedford School, June 22, 1960.

12. Oxford dons are notoriously nicer to students whom they like than to fellow dons whom they do not like. See Harrod, *op. cit.*

13. The assumption also covered recruits from the Dominions. A number of Australians, Canadians, South Africans, and New Zealanders entered the C.S. All took the C.A.S. course.

14. Interestingly, the C.O.'s dependence on the Oxford University Appointments Committee, which, as we have seen, antedated Furse at the C.O., resumed after 1948, when Furse left the selection work. See the committee's 1954 report, p. 6.

This is not to suggest that Furse ignored the Oxford or Cambridge appointments committees. In fact he insisted that candidates apply through them. But he understandably did like to have dons and others at the two universities who were personally known to him act as talent scouts who would then direct promising candidates to the appointments committees for reference to the C.O. Still other candidates applied direct to appointments committees.

15. Italics mine. Letter, Furse to me, Aug. 22, 1960.

16. Testimony before the Parliamentary Committee on the Estimates, *loc. cit.,* p. 462.

17. This is the considered judgment of no less a career expert than C. E. Escritt, secretary of the Oxford University Appointments Committee (interview, Oxford, Dec. 22, 1960).

18. There is unanimous agreement on this point among specialists at Oxford who participated in selection in various ways during the interwar years. Sir Douglas Veale, Sir John Masterman, K. D. D. Henderson, Miss Perham, Sir Maurice Bowra, the bursar of Pembroke (George Bredin), and P. A. Landon are among those who supported the impression. Ernest Greswell, who was secretary of the Oxford University Appointments Committee in the period, also agrees (letter to me, Dec. 4, 1960).

19. Cf. Memorandum by Veale, June 17, 1936 (registry files).

20. Interview, Dec. 6, 1960.

21. Interview with Sir Maurice Bowra, Oxford, Nov. 24, 1960.

22. Interview.

23. Dr. David Mullins, Oxford.

24. Letter, Sir Charles Jeffries to Harold Ingrams (copy to me), Oct. 22, 1960.

25. Trinity was host to the Queen at luncheon in November, 1960, for example. Undergraduates meet such people.

26. Interview.

27. E.g., R. E. Luyt, a South African student of Landon's at Trinity, was sent to Rhodesia in 1940.

28. Interview.

29. Interview, Oxford, Nov. 29, 1960.

30. *Ibid.*

31. Stallybrass came to England during the present century, changing his name from Sonnenschein. His family still operates a printing firm in the Netherlands.

32. See *Historical Notes on the Oxford University Appointments Committee,* 1892–1950, p. 8.

33. Interviews, P. A. Landon, Oxford, Dec. 6, 1960, and S. H. Smith, Oxford, Sept. 16, 1960.

34. The number was 45 (records of the Commonwealth Services Club).

35. Interview, S. H. Smith, Oxford, Sept. 16, 1960.

36. Heath Harrison bequests, Brasenose College bursary.

37. *Ibid.*

38. Interview, S. H. Smith.

39. *The Brazen Nose* (alumni publication), 1960, p. 42.

40. *Ibid.*

41. Letter, E. A. Greswell to me, Dec. 4, 1960.

42. Interview, K. D. D. Henderson, Oxford, Dec. 8, 1960.

43. *Ibid.*

44. Incidental checks were made on the records of other colleges. It was not felt necessary to make exhaustive examinations of the records of more than one college, since, in the opinion of all Oxford and C.O. sources consulted, Brasenose was typical. The numbers of men entering the C.S. from Oxford colleges contributing the most probationers in the interwar years are: (1927–40) Brasenose—45; Balliol (Furse's college)—39; New College—35; Trinity (P. A. Landon)—31; Queens—29; Wadham (Sir Maurice Bowra) —28; Worcester—28; Christ Church (Sir John Masterman) —26. It has been stated elsewhere that Dr. Stallybrass was principally responsible for Brasenose's top showing. Among officials consulted in other colleges were the president of Corpus Christi, W. F. R. Hardie, Sir Christopher Cox, dean of New College, and Sir Douglas Veale, registrar of the University, a member of Corpus Christi College.

45. *Oxford Magazine Supplement,* Nov. 7, 1906, p. 4.

46. Interview.

47. Interview, Oct. 13, 1960.

48. Interview with George Bredin, bursar of Pembroke, Oxford, Dec. 5, 1960.

49. Interview with A. D. Garson, the C.O., July 27, 1960.

50. Interview, Lusaka, Feb. 17, 1960.

51. Letter, Truslove (course secretary) to the Oxford registrar, Sept. 18, 1928 (registry files).

52. Letter, Veale to Sir Ralph Furse, Feb. 27, 1942 (registry files).

53. Interview, H. P. W. Murray, Commonwealth Services Club, Oxford, Sept. 18, 1959.

54. Letter, E. A. Greswell to me, Dec. 4, 1960.

55. Interview, London, Nov. 3, 1960.

56. Minutes, C.A.S. committee, Feb. 5, 1937.

57. Memorandum by the Oxford registrar, June 17, 1936, (registry files).

58. Letter, Furse to Veale, Nov. 18, 1941 (registry files).

59. Letter, Veale to Furse, May 25, 1943 (registry files).

60. Letter, Sudan Office, London, to Oxford registrar, Oct. 12, 1929 (registry files).

61. Minutes, T.A.S. committee, June 10, 1932.

62. E.g., W. G. Morison, 1938.

63. Furse visited and formed regular liaisons with all the important universities in Canada, Australia, and New Zealand.

64. Letter, Kenneth Johnston of the Foreign Office to the Oxford vice chancellor, Oct. 18, 1937 (registry files).

65. *Ibid.*

NOTES TO CHAPTER VI

1. See "University or Industry for Oxford," *The Times* (London), June 16, 1960, p. 16.

2. Interview, J. T. Saunders, Cambridge, July 30, 1960.

3. This is, again, quite natural. He was an Oxford man.

4. 44 in 1939 and 35 in 1940.

5. Letter, Furse to Veale, March 6, 1941.

6. Cf. letter, Furse to Veale, Feb. 14, 1942.

7. Letter, Oct. 8, 1942, from Veale to the under-secretary of state.

8. Cf. Ian Morrison, *Malayan Postscript* (London: Faber, 1942), Ch. III.

9. Letter, Perham to Furse, Oct. 8, 1942.

10. Letter, Furse to Veale, Feb. 14, 1942.

11. Feb. 20, 1942.

12. *Ibid.*

13. *Ibid.*

14. Cf. Sir Andrew Cohen, *British Policy in Changing Africa* (London: Routledge, 1959), pp. 26 ff.

15. Miss Perham had received requests for information on colonial studies from many British colonial governments as well as from such non-British institutions as l'Institut Français de l'Afrique Noire. See her letter to Veale, Sept. 9, 1943.

16. Hebdomadal Council Papers, Oxford University, May 22, 1942, pp. 121–30.

17. *Ibid.*

18. Hansard, Lords, 122, 943, May 6, 1942.

19. Cf. Sir Alan Burns, *Colonial Civil Servant* (London: Allen & Unwin, 1949), p. 309, and Jeffries, Sir Charles, *The Colonial Office* (London: Allen & Unwin, 1956), pp. 40 and 183.

20. Circular Memorandum, Nov. 28, 1942.

21. Nov. 12, 1943.

22. Excerpt, The Acts, Hebdomadal Papers, July 27, 1942.

23. Note by Veale, Oct. 14, 1942.

24. Letter, Nov. 13, 1942.

25. Letter, secretary of the faculties, Oxford, to Veale, June 19, 1942, and letter, June 25, 1942, Veale to the secretary.

26. Veale note to Hebdomadal Council, Nov. 5, 1942; letter from Sir Charles Jeffries to Veale, Dec. 31, 1942.

27. Letter, Veale to Furse, July 5, 1943; letter, Sir William Goodenough to Veale, Sept. 14, 1943; letter, Veale to Professor Forde, Sept. 21, 1943; Forde's answer, Sept. 23, 1943.

28. Letter, Lord Simon to the secretary of state, Jan. 26, 1944.

29. Cf. Georges Hardy, *Histoire de la Colonisation Française* (Paris: Librarie Larose, 1928), chapters XIV, XV, and XVIII; Van der Kerken, G., *La Politique Coloniale Belge* (Antwerp: Zaire, 1943) Part III; A. Vandenbosch, *The Dutch East Indies:* Its Government, Problems and Politics (Grand Rapids: Eerdmans, 1944); M. Frochot, *L'Empire Colonial Portugais* (Lisbon: Editions SPN, 1942); Lord Hailey, *An African Survey* (London: Oxford, 1957), chapters V, VI, and VIII; W. R. Crocker, On Governing Colonies: *Being An Outline of the Real Issues and a Comparison of the British, French and Belgian Approach to Them* (London: Allen & Unwin, 1947).

30. May 29, 1943.

31. Cmd. 6647, 1945.

32. Jan. 24, 1944.

33. Memorandum by Veale, Feb. 10, 1944.

34. Report of the Special Committee of the Imperial Forestry Institute, Oxford, Minutes, Nov. 3, 1936.

35. Extract, Hebdomadal Papers, Oxford, undated, but the position of the document in the file indicates that its date was around Nov. 15, 1943.

36. Veale to Malcolm, Nov. 24, 1943.

37. Veale to Furse, Sept. 11, 1942.

38. *Ibid.*

39. *Ibid.*

40. *Ibid.*

41. Furse to Veale, Sept. 25, 1942.

42. *Ibid.*

43. Note 29 *supra.* I have many times heard French *commandants du cercle* voice this aim. For example, M. Michel, *administrateur* at Tombouctou, March 1953, and M. Tessier, *administrateur* at Boutilimit, same month. A French district officer in former French Equatorial Africa, M. Jean-Pierre Lacour, also verified to me that this was an expressed aim covered in special courses for administrators in Paris. Lacour attended the Devonshire course at Oxford in 1959.

44. Veale to Furse, May 25, 1943.

45. Perham to Veale, Nov. 12, 1943.

46. Minutes, Oxford-Cambridge-London Conference, at London, Sept. 29, 1942.

47. Veale to Furse, Nov. 13, 1942.

48. Extract, Minutes, Oxford-Cambridge Joint Committee meeting, Jan. 12, 1943.

49. Letter, Veale to Furse, May 10, 1943.

50. Letter, Furse to Veale, March 6, 1941.

51. Veale, quoting Furse, in a letter to the Oxford vice-chancellor, March 24, 1941.

52. Veale to Furse, May 12, 1941.

53. Interview, F. J. Pedler, London, July 27, 1960.

54. Col. 198, *Postwar Training for the Colonial Service* (Devonshire Report) (London: HMSO, 1946), pp. 20 ff.

NOTES TO CHAPTER VII

1. Letter, Feb. 10, 1944.

2. Devonshire Report, p. 20.

3. This was not quite the case in actual fact. Cf. Perham, *Lugard,* especially Vol. I, and Robinson, R., Gallagher, J., and Denny, A., *Africa and the Victorians* (London: Macmillan, 1961).

4. On the Carnegie grants, see Jeffries, *The Colonial Empire and Its Civil Service,* p. 126.

5. Furse deals with this in *Aucuparius,* p. 160, pointing out that members of the technical services were occasionally considered "poor whites" by administrators.

6. *Loc. cit.,* pp. 25–6.

7. *Ibid.,* p. 26.

8. Letter, Furse to me, Dec. 8, 1961.

9. *Ibid.* "I have since been told that I was wrong about this," Furse adds.

10. B. J. Dudbridge, Dar es Salaam, Feb. 25, 1960.

11. *Loc. cit.,* p. 29.

12. Letter, M. R. Crocker to me, Aug. 16, 1960.

13. Cf. Hansard, Lords, 122, 943, May 6, 1942.

14. Crocker, *loc. cit.*

15. Copy provided privately to me.

16. Col. 231, *Report of the Commission of Inquiry Into Disturbances in the Gold Coast,* 1948, pp. 7–8.

17. *Loc. cit.*

18. Interview, Sir Christopher Cox, the C.O., Nov. 16, 1960; cf. letter, Prof. Fortes to Veale, Nov. 10, 1945 (registry files). Further material in the registry files, Oxford University, cited in this chapter will be identified by date and type of document only.

19. Letter, Perham to Veale, Feb. 5, 1945, quoting correspondence with colonial officials. Some of the correspondence quoted hereunder was dated in the mid-1940's, some earlier. There is a distinct pattern and continuity of theme, based on continuous service of the officials quoted, which justifies use of letters to support statements in the text, regardless of whether dated in the late 1930's or early or middle 1940's.

20. Quoted by J. T. Saunders, Cambridge, July 30, 1960.

21. Cf. Perham to Veale, Feb. 5, 1945 and July 28, 1944.

22. E.g., Giles (D.O., Sokoto, Northern Nigeria) to Veale, March 24, 1946.

23. W. G. M. Lugton, formerly of the Northern Rhodesia Service, quoting a scholar, in a letter to me, July 17, 1960.

24. Letter, L. L. K. Richards, D.O., Nigeria, to Veale, June 6, 1946.

25. Letter, Giles to Veale, March 24, 1946.

26. Diary of W. R. Crocker, included in *op. cit., Nigeria,* 1936. The diary covers the year 1933.

27. Note 25 *supra.*

28. John Watson, private secretary to Sir Milton Margai, Prime Minister of Sierra Leone, interviewed at his post, Feb. 4, 1960.

29. Letter, S. White, D.O., Nigeria, to Veale, April 6, 1947.

30. Letter, S. White to Veale, April 10, 1946; cf. Crocker diary, *loc. cit.*

31. The governor of Northern Rhodesia remarked to me on Feb. 15, 1960, in Lusaka that he was about to lose his invaluable chief secretary, G. S. Jones, who was leaving that night for Zomba in Nyasaland. Sir Glyn Jones is now governor of Nyasaland.

32. Letter, J. Farmer, D.O., Nigeria, to Veale, Oct. 1, 1946.

33. Minutes, 4th Devonshire meeting, May 11, 1944.

34. Minutes, informal (Oxford) committee, meeting in conjunction with the Devonshire meetings, May 27, 1944.

35. Letter, Prof. Fortes to Veale, March 2, 1946.

36. Cf. *Awo, The Autobiography of Chief Obafemi Awolowo* (Cambridge: Cambridge University Press, 1960), pp. 249 ff., Joyce Cary, *op. cit.;* G. Jahoda, *White Man* (London: Oxford University Press, 1961).

37. Letter to Veale, March 27, 1946.

38. Woodruff, *op. cit.,* II, p. 257.

39. Minutes, 1st Devonshire meeting, March 14, 1944.

40. Minutes, 6th Devonshire meeting, Nov. 2, 1944.

41. Letter, Veale to Furse, Dec. 7, 1946.

42. Minutes, 1st Devonshire meeting, March 14, 1944.

43. Interview, J. T. Saunders, Cambridge, July 30, 1960.

44. Minutes, 3rd Devonshire meeting, April 12, 1944.

45. Letter, Perham to Veale, Feb. 5, 1945.

46. Letter, Furse to Veale, July 21, 1944.

47. Letter, Veale to Carr-Saunders, Aug. 28, 1944.

48. Letter, April 24, 1946.

49. Minutes, 5th Devonshire meeting, June 7, 1944.

50. Interview, Sir Christopher Cox, the C.O., Nov. 16, 1960.

51. Minutes, 5th Devonshire meeting, June 7, 1944.

52. Minutes, 1st Devonshire meeting, March 14, 1944.

53. Interview, D. S. O'Callahan, Morogoro, Tanganyika, Feb. 29, 1960.

54. Interview, Sir Maurice Dorman, Freetown, Sierra Leone, Feb. 5, 1960.

55. "The British Problem in Africa," *Foreign Affairs 29,* 4 (July 1951), p. 649.

56. Minutes, Summer School Sub-Committee, Oxford, June 21, 1947.

57. Cf. Sir Charles Jeffries, *Partners for Progress* (London: Harrap, 1949), p. 19. Although this was written in 1948 the author told me that it refers to pre-1939 conditions.

58. Letter, Stallybrass to Perham, Feb. 15, 1947. In Furse's own words liaison training meant "teaching one branch of the service what were the functions, objectives and methods of the other—and how they could help each other." His letter of Dec. 8, 1961, to me.

59. Letter to Veale, March 27, 1946.

60. Interview, W. J. R. Wright, D.C., Bo, Sierra Leone, Feb. 3, 1960.

61. Minutes, 6th Devonshire meeting, Nov. 2, 1944.

62. Veale's Diary, *loc. cit.,* pp. 36–7.

63. Sir William Goode to me, April 28, 1961.

64. Minutes, 4th Devonshire meeting, May 11, 1944.

65. Minutes, 3rd Devonshire meeting, April 12, 1944.

66. Minutes, 9th Devonshire meeting, July 19, 1945.

67. Minutes, 4th Devonshire meeting, May 11, 1944.

68. Minutes, 3rd Devonshire meeting, April 12, 1944.

69. Extracts, comments of governors received by the C.O., sent to Oxford by Mrs. K. Beamish, secretary to the Devonshire Committee.

70. Minutes, 3rd Devonshire meeting, April 12, 1944.

71. Minutes, 6th Devonshire meeting, Nov. 2, 1944.

72. Minutes, 3rd Devonshire meeting, April 12, 1944.

73. Minutes, 4th Devonshire meeting, May 11, 1944.

74. Minutes, 9th Devonshire meeting, July 19, 1945.

75. Minutes, 4th Devonshire meeting, May 11, 1944.

76. Letter with large sheet enclosure, the Duke of Devonshire to Veale, July 10, 1945.

77. Letter, Sir A. Richards to Veale, April 25, 1945.

78. Memorandum by Veale, undated, in Col. 16 16/1, 1952–53.

79. Minutes, 3rd Devonshire meeting, April 12, 1944.

80. Letter, Jan. 29, 1946.

81. Nuffield Report, p. 65.

82. Crocker, *loc. cit.* See also *Nigeria,* pp. 119, 149, 151–52, 201, 251.

83. *Ibid., Nigeria,* p. 201.

84. Crocker, *loc. cit.*

85. Minutes, 5th Devonshire meeting, June 7, 1944.

86. Letter, March 17, 1944.

87. *Ibid.*

88. Cf. Bertrand Russell, *Power* (London: Allen & Unwin, 1939), p. 213.

89. Letter, March 20, 1944.

90. Minutes, 4th Devonshire meeting, May 11, 1944.

91. Minutes, Nov. 2, 1944.

92. Letter, Sir Alexander Carr-Saunders to Sir David Ross, March 17, 1944.

93. T. S. Simey, *Welfare and Planning in the West Indies* (London: Oxford, 1946), pp. 110–14.

94. Minutes, 1st Devonshire meeting, March 14, 1944.

95. Privately provided.

96. *Ibid.,* paragraph 7.

97. *Ibid.*

98. Letter, Feb. 13, 1947.

99. Interviews: Sir Alexander Carr-Saunders, London, Nov. 3, 1960, and Sir Christopher Cox, the C.O., Nov. 16, 1960.

100. The duke: 1st Devonshire meeting, March 14, 1944; the secretary of state: Oliver Stanley, "Britain's Colonial Policy," *United Nations Review* 5, 2 (March 15, 1945).

101. Cf. minutes, Oxford-Cambridge-London meeting in C.O., June 14, 1946.

102. On Sept. 19, 1945, C. Y. Carstairs of the C.O. wrote to Veale that Oxford must not suddenly confront the C.O. with a request for grants, but must present detailed outlines of what programs will involve, how the grant is to be expended, and how the program fits in with over-all objectives of legislation establishing the grants.

103. Letter, Feb. 5, 1945.

104. Carstairs to Veale, Sept. 19, 1945.

105. The British Resident at Mukalla, commenting on an

article I had written, said, "You must galvanize American opinion and make your countrymen see the light on colonialism." This was in Oxford in 1960. Some years earlier in his residency on the Arabian coast he had not cared what outsiders thought and had expressed amazement that a foreigner would ever bother to visit his area.

106. Cf. a note written by Veale on the need for new texts on Africa and Asia, Sept. 8, 1944.

107. Letter, Oct. 24, 1944.

108. Minutes, 6th Devonshire meeting, Nov. 2, 1944.

109. Cf. letter, Perham to Veale, Nov. 5, 1944.

110. Draft Report, Sub-Committee on Economics, Oxford, Jan. 25, 1946.

111. The Foreign Office so advised the standing joint (Oxford, Cambridge, London) committee at its London meeting, June 10, 1947 (Minutes).

112. "The Labour Party has . . . pressed for independence for the colonies more rapidly than the Conservatives." Lord Stansgate (Mr. Anthony Wedgwood Benn) to me, April 1, 1958. He was then shadow under-secretary of state for the colonies (Labour).

113. Interview, Sir Charles Jeffries, London, June 22, 1960.

114. Minutes, 3rd Devonshire meeting, April 12, 1944; minutes, Oxford-Cambridge-London meeting, June 20, 1944.

115. As it turned out, all postwar administrative probationers went to Oxford and Cambridge, and London drew the majority of specialists in such subjects as education and medicine.

116. Cf. letter, Furse to Veale, Oct. 24, 1945.

117. B. J. Dudbridge, Dar es Salaam, Feb. 22, 1960.

NOTES TO CHAPTER VIII

1. John Masters, *Bhowani Junction* (New York: Viking, 1954), p. 353.

2. African proverb, quoted by S. H. Frankel, *The Eco-*

nomic Impact on Underdeveloped Societies (Oxford: Blackwell, 1953), p. 81.

3. Letter from Veale to Furse, May 16, 1946, refers to Furse's request for arguments which could be used by people at Oxford "to tempt men into the Colonial Service."

4. Miss F. H. Gwilliam, Woman Educational Advisor to the secretary of state, in a talk with me, Singapore, March 8, 1960.

5. "We made much more progress in the last few years under Regional Nigerian ministers and with a rapidly Nigerianizing service than under a central European secretariat." F. J. Lattin, ex-Uganda and Nigeria service, letter, July 17, 1960, to me.

6. *Ibid.;* and cf. W. T. Stace (ex-Ceylon service), "British Colonialism," *Yale Review,* XLIII, 3, (Spring 1954), pp. 373–84.

7. I am not at liberty to cite the name of the person who wrote this letter.

8. In September, 1949, the mayor of a town in Bataan said to me in Manila, "We are only a banana republic now. When you were here we were part of a great country."

9. The Fisher Committee did not touch the entry system for the Home Civil Service officials in the C.O., however. And see Cmd. 3909, *Report of the Royal Commission on the Civil Service,* 1929–31, especially pp. 68 ff. and Chapter IX.

10. Thomas Sterling, *Stanley's Way* (London: Hart-Davis, 1960).

11. *Abinger Harvest* (London: Arnold, 1953), p. 13.

12. John Plamenatz says this was deliberate on the part of the British official, in *On Alien Rule and Self-Government* (London: Longmans, 1960), p. 7.

13. Cf. Sir Philip Mitchell, *African Afterthoughts* (London: Hutchinson, 1954), Chapter 7.

14. This was true even though basic "long scale" salaries were the same for all four West African colonies, in general, during the interwar period. Even though Furse always tried to send a sprinkling of his best recruits to the poorer colonies,

it was the bigger and more important places that had more superscale posts to offer, and they naturally attracted to their services, eventually, the best men from poorer colonies who had gone as far as they could go in the latter. Moreover, the whole atmosphere of government in a place like the Gold Coast under Guggisberg was more alive than that in, for example, the Gambia where there simply was not enough money for administrators to do progressive things with. By the 1930's each colony had a reputation in Oxbridge. It was entirely natural that the best recruits would prefer Nigeria to Sierra Leone, just as previous generations had preferred India to Africa. Although the C.O. was scrupulously fair in its original allocations, in the long run the bigger and richer colonies thus had more impressive administrative machines and progressed faster. The date of independence in each case could of course be affected by still other considerations such as the presence of more dynamic native leaders in one colony than in another, the degree of colony-wide unity in each, etc.

15. See memorandum to the Oxford Town Clerk from his deputy, Oct. 13, 1947 (registry files).

16. Sir Keith Hancock, *Colonial Self-Government* (Nottingham: Nottingham University Press, 1956), p. 19.

17. Mrs. P. J. Bohannan.

18. Letter, H. E. Newnham to me, July 26, 1960.

19. *Ibid.,* cites the sense of shock and horror that went through the I.C.S. when the secretary of state for India said, "If the Indians want corruption they are entitled to have it."

20. Mrs. Martin Page, Bo, Sierra Leone, Feb. 3, 1960.

21. Cf. Chief Obafemi Awolowa, *op. cit.,* Chapter 15.

22. *The Observer* (London), July 24, 1960, p. 26.

23. Dr. Nkrumah said, of his experience with the British, "We are not ungrateful." He is quoted in Sir Alan Burns, *In Defense of Colonies* (London: Allen & Unwin, 1957), p. 295.

24. W. G. M. Lugton, former Northern Rhodesia service, to me, July 17, 1960.

25. When asked what ought to be done for East Africans by American and British universities, a Uganda civil servant,

E. B. Cunningham, answered (in 1961), "Leave them alone."

26. Is it fair to say that the C.S. was representative of British society, since it was drawn from one class only? At a time when Britain had a class system that was accepted, generally speaking, throughout society, it is reasonable to say this. Most Englishmen, whatever their class, would have said that the men of the C.S. had every right to represent Britain in the colonies during the interwar period. It is mainly through the disapproving glasses of post-1945 social criticism that the C.S. appears unrepresentative.

27. "There is neither public nor private hatred nor distrust of the French." Reported by a British correspondent in Brazzaville, *The Times* (London), September 27, 1960, p. 7.

28. The French were by no means unaware of the shortcomings of selection by examination. An author who served for twenty years in the French colonial service writes, ". . . tel brillant élève de mathématiques spéciales ne fera jamais qu'un médiocre officier. . . ." (Delavignette, R., *Service Africain,* Paris: Gallimard, 1946, p. 63.) And again, life in the colonial service "ne convient pas . . . à ceux qui ne sont pas absolument maîtres d'eux-mêmes" (pp. 80–81).

29. *On Governing Colonies,* pp. 123–26.

30. *The Observer,* London, September 25, 1960, p. 5. The former director of the Ecole Coloniale, M. Hardy, writes, "Le but à atteindre aux colonies devrait être la création de véritables départements français." (Delavignette, *op. cit.,* p. 89).

31. Cf. James Duffy, *Portuguese Africa* (Cambridge: Harvard University Press, 1959); M. Frochot, *op. cit.,* chapters IV, VI.

32. *The Times* (London), Dec. 1, 1960, p. 10.

33. Lord Hailey in *An African Survey,* p. 378, gives a breakdown of the origins of Guinea administrators in the mid-1950's.

34. See Vandenbosch, *op. cit.,* Chapter X.

35. Minutes of the 6th meeting, Nov. 2, 1944. See also *Aucuparius,* pp. 200–04.

36. Sir H. Bell, *Foreign Colonial Administration in the*

Far East (London: Arnold, 1928), chapters III, X and XIII; see also Cmd. 3235, *Report by the Hon. W. G. A. Ormsby-Gore on His Visit to Malaya, Ceylon and Java in the Year 1928.*

37. See G. Van der Kerken, *op. cit.,* pp. 116 ff.

38. The best published example of this I know of is M. F. Perham, *Major Dane's Garden* (Boston: Houghton Mifflin, 1926). In one place the author has a D.O. in Somaliland say, "It's a funny old show, the British Empire" (p. 152). See also pp. 230–31.

39. F. C. Lander, formerly of the Cyprus and Gold Coast services, in a letter to me, July 17, 1960.

40. See Michael Oakeshott, "Political Education," in Peter Laslett, ed., *Philosophy, Politics and Society* (Oxford: Blackwell, 1956), p. 11.

41. *Journal of the Royal Commonwealth Society* III, 6 (Nov.–Dec., 1960), p. 226.

Index